OBJECT LESSONS

SUNY Series in Psychoanalysis and Culture

Henry Sussman, Editor

OBJECT LESSONS

HOW TO DO THINGS WITH FETISHISM

E. L. McCALLUM

STATE UNIVERSITY OF NEW YORK PRESS

Published by
State University of New York Press, Albany

For information, address State University of New York Press,
State University Plaza, Albany, N.Y., 12246

Production by M. R. Mulholland
Marketing by Dana E. Yanulavich

Library of Congress Cataloging-in-Publication Data

McCallum, E. L. (Ellen Lee), 1966–
    Object lessons : how to do things with fetishism / E.L. McCallum.
        p.   cm. — (SUNY series in psychoanalysis and culture)
    Includes bibliographical references and index.
    ISBN 0–7914–3979–8   (hardcover : alk. paper). — ISBN 0–7914–3980–1
(pbk. : alk. paper)
    1. Fetishism (Sexual behabior)   2. Freud, Sigmund, 1856–1930—
Views on fetishism.   3. Feminist theory.   4. Postmodernism.
I. Title.   II. Series.
HQ79.M39   1999
306.77—dc21
                                                                    98–13179
                                                                    CIP

10 9 8 7 6 5 4 3 2 1

FOR MY PARENTS,
HERBERT AND DOROTHY MCCALLUM

CONTENTS

ACKNOWLEDGMENTS

I would like to acknowledge the debts I owe to the colleagues and friends whose help enabled me to complete this project. Foremost in my gratitude is Jane Gallop, for all that she has taught me, but particularly for her insightful reading of this project when it was a dissertation. Her comments could bring out points in my own work I had not recognized, yet her direction consistently provided ample scope for me to be productively stubborn as I worked out my ideas independently. I also greatly appreciate the broader perspective of Kathleen Woodward, Lynne Joyrich, Bernie Gendron, and Paul Brodwin, who pushed me to think of this project in relation to the fields and discussions contiguous to it. I would especially like to thank Kathleen Woodward and Carol Tennessen at the Center for Twentieth Century Studies for generously providing an intellectual home while this project became a book. Finally, I am indebted to my writing group for consistent emotional as well as critical support throughout this process: Rachel Baum, Carmen Cavallo, Mary Elliott, and Liana Odrcic. Their friendship extends well beyond collegiality and has made this long road much less trying.

Portions of this project also benefited from readers beyond the UWM community. I would like to thank Naomi Schor, who kindly took the time to read and respond to the first two chapters, and pointed me to further reading that proved most helpful. I am also grateful to her and Elizabeth Weed for including a portion of the first chapter in the fall 1995 issue of *differences* journal. My colleagues at the School for Criticism and Theory in the summer of 1994 also deserve some credit for helping jump-start my brain at a crucial stage in the writing. In particular I would like to thank Elizabeth Constable and Matthew Potolsky, whose readings and commentary on very early drafts were most helpful. I am also grateful to Ladelle McWhorter, not only for reading nearly everything but for ongoing encouragement that extends beyond the boundaries of this one text and into my everyday life.

The hardest people to thank are the ones without whom this book would be inconceivable. Judith Roof's unflagging critical generosity and support proved invaluable in the final revision. I am also beholden to Ben Singer, for his insight and friendship; the kernel of this book is rooted in our conversations over tea years ago, and its eventual direction is certainly marked by his influence. Finally, I am deeply grateful to Ann Veronica Simon, for her tireless and daily support on every imaginable level.

INTRODUCTION

What we perhaps need to think about here is fetishism . . .

—Thomas Yingling

Fetishism stands at the heart of modernity. Exhibiting a remarkable tenacity and flexibility, fetishism emerged on the commercial edges of the West at the dawn of the modern age in the sixteenth century and continues to hold sway in sexual subcultures at the close of the twentieth century. Along the way, fetishism has played a role in definitive issues for Western culture, from the rise of scientific knowledge and rationality as the basis for individual identity to increasing imperialist expansion as the basis for national identity, from contests over religious belief to the anxious definition of proper sexuality, from the emerging importance of commodity exchange to questions of aesthetics. The definition of fetishism has consistently boiled down to the use of an object to negotiate (usually binary) difference to achieve an immaterial end, whether it be economic gain, cultural prestige, or psychical satisfaction. Key philosophical concepts, such as the Cartesian split between subject and object or the Kantian divide between reason and emotion, have reinforced the breach fetishism seeks to overcome, enshrining as disciplinary truths the distinctions, such as the subordination of the object to the subject, that make fetishism conceivable.

Although a variety of disciplines converge on fetishism, their attention consistently puts fetishism in a bad light; as a result, fetishism has been maligned as a sexual perversion, a symptom of our alienation from each other under capitalism, or an example of irrational, primitive thought. Despite the significance of the issues which fetishism engenders, fetishism itself remains relegated to the status of a minor if not aberrant phenomenon. When critical scrutiny has attended to so many of the issues pertaining to fetishism, we need to think about fetishism itself.

The first step is to take fetishism seriously, not as a threat but as a promise. This study thus begins with the question, what can fetishism teach us? One answer, as this examination will make clearer, is that fetishism is a form of subject-object relation that informs us about basic strategies of defining, desiring, and knowing subjects and objects in Western culture. More importantly, in the way that it brings together peculiarly modern anxieties—especially those about sexuality, gender, belief, and knowledge—fetishism reveals how our basic categories for interpreting the world have been reduced to binary and mutually exclusive terms. The most intransigent reduction has been in the definitions of sexual difference, where the divisions between masculine and feminine, or homosexual and heterosexual, are now pursued at the level of gene and brain structure, as if the biological architecture could refute the diversity of individual practices and cultural differences. By foregrounding concerns about sexual differences in examining fetishism's unique intersection of desire and knowledge, this study seizes the promises fetishism offers to those who want to call into question the resurgence of conservative and even reactionary drives to lock down absolute definitions of sexual differences through either biological or cultural essentialism.

We need to know first what fetishism is. The term is hardly a simple one. Even though the idea has had currency in marxist, religious, and anthropological discourses for a longer time, the most commonly recognized definition of fetishism comes from psychoanalysis. This is particularly true outside the academy, where radio advertisements for a local nightclub's "Express Your Fetish" night are hardly expecting patrons to bring African tribal religious icons, much less commodities that embody modern subjects' alienation under capitalism. In common as well as psychoanalytic parlance, fetishism has come to mean the sexual fixation on an overvalued object, an interpretation that derives most clearly from Freud's essay on fetishism.

The psychoanalytic definition took shape from the sexology of the late nineteenth and early twentieth centuries, and is widely presumed to apply only to men. Yet this understanding gives fetishism short shrift on a number of fronts. Not only is the phenomenon not strictly limited to men, but it has a history reaching back much further than the late nineteenth century, one that is arguably coextensive with the emergence of the modern West. The notion of fetishism is, in fact, an interdisciplinary notion par excellence. As William Pietz has shown in his extensive discussion of fetishism's history, the term first came into use in the sixteenth century as Portuguese sailors and West African societies encountered one another and began to establish trade relations; in that context, technological and economic changes were transforming the boundaries that delineated national interests and identities.[1] The term that emerged in this cross-cultural space has accrued significance in a rather astoundingly vast number of contexts: religious, aesthetic, cinematic, commercial, and sexual.

This history suggests why we should pay attention to fetishism now. Pietz notes that "the emergence of a distinct notion of the fetish marks a breakdown of the adequacy of earlier discourse under quite specific historical conditions" (I: 6). If we find ourselves needing to think about fetishism, perhaps this is because history is repeating itself and the current discourses are inadequate for meeting our needs. The last twenty-five years of this century have seen a great upheaval in gender and sexual roles, and it now seems particularly appropriate to try to integrate the psychoanalytic emphasis on the sexual aspects of fetishism with the term's interdisciplinary history.

As with the moment of fetishism's intercultural emergence four centuries ago, our specific historical situation is similarly figured in the confluence of economic, political, and cultural change. In the present case, however, recent significant economic and political shifts have eroded the traditional boundaries that defined and regulated sexual identities rather than national ones. The narrow constraints of gender and sexuality in the public imaginary have been challenged and broadened; states, for example, find themselves confronting the novel issue of gay marriage, although this challenge has not gone unanswered by a conservative backlash and legislatures now are specifically outlawing same-sex unions. Changes in the public imagination about the proper roles and capabilities of men and women, gays and straights, have their basis in social practice, in the labor force as well as in the interpersonal social connections that comprise communities. For example, as many of the more highly rewarded forms of labor involve mental rather than physical resources, biological sexual differences become less relevant; as heterosexual marriage and reproduction has become less pressing as a requirement for economic survival, sexual expression becomes more of a choice and more central to building one's identity. The transition in the economic sphere from a commercial, goods-based capitalism to the "postcapitalism" of the service and information-based economy joins with the promise in the political realm to make good on the guarantee of liberty and equality for all to change how individuals can imagine themselves in relation to their culture. Together, these transformations have made it possible for nontraditional interpretations of sexual difference to emerge—be it the independent, heterosexual "liberated" woman, or the queer radical, or even the fetishist. The current disintegration of earlier discourses about subjects—their political rights, their economic possibilities, their philosophical identities, their individual proclivities or pathologies—is situated on the divisions between public and private, knowledge and desire, that are loaded with sexual difference—all key elements that fetishism addresses.

Because of the challenges to traditional sexual and gender configurations, a persistent theme of late twentieth-century Western thinking reflects on how categories of sexual difference seem to be in crisis. In the academy, feminist studies and queer theory have both instigated and emerged from the struggle over attending to sexual differences. And yet the key terms are not static; this "crisis" has proved an opportunity to rethink sexual differences. In renewing attention to fetishism, and particularly fetishism in the form that most clearly addresses issues of sexual difference, I want to respond to that categorical instability; this study is an effort to amend the breakdown of the adequacy of discourses about sexual differences. This breakdown connects to a kind of epistemological crisis, since when our basic categories for understanding the world are fundamentally challenged, so too is our sense of certainty about what we know. Thus, there is a firm but complex connection between sexual differences and knowledge.

This study, however, is not a comprehensive examination of fetishism's history, nor is it a wide-ranging catalog of its impact in various disciplines. It is, rather, a strategic analysis of the depiction of fetishism in particular theoretical texts, a study of the conditions and assumptions that undergird how fetishism has been interpreted in Freud's and psychoanalytical feminist theories. This study is also an attempt to overcome the limitations those assumptions have imposed on our ability to see fetishism as a potential source for productive answers to questions about how subjects negotiate difference, knowledge, and loss. I believe that the psychoanalytic account of fetishism has more to offer our thinking than simply an informative catalogue of the various objects taken as fetishes, or an abstract label for poor reasoning. For this reason, I tackle the psychoanalytically informed theoretical notion of fetishism, which has become isolated from the historical and multidisciplinary senses of the term. My analysis aims to come to terms with how the many aspects of fetishism work in concert and to explore what insights open up about the connections between desire and knowledge, sexual differences and epistemology, when we work from a more rig-. orous account of fetishism. Examining how fetishism subtends our knowledge of sexual difference is the first step in coming to see how fetishism provides a more general alternative epistemological model.

My exploration of fetishism addresses feminist and queer theories, certainly, since those are the theories most concerned with sexual differences. But this study also seeks an audience among those who are thinking through the challenges offered by postmodernism and recent antifoundationalist philosophies. While much postmodernist thought has focused on the changes in the meaning and constitution of subjects, and some—particularly that concerned with cyberspace and virtual reality—has examined changes in the meaning and constitution of objects, this study uses fetishism to focus on the meaning and constitution of the *relation* between subjects and objects, a relation that is clearly under redefinition in the shift to postmodernity. Insofar as postmodernism also addresses issues of loss—loss of center, loss of meaning, loss of transcendent Truth, etc.—this study of fetishism responds to postmodernism by outlining a possible strategy for negotiating loss and partiality. In responding to the crisis of representation, postmodernism emphasizes fluidity, fragmentation, partiality, and the transgression of boundaries. Fetishism, generally construed as a fixation, would hardly seem to be the answer to this crisis; indeed, it seems to be a retrenchment, a symptom of the resistance to change, a refusal to meet the postmodern challenge. This view reflects the fact that fetishism itself has come to be fetishized—it is used now as a charge against an interpretive approach that fixes meaning. The weight of this charge derives circularly from a narrow understanding of fetishism as focused on fixed meaning, however, and not from a broader grasp of the phenomenon of fetishism itself.

This study, then, is an effort both to redefine fetishism as an instructive strategy for postmodern thought and to examine the implications fetishism holds for modern assumptions about the nature of the world and its inhabitants. It is a serious effort not just to think *about* fetishism, but more importantly to think *through* fetishism, using it as a strategic perspective for analyzing assumptions about subjects and objects, desire and knowledge, identity and difference. By positing how a fetishist would look at certain pressing questions of today—such as identity politics, the ways we define gender and other sexual differences, the question of how to know things when there is no absolute standard of truth, or indeed how to read and interpret at all—this analysis hopes to demonstrate fetishism's epistemological possibilities, particularly for feminist analysis and queer theory in the confrontation with postmodernism.

My analysis sprang from observing that fetishism often is used synecdochically to mean any number of things that comprise it: overvaluation, fragmentation, fixation, repudiation of difference, or rigidity. This synecdoche has often occluded the interconnections between these elements and deeper motives in fetishism, some of which are potentially quite productive or interesting. Fetishism, for example, helps a subject negotiate the difference between self and other(s). It is also a strategy for dealing with anxiety and contradiction in order to reach satisfaction. Most importantly, it is a strategy which uses ambivalence in order to achieve a coherent and even creative interpretation. Fetishism is, at heart, a hermeneutic strategy, one which aims to interpret the world by negotiating the difference between self and other.

Usually, a reference to fetishism carries negative connotations, disapproval if not outright condemnation. Most often this critical attitude uses fetishism in its verb form, and "to fetishize" seems to have become the modern theoretical equivalent of "to misapprehend." But stripped of its evaluative trappings, the phenomenon of fetishism is clearly and simply a particular relation between subjects and objects. This subject-object relation, however, is special because although it involves ambivalence, indeterminacy, contradiction, it remains reassuring or satisfying. Indeed, the central conflict of fetishism, whatever form it may take (commodity, sexual, anthropological) is between belief and knowledge; this conflict necessarily engenders competing interpretations of the world, particularly because it is the belief that the fetishist acts upon, not the knowledge alone. In this light the fetishist could be construed as the prototype of the political activist, acting on a belief about how things should be rather than on a knowledge of how the world really is. The important point here is that neither belief or knowledge alone is sufficient, for without knowing how the world is, belief would not compel us to reinterpret it. Thus, changing to a more positive appraisal of fetishism coincides with a more explicit emphasis on the epistemological dimension of the phenomenon as well as on its hermeneutic effects—that is, an emphasis on how fetishism helps us creatively to know and interpret the world through the things around us.

The change from thinking *about* fetishism to thinking *through* fetishism calls for a change in attention, from fetish objects to the use subjects make of fetishes and fetishism. Thus, this study is not a catalog of fetishes, for that would reinscribe us in the familiar problem—the very one fetishists are classically faulted for—of attending to the object rather than clearly confronting the issue at hand. Rather, the aim is to show how thinking as a fetishist leads us to a more complicated and nuanced view about sexual and ontological differences, and that through this complication, more creative and productive interpretations of subjects and objects can emerge. The end result is an epistemology of fetishism, its effects on the subject and on the constitution of the subject's view of the world.

To make such a claim, however, raises the question, for whom is this reinterpretation of fetishism? My hope is that the epistemological dimensions of fetishism will abet pragmatic cultural critics who are skeptical of the promises of postmodern fragmentation and the threat of partiality, but who know that the reign of absolutes—of Truth, authority, universally shared definitions—is bankrupt. It is also a strategy for those who are still looking for how to implement pragmatically a politics of idealism—the progressive promises of feminism, civil rights, gay and lesbian liberation—when we know all too well the limitations of identity politics and strategic essentialism, and how they lead to further fragmentation and division rather than progressive action and less discrimination. This epistemological strategy acknowledges that we are all not only very interested but deeply invested in differences, particularly those differences of sex, race, class, and desire. These are not simple distinctions, nor are they merely individual differences (though they may be coded as such in order to place responsibility on the victim's shoulders) but are interpersonal and intrasocial relations that are loaded with disparities in power. To change the social distribution of power requires that we embrace rather than efface the spectrum of difference and transform its cultural meaning. To some extent, identity politics—making claims on behalf of people because of who they are—has sought to address this; and yet this strategy backfires by working on the basis of exclusion.

To illustrate this problem, let me take an example from feminist theory, which struggled in the 1980s with the problem of recognizing multiple differences. Having gained a foothold in the academy, feminists were realizing or being called on to realize that bringing sexual difference to bear on academic study was only the beginning of the work that lay ahead. Women who were not white, heterosexual, or middle class found that the paradigms predominantly used by feminists failed to integrate their experiences or allow for their differences. The result, as the title of an early African American women writers anthology suggests, was that all the women were white, all the blacks were men, but "Some of Us Are Brave."[2] And so feminist theory turned to the challenge of how to understand the ways that a social fact—gender—was inflected by differences of race, sexuality, class, religion, and region. The result, however, was often unwieldy lists of identity categories that seemed endless, maintained the separations between the terms, and almost always failed to include the brave. Trying to think in terms of the list led to further binary divisions: for example, speaking of women and race too often meant speaking in terms of only black and white women; speaking in terms of class and women would boil down to working-class and middle-class white women; speaking in terms of sexuality meant talking about lesbians and straight women. To think of anything more complicated—like the connections between middle-class heterosexual black women and working-class Chicana lesbians—started to seem like hairsplitting. The larger aim of the feminist movement was lost in the struggle over who is recognized and how. What was needed was a model for thinking about political and cultural identities as multiple layers rather than a laundry list that overwhelms us with specificity and thereby trivializes differences. This was not only a political problem, but also an epistemological and hermeneutical one, a question of knowledge and interpretation.

The epistemological and hermeneutical implications of fetishism devolve most clearly from its psychoanalytical formulation, since it is that incarnation of the notion that brings together questions of knowledge and belief with issues of difference, otherness, and desire. Therefore, rather than take the historical, multidisciplinary approach to reexamining fetishism, as Pietz has already done, or pursue the widely deliberated line of thinking about fetishism instigated by Marx, I will focus on the psychoanalytic construction of the term, beginning with the texts of Sigmund Freud. Reading Freud brings us directly to important questions of sexual difference and desire, questions that some feminists and gay theorists have faulted him for providing harmful answers to. I find that, like fetishism, Freud's texts still have something to offer, despite the critical disparagement.

From Freud the investigation proceeds to consider feminists' treatments of fetishism, since feminists are particularly concerned with discussing sexual differences and this study is committed to intervening in those discussions. I am especially interested in the feminist theories that are searching for the good or the useful in fetishism. While not all of them find an unequivocal good, they nonetheless open new dimensions. The feminist work I examine does more than attend to strictly binary forms of gender differences; it brings our attention to other differences, of class, race, and sexuality. Finally, the third chapter closes with a reading of feminist theorists who are not directly addressing fetishism but melancholia. Because my investigation of fetishism leads me to claim loss, rather than lack, as the origin of fetishism, examining their work on melancholic loss provides informative parallels to the analysis of fetishism. The coda then emerges from the melancholia comparison to situate the fetish-relation in the field of epistemology and its questions of knowing an object, rather than the field of psychoanalysis and its questions of desiring an object.

This study thus begins with a close reading of Freud's 1927 essay on fetishism, the text which has been the touchstone for so many subsequent discussions of fetishism. The very strength of the theoretical fixation on the interpretation of the fetish as a substitute for the penis suggests that more is going on in fetishism than first meets the eye. And, indeed, what a close reading of "Fetishism" reveals is that not only is more going on in fetishism, but that there's quite a lot of potentially productive instability in the way Freud employs the term "penis" as well. The chapter's title, "How To Do Things with Fetishism," reverses the usual formula for the perversion—how to do fetishism with things—to signal that this reading will seize on the instabilities of meaning in fetishism's supposed anchor, the penis, in order to negotiate satisfactorily the contradictions about sexual difference in fetishism theories; this strategy is analogous to how the fetishist employs the ambivalence inherent in the fetish to resolve his own contradictory interpretations of sexual difference.

One of the things to do with fetishism is to use the connection between the two terms, fetish and penis, to show how Freud's formulation of fetishism productively disrupts assumptions about sexual differences. The next thing to do with fetishism is to turn from a close attention to sexual difference in "Fetishism" to the function of fetishism in Freud's other works about sexuality and sexual difference—in short, to look at what things Freud does with fetishism. One motivation for this chapter is the question of why women were excluded from consideration as fetishists (how can women do things with fetishism, or more to the point, what prevents women from doing things with fetishism?), and what that might say about how sexual difference is understood in Freud and in the culture at large. Juxtaposing Freud's essays on "Fetishism" and "Femininity" elicits a striking parallel in the development of these two sexualities, and raises the question of whether women were excluded from being considered fetishists because Freud saw it not as a perversion for them, but as a norm.

But Freud is not the only one doing things with fetishism. Even if women weren't taking a shine to fetishes, that hasn't stopped feminists from focusing on fetishism. The second chapter turns to recent feminist appropriations of Freud's formulation of fetishism. While Freud has been blamed for the exclusion of women from fetishism, in fact he never said that women cannot be fetishists; indeed he asserted in a 1909 lecture that "all women are clothes fetishists." As this chapter's title, "The Travesty of Clothes Fetishism," intimates, this specifically sartorial sort of fetishism resonates with a striking tendency in feminist theories of fetishism to emphasize clothing fetishism, dressing, and cross-dressing, despite the whole spectrum of phenomena that fetishism presents and the range of objects taken on as fetishes. This chapter examines how the seemingly inevitable conjunction of female fetishism, clothes, and travesty offers a productive view of fetishism as a strategy subjects use to define themselves. I show how fetishism in feminist theory challenges the tendency to think of categories of racial, class, and sexual differences as sets of binary pairs. The travesty of feminists' attention to fetishism is that feminists have not fully appropriated fetishism in order to support these insights, but instead have allowed the negative valence on fetishism to dissuade them from reaching more fruitful conclusions. Fetishism goes unrecognized as a useful tool for complicating narrow assumptions about difference, partly because its interpretation has been dominated by the idea that fetishism is used to avoid confronting difference. Yet it is precisely because thinking about difference in strictly binary terms is so entrenched that such a complicating tool is so imperative.

Once clothes fetishism is understood less as a fixation on a type of object and more for its insights into how subjects use clothes-fetishes to construct their identities, we can see how negotiating one's inner concept of self and the often contradictory readings of that self by the outer world provides a model for a more nuanced and effective feminist politics that emphasizes an openness to interpretation, revision, and recognition. Just as individual subjects can use *fetishes* to become more active and creative individuals, so too can feminist theorists use *fetishism* to become more rigorous and creative thinkers. Fetishism should be viewed more positively for providing a complex way to negotiate differences as contingent upon a network of often conflicting meanings and contaminated by the oppositional element. This field of interpenetrating elements includes not merely the opposition between masculine and feminine, but between subjects and objects, materiality and psychic reality.

The critics' choices of examples point us towards this positive interpretation. Much of the evidence for female fetishism in feminist theories focuses on literary examples, and most of these examples are masculine women. While these examples certainly reinforce the theme of cross-dressing and travesty that seems inextricable from feminist theorization of fetishism, it also provides clear insight into how fetishism is used to construct gender identity, a core element of subjectivity. In line with this critical tradition, this chapter also draws on a literary example, ending with a reading of the novel *Stone Butch Blues*. However, this example pushes us in a new direction for thinking about the relationship between fetishism and sexual difference, since the masculine protagonist provides an example of fetishism that is not oriented toward signs of either masculinity or femininity. Instead, this protagonist carves out a third, transgender identity.

The third chapter, "The Language of Loss," moves into a wider-angled view of fetishism that will dominate the conclusion of the investigation. The first two chapters' concern with how fetishism shakes up assumptions of polarized, binary sexual differences gives way to the third chapter's focus on how fetishism shakes up assumptions about polarized, binary ontological differences. This ontological difference may be figured as the distinction between presence and absence (loss) or between subject and object. By moving away from the notion of fetishism as perversion, we can see more clearly how fetishism is a subject-object relation that violates the modern, Western assumption that subjects and objects are mutually independent. This broader perspective thus directs our attention away from the fetish subject to bring the fetish relation into view. The trajectory of the interpretation of fetishism changes from how fetishism has been understood historically as an essentially modern "problem" to an exploration of the possibilities for a postmodern fetishism. However much the categories within which fetishism operates change as postmodernism supersedes modern conceptions of the world, what remains consistent is fetishism's foundation in loss.

The third chapter draws on feminist theorists who work on both the constitution of sexual differences and the ways in which these differences are tangled up in broader philosophical questions about personal identity or cultural and epistemic authority. The two theorists, Julianna Schiesari and Judith Butler, are chosen because their models for sexual difference are intricately tied in with the notion of loss and its function in melancholia. Like fetishism, melancholia breaks down proper boundaries between subject and object; also like fetishism, melancholia emerges as a subject deals with loss. Unlike fetishism, however, melancholia has occupied a privileged position in Western culture. "The Language of Loss" thus brings together fetishism and melancholia as two expressions of loss, situating them in semiotic relation to one another as if they were part of the same language, and teasing out what their differences might be. This "teasing" follows the pattern set at the beginning of the investigation: whereas the first chapter worked through the question of whether it was only norms of sexual difference that excluded women from being considered fetishists in order to show how fetishism usefully complicates binary conceptions of sexual difference, this last chapter works through the question of what holds apart melancholia and fetishism, in order to show that fetishism offers a positive result, by enabling differences to emerge through loss. Because it is able to mark differences in kinds of losses as well as different expressions of the same kind of loss, fetishism emerges as its own sort of language about loss. Viewing fetishism in this light, as a language about loss, underscores the hermeneutic aspect of fetishism, its interpretive capabilities. Furthermore, the comparison with melancholia ultimately facilitates the move from sexuality to epistemology by clearly aligning fetishism within a system of subject-object relations.

Fetishism inevitably relies on the subject-object distinction. This split is fundamental not only to fetishism but also to the modern world view, which presumes that the object is subordinate to the subject's mastery. The move into postmodernity does not free us from this desire for mastery, or from negotiating the necessary restrictions imposed on our will to power or our will to know. What we need, therefore, are epistemological paradigms that account for a degree of agency and communicability but also that can productively withstand the loss of certainty, of absolute Truth. The analysis concludes by proposing how fetishism offers just such an epistemological paradigm, in part through comparison with Lorraine Code's feminist epistemology, which takes friendship as the model for knowing. Her argument establishes how we can—and do—have an ambivalent form of knowing in how we relate to other people as friends. We can reasonably say that we know a person, and yet that same person may surprise us by what we do not know about her. This sort of model shows how ambivalence is not necessarily an impediment to action.

The comparison to friendship also elicits the aspect of care in fetishism, for like the friend's attention to the object of affection, the fetishist's attention to the object of desire, however ambivalent, is bound up in caring about the object. At the same time, fetishism recommends itself over friendship because of its emphasis on desire; it is the passion of fetishism that makes it so compelling as an alternative epistemological model. Moreover, fetishes can be known in ways that friends necessarily cannot; we can often communicate our relations to objects better than we can our relations to other subjects, precisely because other subjects must be treated like other subjects and not objects. Fetishes offer common ground, convergences of interest, that can be understood both on the level of the particular—e.g., the fetishist's special relation to *that* shoe—and the level of the general which need not be corroborated by the object itself—e.g., Freud's recognition of the specialness of that relation, without having to experience it himself.

In the end, fetishism provides an epistemology of the object, a way of coming to know a thing. But this epistemology has something to teach us too, for fetishism is a two-way street: the subject not only relates to the object but also believes—knows, even—that the object relates back. The title of this study, then, is an attempt to make good on the epistemological promise fetishism offers. We make our objects from what we make of our world, and in return they teach us: this is fetishism's object lesson.

1

How to Do Things with Fetishism

Fetishism bears upon our thinking wherever we broach questions of difference, the exercise of power in a heterogeneous field, or the intersection of knowledge and desire. The version of fetishism developed by psychoanalysis shows fetishism to be an act of interpretation that serves as a theory about sexual difference. In this light, fetishism is not only a sexual practice, but it also has epistemological consequences, insofar as it frames knowledge and belief about sexual difference for the fetishist. Through this interpretive framework, the fetishist comes to know the world and to construct a sense of self in relation to that world, since sexual differences are a fundamental category for how humans organize their knowledge of the world. These epistemological consequences redound upon the fetishist as well, for fetishism's contribution to the interpretation of sexual differences is not only a new theory of relating to objects but a new identity for those doing this relating. Yet as this analysis will show, this new identity is one which cannot simply assimilate to one side or the other of a binary system of sexual differences. This chapter will examine how fetishism operates rhetorically in Freud's texts in order to demonstrate that fetishism's inability to assimilate into binary sexual differences provides both a broad insight on an alternative model for knowledge and a particular theory of sexual differences which moves beyond dualistic thinking.

Psychoanalysis's gloss on fetishism is not only relatively late in relation to the term's overall history, but fetishism as psychoanalytic concept at first glance appears to be a relative latecomer in Freud's thinking. His article on "Fetishism" dates from 1927, two years after "Some Psychological Consequences of the Anatomical Distinction between the Sexes," and a few years before "Female Sexuality" (1931) and "Femininity" (1933), which both pick up on themes set out in the 1925 essay. This chronology prompts us to explore how his ideas on fetishism connect to his concern with issues of sexual difference, since his theories of both fetishism and sexual difference are explicitly formulated in the later years.

Given the historical lineage of the term, we might expect to find Freud considering fetishism in his works about "primitive" man and the idea of civilization. But there is no discussion of fetishism as such in either *Totem and Taboo* (1913) or *Civilization and Its Discontents* (1930). However, fetishism does appear in a number of Freud's earlier works—most notably in the first essay of his *Three Essays on the Theory of Sexuality* (1905), but also in his analysis of Jensen's novel *Gradiva* (1907), his case study of the Rat Man (1909), a 1909 lecture given to the Vienna Psychoanalytic Society, and his essay on Leonardo da Vinci (1910). These are all works which address issues of sexuality, and thus to see fetishism as a late-developed concept is a mistake. Rather, this context supports the idea that fetishism is at the root of Freud's thinking not only about sexual difference but also sexuality (or what might now be called sexual identity); fetishism is thus not only a theory of sexuality for the fetishist, but may also be instrumental in Freud's theories of sexuality and ideas about the development of subjectivity.

Freud fundamentally shifted the study of sexuality from the problem of how to account for deviance, with the implication that we would thereby learn to correct it, to the question of how "normal" sexual identity and practice are achieved. This shift challenged the corrective bias and led to understanding deviations from the norm as interpretations of that norm. We would thus do well to question how fetishism fits in with his challenge to interpretations of sexuality and sexual difference. Indeed, Freud's emphasis on variation rather than deviation in his descriptions of sexuality and sexual difference provides an important model for how we can understand difference differently, through some nonbinary pattern like a spectrum. Yet Freud's texts display a peculiar ambivalence around the formulation of difference, and it is this ambivalence that most interests me. Freud's texts vacillate between being progressive—offering a fundamental challenge to how we think about ourselves—and conservative—failing to follow through on that basic challenge of our assumptions and lapsing instead into the accepted wisdom of the day.

This vacillation is clearest and most tightly interwoven in his discussions of sexual difference, a division he both emphasizes and ignores. "Fetishism" replicates that logic; contrary to its simple or straightforward appearance, the text explicitly and complexly foregrounds questions of sexual differences and Freud's ambivalent handling of them. Through Freud's work we come to understand sexual difference not just as the binary gender difference of masculine and feminine, but also as the differences apparently within one gender, between straight and queer, perverse and normal, chaste and promiscuous. Freud's texts do tend to undermine the rigid boundaries delineating these differences—most famously, they deconstruct the separation between normal and perverse and thus make it possible to perceive homosexuality as neither criminal nor pathological. At the same time, however, there are moments in Freud's texts that obstruct this undermining force and tend to reinforce the conservative cultural assumptions which hold these binaries together. Which of these readings, progressive or conservative, comes to the fore is very much a matter of interpretation.

This tension between Freud's radical interrogation of certain categories and unquestioning reliance upon the context in which those categories are constructed thus provides an important reason for turning to the work of Freud. "Fetishism" (Freud's lecture) and fetishism (the practice or concept) foreground the issue that lies at the heart of psychoanalysis: the question of interpretation and the relation of interpretation to knowledge, belief, desire, and truth. Psychoanalysis's concern with the unconscious raises the problem of the representability of the unrepresentable, tapping directly into the basic hermeneutic problem of how one can grasp, or even approach, the radically different, and communicate it to those like oneself without compromising the difference of the other.

Fetishism is a dense metaphor for this hermeneutic problem. At a basic level, fetishism is one strategy for negotiating the unsettling otherness of sexual difference through the interpretive act of giving the mother a penis. This attribution both admits and denies the mother's sexual difference; it makes the mother's sexual difference representable through the fetish, and yet at the same time also renders that difference unrepresentable by denying or disavowing its specificity. At a different, epistemological level, fetishism operates like an open secret. While fetishism conceals its private significance, its otherness, from the world at large, thereby denying difference or impeding interpretation, it is never entirely categorically indecipherable: the objects of the fetishist's attention are commonly known and available for interpretation. Thus fetishism itself is both representable as publicly available knowledge that certain objects may contain a private and titillating significance, and unrepresentable insofar as the public never knows precisely for whom, and for which items, that significance exists. This aspect of interpretation in fetishism is consistent with fetishism's history, where the fetish provided the hinge of translation between incommensurable European and West African languages, enabling exchange to take place based on provisional and partially public knowledge of the other.

In the psychoanalytic formulation, this hermeneutic sense is foreclosed; the fetish object is simply and narrowly taken to be a penis or phallus substitute. The fetishist seizes on the fetish to guard against acknowledging his mother's difference from him—that is, her lack of a phallus. From this reading, fetishism has been formulated as the refusal to jump into the semiotic stream of ever-changing interpretations; the fetish guards against the instability of meaning and the threat posed by difference. The dominant psychoanalytic reading of the fetish thus emphasizes fetishism's negative aspects: the overvaluation of an object at the expense of another subject or a fluency of interpretation. Marcia Ian describes fetishism as "characterized by the refusal to individuate, the lack of ego development, and an inability to use symbols to represent rather than embody" (177). In this view, fetishism is precisely that which is antithetical to language, to the symbolic, to interpretation, insofar as it closes down the inherent openness of language to interpretation.

I do not want to deny the need for a label for the regressed state of refusing to "use symbols to represent rather than to embody" and for the desire for the return to an imaginary fusion with the mother. Nor would I want to deny that such a position exists. Yet this understanding, as Ian points out, is one which fetishism has accrued since Freud, and indeed differs from the Freudian interpretation. I believe there are interesting complexities in Freud's discussion of fetishism that deserve to be explored. By returning now to Freud's text we can move to de-fetishize fetishism, unloosen its fixed meaning, examine its internal contradictions, and release the fetish from its overdetermined and overdetermining interpretation as the very pinnacle of the Thing, an object the fetishist is stuck on as the embodiment of substance and meaning. We can, for instance, come to see how the dominance of the penis-substitution definition gives fetishism a negative connotation that eclipses the potentially productive aspect of fetishism as a way of holding the contradiction between belief and knowledge together in tension. Indeed, once we begin to interrogate the larger framework of fetishism, we find that the notion brings together a number of complicated understandings of gender, knowledge, and desire.

Finding the value in fetishism is a matter of interpretation. By shifting perspective from a masterful, distant epistemology to a more sympathetic epistemology, we will see that in what outsiders view as the overvaluation of an inappropriate object, the fetishist finds an adequate solution to his or her needs. The fetishist's viewpoint focuses attention on fetishism's positive aspects as a combination of pragmatic and creative responses to the demands of the situation and the subject's needs. In this light, two faces of fetishism emerge. One is antithetical to language by dint of its investment in fixity and stasis. The other is an instrumental strategy for symbolic exchange, epistemology, and political imagination by virtue of its investment in ambivalence, particularly in the ambivalent tension desire sets up between belief and knowledge. Where the negative side has been too long emphasized in psychoanalytical interpretations of fetishism, this study prefers to draw upon the positive offerings, the insights fetishism holds as a strategy for understanding sexual differences and the connections between desire and knowledge.

It may seem strange to call fetishism a strategy, since this move takes fetishism out of the context of the unconscious, rationalizing it by relating it to notions of agency, consciousness, and choice. Yet, while I do not want to sever the unconscious aspect of fetishism from my reading, I do want to retain this notion of strategy, precisely because it emphasizes provisionality and usefulness over the finality of proclamation and reminds us of the contingency of interpretation within a given context. The irony of an unconscious strategy—which is what is suggested by the very notion of fetishism as an epistemology—is intended to emphasize Freud's most basic lesson: that our conscious actions contain unconscious wishes. Rationality can never shake itself free from desire; fetishism as an epistemological strategy may help us better employ reason and desire.

To reexamine this general understanding, we must return to its point of departure, the text "Fetishism" by Freud. In this examination of Freud, I want both to impose the rigor of the text onto the rather loose interpretation of fetishism that currently holds ascendance—that is, fetishism as sexual overvaluation of an object—and to try to exploit that text's interpretation as a way of pushing our thinking about what fetishism is, and how it operates in modernity and postmodernity. What follows, then, will be a reading of Freud that mines the text for its instabilities not only in order to question the underpinnings of the formulation of fetishism, the assumptions which enable it to come into being, but also to see how this notion can be transformed, worked over, to provide a more productive understanding of how we can relate to the world. This reading mimes fetishism not only by being "true" to the text by minding what's there, but also by adventurously blowing things out of proportion for a strategic purpose.

Symptoms of an Analogy in the Construction of a "Penis"

I will begin at the end, at the point in Freud's essay on "Fetishism" which seems to sum up the foundation of this perversion. In the last sentence, which is itself the last paragraph—and thus clearly intended to strike the reader's attention—Freud asserts that

Schießlich darf man es aussprechen, das Normalvorbild des Fetisch ist der Penis des Mannes, wie das des minderwertigen Organs der reale kleine Penis des Weibes, die Klitoris. (*GW* 14: 317)

In conclusion we may say that the normal prototype of fetishes is a man's penis, just as the normal prototype of inferior organs is a woman's real small penis, the clitoris. (*SE* 21: 157)

The normal prototype of all fetishes is the penis of the man, just as the normal prototype of an organ felt to be inferior is the real little penis of the woman, the clitoris. (Rivière translation, 219)[1]

Quite apart from its position at the end of the essay, the phrase "Schießlich darf man es aussprechen" or "In conclusion we may say" emphasizes the decisiveness of the sentence. The finality of this pronouncement may be in large part responsible for the prevalence of the penis-substitute definition of fetishism, although the phrase is elided in the mass-market translation by Joan Rivière.

This penis-substitute theory, read too glibly, invites an interpretation of Freud as a biological determinist or essentialist when he thus portrays the link between penis and fetish, reducing the latter to the former. Yet it is not Freud who is being so reductive but those who would hold to this interpretation, reaffirming what they already thought about fetishism. Such a reading narrows the myriad interpretations of "penis" that fetish objects provide to a single, simple, even patently obvious, base. The fact that this assertion comes at the end of "Fetishism" gives this reductive reading the weight to close off interpretive openness in favor of what seems to be anatomically evident. By taking anatomy as the unquestionable foundation for the model of the fetish, we complacently accept a certain biological determinism. Such a reading in fact functions at odds with the practice of fetishism, which at a basic level refuses to distinguish between anatomical and other objects. The biological given that anatomy seems to provide is not interrogated further as to the extent to which it is itself an interpretation, and contingent, not absolute. Furthermore, an interpretation of fetishism that makes the fetish strictly dependent upon the man's penis plays into the assumption that one has to have the latter in order to have access to the former. Such a view makes anatomy seem to be self-evident but still significant: beyond interpretation, but not beyond meaning.

Just this sort of reading has contributed to the view of fetishism as an exclusively male perversion in psychoanalysis; it is easy to make the logical error of slipping from "man's penis is the model" to "therefore it is men—as people with penises—who become fetishists." This slip renders the fundamental gesture of fetishism the act of attributing what you have to someone who doesn't have what you have. Indeed, this is the very gesture that Freud makes in this sentence, albeit at a very different level and thus with different rhetorical effects, when he uses the word "Penis" to describe both men's and women's genitals. While this gesture—whether Freud's or the reductive reading's—does illuminate the dynamic of fetishism that seeks to efface difference, it causes us to overlook another key aspect of fetishism: the implied inadequacy of the fetishist's own penis (or else why would it need a supplement in the form of the fetish object?). The inadequacy may best be understood as a precarious possession of the penis, threatened as it is with castration; this precariousness is the flip side of the refusal to recognize sexual difference. More importantly, the interpretive slippage between the man's penis as the model and the idea that only men are fetishists forecloses the disturbance produced by Freud's naming the clitoris the woman's penis, thereby introducing a striking ambiguity of sexual difference.[2]

In this last sentence of "Fetishism," there are implicit parallels made possible through the structure of an analogy. The explicit analogy between the normal prototype of the fetish and the normal prototype of an inferior organ—penis is to fetish as woman's penis is to inferior organ—permits the following: man is to woman as penis is to clitoris as fetish is to inferior organ. These parallels construct a matrix through which we can compare the elements of the analogy by tacitly acknowledging the difference within the pairs (man:woman or penis:clitoris) while focusing on the similarities between the pairs. Although the analogy is not forced, the force of the analogical form conceals the failure of the parallel on the rhetorical level. Notably, this failure is not a problem of translation; even in the German the parallel fails on the rhetorical level.

Freud labels the clitoris as fetish-counterpart a "minderwertigen Organs." The German for "inferior" or "inferior quality" is "minderwertig," so the translation is fairly direct; however, what is lost in the translation is the sense of value or worth—in German "wert"—that is literally written into the term. The clitoris-organ has a distinctly lesser value and is compared here to the penis-fetish, which has no particular value. The comparison is thus rather lopsided, since the points of comparison are not, as might be expected, between something lesser and something of superior or "hochwertiger" quality. This imbalance is evident in the grammar as well. The significance of the phrase is carried by the adjective "minderwertigen," rather than by the noun, as we would expect. Otherwise, the clitoris would be the normal prototype of an organ, in contrast to the penis as a normal prototype of a fetish. It is not two nouns being weighed in comparison, but an adjective and a noun. To compound this grammatical asymmetry, the descriptive work done by the word "minderwertigen" cannot be separated from its evaluative force, which contrasts to the unmodified term "fetish."

It is not only with the comparison between the fetish and the "minderwertigen Organ" that the parallel is strained; Freud's parallel between the penis and the clitoris is also complicated. While the term "Normalvorbild" is implicitly repeated in the sentence, the term "Penis" is explicitly repeated. Once again, the noun on the male side of the analogy is neutral and unmodified, while the noun on the female side is modified and evaluated as lesser. This time, however, the adjectives are doubled, and they do not overwhelm the modified noun to the point of substituting semantically for it. Whereas on the one hand we have "the penis of the man," on the other hand we have "the woman's real small penis, the clitoris." If the woman's penis is "klein," we might expect the man's penis to be "groß." In such a comparison, each term would be evaluated against the standard of its opposite. Instead, there is this doubled emphasis on smaller and lesser, and thus a strong sense of the female falling short of the standard. In English the doubled adjectives resonate with colloquial emphasis—the woman's penis is real[ly] small, though of course this is only a trick of translation.

What is further remarkable is the vocabulary Freud uses to describe this woman's penis. Instead of using the common German word "wirklich" or even "wahr" to describe the "real, little penis," Freud uses the Latinate term "reale."[3] This word choice is all the more suggestive when we realize that earlier in the text, Freud refers to the "real female genitals" (*SE* 21: 154) as "das wirkliche weibliche Genitale" (*GW* 14: 313). This difference may seem unremarkable, yet it subtly underlines the oddity of calling the clitoris a penis by evoking a different cultural-linguistic framework. At the same time, in the same gesture, the choice of term covers over difference in its insistence that the woman's penis is "real" and marks the difference that is being suppressed. This importation serves as a reminder of the inadequacy of the available terminology, as if to signal the inadequacy of available anatomical interpretations.

Throughout this last sentence, then, Freud slips from a descriptive, positivist, scientific mode to an evaluative one. In the Rivière translation this shift is most apparent, though it is detectable in Strachey. Rivière renders Freud's account of the relation between the penis and the fetish as all-encompassing formula: *all* fetishes have a penis prototype. In the German, Freud only says "of the fetish" [des Fetisch], which Strachey gives as "of fetishes," mysteriously making it plural—notably the only time the term appears in the plural in the translation. Likewise,

Strachey makes the "inferior organs" plural too, but manages to convey Freud's "minderwertigen Organs" equally concisely. In the Rivière translation, however, the account of the relation of the clitoris to its fetish-equivalent is much more verbose: "an organ felt to be inferior." There is no handy, single-word term in English that adequately names that to which the clitoris is to be compared, unlike the case of the penis and fetish. Thus Freud's translator appeals to a sort of circumlocution, as well as to a passive voice construction.

The latter aspect, the introduction of the passive voice, might further be read as an implicit critique: felt to be inferior by whom? Perhaps not by Joan Rivière, whatever Sigmund Freud and James Strachey might think. It is a striking difference, this circumlocution of Rivière's in contrast to Strachey's direct "inferior organ"; the former distances the reader from the evaluation of inferiority, whereas the latter seems to take the evaluation as truth, or at least as neutral assessment. Rivière's rewriting of Freud loses the declarative force of Freud's pronouncement on fetishes by implicitly questioning this pronouncement. Strachey maintains that declarative momentum, and thereby lulls the reader into accepting that the clitoris is indeed inferior, as if "inferior" were a neutral rather than a value-laden description. But if Rivière's translation raises the question, for whom?, Strachey's version more directly raises the question, inferior to what?—is the clitoris inferior as an organ, or as a penis?

Thus the parallel structure is not, in fact, parallel; indeed, the very basis for the comparison falls apart, as we are unable to compare penises and clitorises or fetishes and inferior organs because they are collapsed into being the same thing—no difference holds them apart to make a comparison interesting or worthwhile. This breakdown in the parallel structure shows us Freud is implicitly and contradictorily arguing much more in the last part of the analogy: both that the clitoris is inferior *and* that it is the equivalent of a penis. This argument is in fact the real model for fetishism and for sexual difference in Freud.

If we reexamine this last sentence, we will see that Freud's ambivalence about sexual difference is critical to setting the stakes for fetishism. This passage suggests that if we are to understand what fetishism is in psychoanalysis, we must acknowledge its relation to the penis, whether or not we agree with Freud that this organ serves as a "normal prototype." The reductiveness and logical slippage invited by the standard reading of this sentence also forecloses upon the disturbance produced by Freud's naming the clitoris the woman's penis, introducing a striking ambiguity of sexual difference. The final sentence of "Fetishism" clearly suggests that the "penis" may not be the sole anatomical preserve of one gender. Thus, the assertion that the fetish in some way relates to or even depends on the penis does not automatically exclude women from fetishism.[4]

The operation of gender in this last sentence is particularly striking once it is extended to include all of the elements: man is to woman as penis is to clitoris as fetish is to inferiority. From this sense of inferiority comes shame. Elsewhere Freud points out that "shame . . . is considered to be a feminine characteristic *par excellence* but . . . has as its purpose, we believe, concealment of genital deficiency" (*SE* 22: 132). In thus articulating this analogy at the end of "Fetishism," Freud connects and contrasts shame with fetishism, implying that fetishism is a masculine characteristic par excellence. This gesture also reinforces gender differences that are culturally expressed as an anatomically based sexual difference between men and women. Indeed the view that female fetishism is an "oxymoron," as Naomi Schor has noted (365), or that documented cases of female fetishism are exceptions, if not impossibilities, buttresses the notion that fetishism is a male perversion or preserve. This final sentence of Freud's, however, is not the last word, even as it may seem to foreclose—or disavow—the possibility of female fetishism.

The point of raising the question of female fetishism is not merely to insert women's bodies into the text, but to open up the space to examine and interrogate the gendered frameworks that structure our knowledge, and to recognize these frameworks as contingent rather than absolute. Thus, in recasting the question in terms of female fetishism, I do not contest the connection between the penis and the fetish, but rather the way this notion of the fetish has been construed to hinge on having a penis, and a narrowly defined one at that. Moreover, the challenge to a narrow definition of penis derives from Freud's own texts, since his definition of what a penis is changes in rather interesting and often ambivalent ways throughout his work, notably in "Fetishism." Sometimes a cigar may only be a cigar for Freud, but quite often a penis is something other than a penis. Thus, even if Freud asserts that the prototype of a fetish is a man's penis, we cannot necessarily take this penis at face value: first, because it is qualified as "the penis of the man," a logical overstatement given the human context (who else would have one?), but second, because it is juxtaposed in the same sentence with the "real little penis of the woman." Here, a penis is not a mark of sexual difference, but of sexuality, which either gender has, though to different effect. Both a man and a woman have a penis—and Freud even specifically asserts that the woman's penis is "real," albeit little. This equivalence may seem to imply a fundamental sexual indifference, as if male and female anatomy or sexuality are basically the same; such a view resonates with Freud's idea that there is only one libido. However a significant difference remains here, one which is not contingent upon presence or absence, but upon both size and what one does with one's penis—that is, whether one bases one's fetish on it or one's sense of inferiority.

This difference is important for aiding our understanding of what a fetish does. If the choices are fetishize or feel inferior, then the fetish could be understood as what enables one to construct a positive—or at least adequate—sense of one's self. In a discussion of the strategic emergence of fetishism in the course of a male's sexual development, Louise Kaplan tells us that

> The fetish is designed to reassure the boy that he has control over the mysterious . . . cycles of erection, ejaculation, orgasm, and detumescence. The fetish also gives him a feeling that he can modulate his hostile aggressive strivings. . . . (39)

This claim leads me to suggest that fetishism may indeed be instrumental in constructing an autonomous subjectivity, enabling one to have control over oneself, a form of subjectivity hardly encouraged in women under patriarchy but certainly crucial for men. Such a reading need not obscure the very real existence of pathological cases of fetishism that in their extremity seek to deny the subjectivity of the sexual partner. Rather, this reading emphasizes that fetishism, far from being a marginal or extreme perversion, in fact is a central route to constructing a sexual subjectivity, or subjectivity in general. This subjectivity may depend on a particular object, and thus be viewed by many as flawed. Nonetheless, because that object is inherently subordinate, this dependence is useful or instrumental rather than threatening to one's creation of a whole, independent self.

Fetishism thus offers a third route between autonomy and dependence, two poles which have been traditionally mapped onto masculinity and femininity, respectively. This reading suggests that the subject-object distinction is a critical difference for fetishism; even if fetishism seeks to obliterate other differences, it relies on the difference between what a subject is and what an object is. In other words, the very ontological difference of the fetish object renders it less threatening than another subject would be, and that enables one to assert oneself as autonomous, however conflicted and ambivalent this autonomy may be. It is perhaps not accidental then that fetishism triangulates not only gender binaries but the binary between dependence and autonomy, two

fundamentally distinct ways of being in the world. As the binary gender matrix is deconstructed, and its grip on our assumptions about sexual difference loosened, the ontological difference at stake in fetishism
may become not only more important, but more productive.[5]

Implicit in these options, as the gendered matrix underscores, is
the fact that context—specifically, what Kaplan calls the social gender
stereotype—is a crucial determinant for the development of fetishism.
Unquestioned in Freud's formulation is the idea that the man's penis
guarantees the ascension to subjectivity (enabling him to feel superior
to objects) while the woman's penis only reminds her of her failure to
achieve that subjectivity (making her feel inferior to subjects). Women
could not be fetishists precisely because they could not be expected to
develop the same form of independent subjectivity as a man, or feel that
their sexuality could achieve the same potency as his phallic penis
seemed to guarantee. But what if the context were to change? What if
this gendered matrix, which affirms only a rigid binary sexual difference and distributes power differentially according to that difference,
were challenged or undermined? What if anyone could potentially
have the penis? The association of the clitoris with inferiority merely
serves to underscore the interpretation of female genitalia as inadequate for setting the standard, indicating, following patriarchal logic,
that women are deviant from men; however, it fails to account for how
that sense of inferiority may have come about.

The parallel suggests that shame is a perverse reaction just as
fetishism is. But the juxtaposition also raises the following question:
why would a sense of inferiority derive from the clitoris? One response
would be that the clitoris is not enough of a penis—in both the sense of
being enough like, and in the more literal sense of not having enough
penis-substance, of skin, nerves, and blood vessels. In order for the clitoris to be perceived as inferior, there must be some sense of commonality with the penis, some point of identity that enables the comparison.
This necessity suggests the interpretation rests on sexual indifference,
rather than a sense of sexual difference which would have focused on
contrast. Given this association, we are prompted to ask whether this
connection, the analogy between penis and clitoris, is any more real or
true than the suggestion that the fetish models itself on the man's penis.
The objects held together here by association are not only not identical,
but may not even resemble each other. (What penis looks like a strip of
velvet or lace undergarment?)[6] The analogy presumes sexual difference
but works through sexual sameness in order to conclude by asserting
both inferiority and fetishism. What enables this move from sameness
to the sharp distinction between inferiority and fetishism? Here it be-

comes clear that the analogy seeks to conceal what it so brazenly reveals: the contingency of interpretations of anatomy.

Despite the distribution of the word "penis" on either side of the analogy, underpinning Freud's description of fetishism is an assumption that morphology can only be interpreted one way, that a penis is always sufficient unto itself and a clitoris can never be sufficient, but rather indicates lack. It is clear that Freud feels no need to clarify anything regarding the man's penis but doubles the number of words to describe the woman's penis. Yet fetishism results from an inadequacy of the penis, a sense that one is not enough and thus a supplement is required. Moreover, this inadequacy is inextricable from the more commonly recognized association of overvaluation with fetishism—setting up an ideal which the penis can never hope to live up to. We must thus look outside of the penis-clitoris analogy to find the distinction that intervenes between fetishism and inadequacy, between overvaluation and undervaluation.

In the construction of the fetish here—grafted from the penis of the man—the apparently equally real penis of the woman is feminized as a prototype of inferiority. This feminization is particularly striking because so often the clitoris figures in Freud's texts as masculine.[7] Freud quite frequently reads the clitoris as the penis, in the essays on "Fetishism" and "Femininity," as well as in his earlier *Three Essays on the Theory of Sexuality.* Freud's doubled strategy of literalizing and metaphorizing these body parts in his text complicates our reading. To metaphorize the clitoris as the "penis-equivalent" (*SE* 22: 118), produces a destabilization of the univocal, literalized hold that "penis" claims as a term referring to male genitalia—in effect, it renders "this penis . . . no longer the same as it was before" (*SE* 21: 154). "Penis" becomes instead a term that signifies the site of pleasure and self-gratification in the phallic stage. However, a consequence of this destabilization is that the penis cannot attain its phallic significance through its purported absence in half the population. That is, if everyone has some version of the penis, some analogous focus of pleasure in the phallic stage, sexual "difference" has to be constituted on some other basis than lack and castration. This understanding of fetishism highlights the fact that the "penis" is not a unique or univocal signifier, as a reductive anatomical reading would posit; instead, structurally and inherently, a "penis" must accommodate and fragment into a number of different interpretations.

Two possibilities, which may be maintained simultaneously, present themselves immediately. On the one hand, the penis in fetishism's primal scene functions as a signifier of difference in comparison to the phallus (as symbol of control or mastery); Elizabeth Grosz works on this distinction in her reading of fetishism, which posits the boy's penis as insignificant in the presence of the mother's phallus. On the other hand, the penis also operates unremarked in Freud's text as a metaphor for sameness, a figure for common ground, but one that elides a certain anatomical or (hetero)sexual difference. These examples suggest that the "penis" is not something that can be taken for granted as obvious; they push us to question how "penis" is being interpreted and put to use.

There is, however, more at stake in this final paragraph of "Fetishism" than a difference between masculine and feminine, or between penis and clitoris, or fetishism and shame. At work in this passage is also the sexual difference between "normal" and "perverse." The paradoxical nature of sexual difference we have already explored is only heightened by Freud's oxymoronic claim that the man's penis is a "normal prototype" of a perversion, which is, by definition, not normal. The use of the word "normal" here raises a red flag for any reader of Freud who is aware of his skepticism toward this category throughout his work, his "reluctance to view matters of human sexuality in terms of normality or abnormality" (Kaplan 47). Although Freud most likely intends for the term "normal prototype" to suggest the standard from which the perversion deviates, the implication remains that some other prototype of this perversion could exist. The contrast of "normal prototype" and the sweeping generalization "all fetishes" (or in German, the abstraction "des Fetisch") makes for an interesting twist. The variety of fetish objects is obscured, reduced down to the penis model.[8] If the non-normal prototype of a fetish were the woman's "real little penis" would female fetishism then be a perverse perversion? Instead of a normal perversion, would it be a perverse normality?

The ambivalence in the term "penis" as something which could belong to either a man or a woman parallels Freud's recurrent ambivalence over the term "normal"—the tension in his work between his drive to interrogate the foundations of our assumptions about the status quo and his resistance to radically disrupting some of those received ideas. Asserting the penis as a "normal prototype" reinscribes it as a standard, counterbalancing the potential disruption to patriarchal hierarchy posed by its equivalence with the clitoris. Both the term "normal" and the term "penis" in this passage seem intended to function descriptively as a standard of comparison, rather than prescriptively through evaluation. By juxtaposing "normal prototype" with the man's and woman's penis, Freud indeed may aim to undermine the prescriptive force behind either "normal" or "penis." But while he may succeed to some extent with regard to "normal" because of its instability throughout his work, he is less successful with "penis."

There is a double edge to Freud's unsettling of the overdetermined and exclusionary claims of biological essentialists. The radical gesture of interrogating how the "norm" is established—the gesture of calling the clitoris a penis—is undercut by the failure to question the penis as a standard. The tension between Freud's use of the term "penis" as a gender-neutral and technical term and the highly gendered significance of the term outside of Freud's texts—the very meaning of which gives his equivocation of the penis and clitoris its radical quality— remains implicit rather than acknowledged. The singularity of the choice of "penis" as the gender-neutral classification is particularly striking, given that the clitoris is never similarly taken up as a technical term but is instead effaced or disposed of. Indeed, there is a thematic insistence, throughout Freud's work on sexual difference, on the clitoris's inferiority, which only comes about through its evaluative comparison with the penis, its thematic masculinization.[9] If the term "penis" is a theoretical, scientific term that includes the clitoris, it suggests that we should have another "real" name for the man's penis, one less sexually indifferent.

Using the term "penis" without explicitly acknowledging this instability presumes that the readers already understand what that designation might mean—that is, that we know what a penis is. But taking Freud's schema here to its radical conclusion suggests that perhaps we do not know what a penis is, any more than we know what normal is: both have to be accounted for, rather than presumed. The final lesson of this final paragraph, then, may well be to apply to the term "penis" the same skepticism we readers of Freud have developed towards "normal." If we take the term penis in the same vein as we take the term normal, then reading Freud will shake up assumptions about sexual difference—that is, by telling us something new, rather than something we already know or would expect.

Penis, Phallus, Fetish

At the outset of "Fetishism," Freud hones the psychoanalytic definition of the fetish: "Wenn ich nun mitteile, der Fetisch ist ein Penisersatz, so werde ich gewiß Enttäuschung hervorrufen" (GW 14: 312). "When I now announce that the fetish is a substitute for the penis, I shall certainly create disappointment" (SE 21: 152). Rivière's translation, "When I now disclose that the fetish is a penis-substitute I shall certainly arouse disappointment" (214–15), comes a little closer to Freud's German at two points: in the more direct rendering of "Penisersatz" as "penis-substitute," but, more importantly, in the translation of "hervorrufen" as "arouse" rather than "create." Rivière's word-choice, perhaps uninten-

tionally, sets up an ironic tension in this clause, given that disappointment tends to quell arousal rather than be arousal's aim. But apart from
the sexual resonances, "arouse" comes closer than "create" to the sense in
the original of there being something already there, merely needing to be
evoked. "Hervorrufen" has as its root the verb "rufen," to call or to send
for; while there may not necessarily be something there to call forth, at
the very least the hope or expectation that such a thing would be there remains implicit in the word. "Create," on the other hand, has no such resonances; indeed, it suggests that nothing was there in the first place, so it
had to be made. My concern in attending to this inevitable slippage of
meaning in translation, however, is not the question of which translation
is better or worse, but rather what is at stake in this disappointment—
where is this disappointment coming from, and what does it mark?

At the very least, Freud's choice of "hervorrufen" supposes that
disappointment is in the air, lurking somewhere. At first glance, this
disappointment is merely a rhetorical move, since if the fetish were only
a penis-substitute, Freud would not need to write this article to explain
further the nature of fetishism. The statement is straightforward, declarative, despite its theatrical overtones; it presumes that everyone
already knows what fetishism is, and certainly implies that the knowledgeable audience might have guessed the answer from the lead-in to
this assertion, in which Freud introduces the well-known case of the
shine on the nose. There is reason to think that at least some of Freud's
audience would not find the penis-substitute theory a revelation, since
Freud has touched on fetishism in quite a few of his writings. Thus,
Freud's belief in his audience's disappointment is not merely an empty
rhetorical device but an acknowledgment of real possibility that they do
already know this much about fetishism.[10] The disappointment thus
seems to mark some anxiety on Freud's part about satisfying the cu-
riosity of his readers; he expects that the penis-substitute answer is no
news flash to them. Since this is his first published article focusing exclusively on the phenomenon after years of commenting on it within
other texts, the anxiety may be attributed to Freud's sense that he ought
to say something new rather than repeat what he has said elsewhere.
Whatever the cause of the anxiety, whatever expectations Freud projects
onto his audience, this much is clear: the disappointment is certain. ("I
shall certainly arouse disappointment. . . .")

After acknowledging this inevitable disappointment, Freud continues: "Ich beeile mich darum hinzuzufügen, nicht der Ersatz eines be-
liebigen . . . Penis." "I hasten to add that it is not a substitute for any
chance penis. . . ." Freud's haste in moving on suggests that he is not
satisfied with this penis-substitution answer. He wants to move quickly

beyond the inevitable disappointment this explanation brings. Interestingly, at the end of this paragraph in the text, Freud has a footnote that states "This interpretation was mentioned in 1910, without any reason given for it, in my study on Leonardo da Vinci." Freud's haste, in this light, turns out to be not so hasty, since he has taken seventeen years to give the reasons for this interpretation. Likewise, what Freud acknowledges as obvious is in fact not so obvious, the disappointment not so certain. There is a discrepancy between how Freud feels about the penis-substitute explanation and how his audience likely feels, since in truth they all cannot be expected to already know everything Freud has said on the subject of fetishism. Let us examine the larger picture, the fuller context of this first revelation of what the fetish is. Here is what Freud tells us:

> Wenn ich nun mitteile, der Fetisch ist ein Penisersatz, so werde ich gewiß Enttäuschung hervorrufen. Ich beeile mich darum hinzuzufügen, nicht der Ersatz eines beliebigen, sondern eines bestimmten, ganz besonderen Penis, der in frühen Kinderjahren eine große Bedeutung hat, aber später verloren geht. (GW 14: 312)

> When I now announce that the fetish is a substitute for the penis, I shall certainly create disappointment; so I hasten to add that it is not a substitute for any chance penis, but for a particular and quite special penis that had been extremely important in early childhood but had later been lost. (SE 21: 152)

> When I now disclose that the fetish is a penis-substitute I shall certainly arouse disappointment; I hasten to add that it is not a substitute for any chance penis, but for a particular quite special penis that had been extremely important in early childhood but was afterwards lost. (Rivière 215)

Freud's anxiety hastens him to substitute the shamefully inadequate explanation of fetishism as a penis-substitute for the more satisfying explanation of fetishism as a substitute for a quite special penis that once was extremely important and has since been lost.[11] In short, at the rhetorical level Freud indulges in the fetishistic move of thinking that the thing he knows is inferior and substituting it with a more satisfactory belief in an illusory object. The special qualities of this recovered penis serve to compensate for the disappointment raised by the penis-substitute explanation.

Yet even this explanation is not sufficient; it must be shored up by two other iterations of the same idea, which only gradually layer their meanings onto the overall significance of the fetish. Freud continues with the second iteration: "Das heißt: er sollte normalerweise aufgegeben werden, aber gerade der Fetisch ist dazu bestimmt, ihn vor dem Untergang zu behüten" (*GW*). "That is to say: it should normally have been given up, but the fetish is precisely designed to preserve it from extinction" (*SE*). The third reiteration is a much more marked repetition of the previous formulations:

> Um es klarer zu sagen, der Fetisch is der Ersatz für den Phallus des Weibes (der Mutter), an den das Knäblein geglaubt hat und auf den es—wir wissen warum—nicht verzichten will. (*GW*)

> To put it plainly, the fetish is the substitute for the woman's (mother's) phallus which the little boy once believed in and does not wish to forego—we know why. (Rivière)

If Freud's certainty of disappointing his audience with his initial announcement of the penis-substitute explanation of fetish is connected to an anxiety about repeating his earlier discussions about fetishism, that anxiety about repetition has clearly dissipated here. Indeed, Freud seems so satisfied by his elaboration on the penis-substitute theory that he spins it out further through repetitive clarification. Yet this elaboration ends with a cagey "we know why," once again playing into the presupposition of shared knowledge, which had undergirded the certain disappointment. It is only in the next paragraph that the nonknowledgeable audience might be let in on the secret of the young boy's ("Knäblein"—a clearly gendered term) emphasis on the mother's penis. This penis is special because it had guaranteed the boy was like his mother, and because its loss promises that the boy could lose his. For Freud, as for the young boy, what makes this second elaboration more satisfying, more adequate, than the disappointing revelation of the penis-substitute is the value put on the quite special penis. This value is derived not from the thing itself, but from the threatened absence of the thing.

In a slightly different reiteration in her essay "Lesbian Fetishism?" Elizabeth Grosz points out, "The fetish is thus the substitute for, the talisman of, the phallus . . . not just any old phallus. . . . but his mother's" (42). Juxtaposing her formulation with Freud's here underscores the slippage between penis and phallus that appears in Freud at the crucial moment: Freud's "particular quite special penis" is in fact also a phallus, and a maternal phallus at that. We have moved from the "disappointing" revelation that the fetish is a penis-substitute to the more satisfying and interesting understanding that the fetish is a maternal phallus substitute. There is much at stake in distinguishing between penis and phallus; while the former refers to a part of the body, the phallus is not a part of any body, but is a symbolic figure through which an individual may claim a degree of power and authority. Freud's substitution of "phallus" for "penis" in this first definition is therefore significant for its lack of rigor.

At first glance, it seems that the facility with which Freud quietly substitutes "penis" with "phallus" is easily explained by acknowledging that it is not so much the penis itself that is substituted here, but rather, what it signifies or guarantees within a phallocentric or patriarchal culture. But such a glib substitution is troubling to twentieth-century readers returning to Freud after reading Lacan, although it would, of course, be anachronistic to insist that Freud maintain the Lacanian distinction between penis and phallus so rigorously. Much psychoanalytic discussion has been directed toward our understanding this guarantee, and the term "phallus" has been introduced as a way of distinguishing between the penis as an anatomical organ and the phallus as the arbiter of what the presence or absence of that organ signifies.[12] But what is at stake is not a simple substitution of arguably interchangeable terms, "penis" and "phallus," as reading Grosz with Freud will show.

At the level of the text in "Fetishism," this slip from penis to phallus serves to avert the shock of saying "the woman's penis," holding off till the end of the article its explicit articulation, but intimating the point nonetheless. In other words, this ambivalence allows the woman to have a penis (but only "a particular quite special penis") and not have the penis (because she has, instead, a phallus). Indeed, this attempt to avert or defer the shocking revelation of the woman's special penis provides a different, though equally plausible, explanation for why Freud feels compelled to present his theory of the fetish through such repetitive rhetoric. Furthermore, it is disappointing only that the fetish would turn out to be a penis-substitute; what is not disappointing, what, indeed, is so shocking that we must ease into this idea through terminological substitution, is that this penis for which the fetish substitutes belongs to a woman, a mother.[13]

Moreover, what this lack of rigorous distinction between penis and phallus reveals is that the fetish cannot be anchored to what Freud concludes to be its prototypical basis, the "penis of the man." When the basis of the fetish is first defined in the text, the penis becomes a phallus—the quite special penis turns out to be a maternal phallus. This phallus is then "lost" in two different ways in this text. First, diegetically, it is lost to the boy-child who will become the fetishist in order to assuage this loss. Secondly, on the level of rhetoric, this phallus is lost in Freud's definition of the fetish prototype, since he resorts in the final sentence to the man's penis. Finally, there is a significant but unremarked shift from the boy's penis, which is endangered by the sight of his mother's genitals (*SE* 21: 153), to the man's penis which now serves as the fetish prototype (*SE* 21: 157).[14]

We can look at the chain of loss and substitution in this initial definition of fetishism even more closely. Is this slippage between "penis" and "phallus" itself a fetishistic substitution, supplementing one inadequate term with a more significant or weighty one that will better ground the meaning because of its private significance? In this case, the "phallus" is the fetish object that bolsters the "penis." If fetishistic substitution is such a part of the discourse, can one write about fetishism without employing the logic of fetishism? In other words, to understand fetishism, do we have to take up the position of the fetishist, or is there an outside to fetishism which still gives us understanding of the phenomenon? This question is important since one of the key aspects in Freud's description of the fetish object is its undetectability, the fact that its significance "is not known to other people" (*SE* 21: 154). In this sense, the fetish object is the very opposite of the penis, which is the thing we all must have knowledge of, whether we "have" one or not. In this light, one has to wonder at the appropriateness of the substitution of the penis by the fetish object, since they are semiotically opposite.

In trying to answer the epistemological question of whether we can understand fetishism without being fetishists, we can examine Freud's exegesis of the term. Freud tells us that he arrived at his definition because the fetish "revealed itself so naturally and seemed to me so compelling" (*SE* 21: 152). ("Sie ergab sich so ungezwungen und erschien mir so zwingend" [*GW* 14: 312].) The fact that he can employ such straightforward and emphatic words as "ungezwungen" and "zwingend" suggests that he believes it is possible to have access to knowledge about fetishism from outside of the fetishistic relation, since a fetishist would be ambivalent, if not equivocal. Freud's certainty here indicates that far from being a purely private language, fetishism is accessible to those who are not fetishists, who are outside fetishism's semiotic economy. Indeed, as Freud's certainty here shows, fetishism can be explained quite directly, its arguments can be cogent and compelling. This not only enables Freud to be definitive rather than hopelessly ambivalent (as a fetishist would be), but it also suggests that the fetish object is not nearly as inscrutable as the fetishist may think.[15]

Yet this passage presents an interesting twist, precisely because the definition of fetishism hinges upon the categorical or the generalizable. Unless we too are fetishists, we cannot understand the significance of the specific fetish object, but only the categorical definition. In the context of reading "Fetishism," this leads to an odd effect: insofar as we know what it signifies, the penis is something to which we all have access, unlike the fetish, whose significance we cannot know. However, unlike the penis—which may be a phallus or a clitoris, which may belong to a man or a woman or a mother—the fetish is by Freud's account clearly discernible, and he manages to list quite a number of them. Oddly enough, in this case definition and significance—the difference between what a thing is and what it does—are mutually exclusive.

This point reminds us how deeply knowledge is structured by the framework of interpretation, because interpretation most deeply affects our understanding of a thing in its function or uses; we can usually pretty much agree on objective descriptions. If we go *into* Freud's account rather than *by* it (and thus think functionally *through* rather than categorically *about* fetishism), the fetish may maintain a certain stability in its categorical qualities, while the penis becomes increasingly unstable and uncategorizable in its trajectory from man to woman and from penis to phallus. Fetishism offers us knowledge that we cannot get by dint of objective observation, by just looking at the evidence head-on; it requires a more oblique, and shifting, strategy of knowing. The shared knowledge of the fetish marks the paradoxical possibility of establishing common knowledge with room for different, perhaps contradictory or conflicting, but equally useful interpretations.

Grosz's reliance on the phallus rather than the penis as the basis for the fetish seems to offer a way out. This clarification may even seem to provide a better perspective on fetishism, because it avoids the fetishistic effect that Freud's indeterminacy around the "penis" and the "phallus"—or indeed, around the "penis" alone—produces. Grosz disposes of any recourse to "real" penises, affirming that the key is the representation of the organ, not the organ itself. Unlike in Freud, where everyone is presumed to know what a penis is, in Grosz's account we have no relation to this real organ and so must work solely within the symbolic order and its organ, the phallus. On this basis, Grosz is able to claim that, "The child's perception of the mother's lack and his symbolic utilization of the last object witnessed before he 'sees' the missing phallus . . . do not adequately explain fetishism because the fetish is a substitute for the phallus" (44). Here then, the fetish is significantly not a substitute for the penis, and the interchangeability between penis and phallus is disrupted. The fetish, by offering the safeguard against the loss of the maternal phallus or the woman's penis (which Freud tells us, both above and then implicitly at the end of "Fetishism," she has "in spite of it all") retroactively confers significance onto this phallus.

Grosz's reading seems to simplify things by clarifying that when we discuss fetishism, we are into the realm of signification. Her distinction between penis and phallus seems a move to apply Occam's razor, to more clearly define the Freudian indeterminacy regarding the penis and phallus by eliminating the unnecessary term. Yet that is not the answer, as her text makes evident:

> From being a real organ, the penis is transformed into an imaginary object dividing the sexes according to its presence or absence, possessed by some and desired by others. Only then can it function as a symbolic object (an object of union/exchange) between the sexes. The phallus distributes access to the social categories invested with various power relations. (44)

This passage is interesting for its marked gap between the discussion of the penis as symbolic object and the commentary on the phallus. There is no account of the difference between the effects of the symbolic penis and those of the phallus, because the penis has been left behind in the process of becoming a symbolic object. By striving to eliminate excess terminology, Grosz has struck the difference between the phallus and the penis from the discussion and ignored the fact that even the "real organ" is loaded with symbolic meaning. This move, which is fundamental to her argument about the basis of fetishism and who might be a fetishist, reinforces rather than eliminates the need for the distinction between penis and phallus, remapping it in the split between the real and the symbolic. Grosz rhetorically transforms the penis into the phallus; however, this transformation is not without loss. The change in terms fails to offer a solution to the problems of the defining basis of the fetish. Rather than clarify by using more precise synonyms, the changes call attention to the inadequacy of these three terms' substitution for each other.

Thus, like Freud, Grosz ends up slipping between the terms, despite her recourse to Lacan's distinction. The fetish and the phallus become indistinguishable as "penis-substitutes." The Lacanian distinction separates out and defines the phallus, but not the complexities of the penis, which in Freud's text is not obviously or consistently a man's genital organ. Shifting to the symbolic realm, insisting on the "phallus" rather than the "penis" does not resolve the problem, but instead it raises the question of whether the fetish (or, for that matter, the phallus) adequately serves as a penis substitute. In the end, the distinction between the penis and the phallus is not as important as the recognition of the constructedness of each. Whether we follow Grosz's line of argument that posits the phallus as the basis for fetishism (where the phallus is not an essential, anatomically determined attribute), or whether we prefer Freud's closing assertion that the fetish is modeled on the penis (where the question of exactly who has a penis radically destabilizes anatomical determinism), the texts open up the possibility for anyone, not just men, to become a fetishist.

Reflecting on this possibility highlights the narrowness of an understanding of sexual difference as binary heterosexual difference. It also shows that fetishism, rather than serving as a strategy to bolster a heterosexual aim (as Freud claims it does [SE 21: 154]), in fact threatens heterosexuality's claim to naturalness—a claim founded in the assumption that anatomy is beyond interpretation or construction. In this important shift from a paradigm that presumes anatomy to be fully evident and overdetermined to a multiply interpretable paradigm, we begin to see how we could think sexual difference differently. Indeed, we must think differently if we are to avoid disappointment, for the disappointment with the mere penis-substitute account of fetishism—the one that would imply any chance penis could be substituted when in fact we would only be satisfied with the quite special penis of the woman—lies with thinking we already know what a penis is. Instead, Freud is strategically ambiguous about what a penis is, and thus the very basis of his exposition challenges binary and mutually exclusive definitions of sexual difference. What he reveals is not so much that the special penis is that of a woman, but that we will have to rethink what we know a penis to be.

Once we understand that the first thing to come into question is the fundamental, defining term, that in fact we cannot say for sure what a penis is, we can see what a problem it is to figure out what could *substitute* for that penis. If the apparent grounds of fetishism—the simple "given" of the penis—are complicated, as indeed Freud's last sentence suggests, we find we have no standard to which to appeal to anchor the process of substitution. We might be better served to think of the penis as the substitute for the fetish rather than the other way around, since the fetish has a clearer delineation in this text, as the thing which provides reassurance and enables difference—sexual or ontological—to be negotiated.

To further interrogate the possibility that these terms, penis, phallus, and fetish, are not simple substitutions, let us look at another important difference raised by these accounts. The juxtaposition of Grosz's

and Freud's definitions of a fetish elicits a contradiction that goes beyond the distinction between the penis and the phallus: what does it
mean if the prototype of the fetish is the man's penis, and yet if it is the
mother's phallus which the fetish substitutes for and sustains? The difference is not only a question of the distinction between the penis and
the phallus, or an issue of whose organ it is—the mother's or the man's.
The difference is also a question of priority and order. The difference between prototype and substitute hinges on order: the prototype comes
first, and the substitute after. Yet because it comes first, the prototype is
inherently less satisfying than the actual thing; it is the model that is put
through the paces to determine what kinks need to be worked out,
what improvements need to be made, what corrections are necessary.
The prototype is a projection of what will come, but because it is the
first model, it is also already marked as not living up to the ideal; it may
be functional, but it may not necessarily work as well as the later models will. This connotation makes Freud's final pronouncement particularly striking, since the man's penis is contrasted with the inferiority of
the woman's penis/clitoris. The substitute, on the other hand, is expected to function as the thing, although it may differ quite a bit from it
in form. The degree to which the substitute functions as well as the
thing itself correlates to the degree to which it is satisfying. When a substitute does not work, it is not so much corrected as discarded.

This simple relation of before and after, prototype and substitute,
becomes complicated in Freud's text because the discussion of the substitute comes well before the disclosure of the prototype at the end. In describing the effect of fetishism in the mind of the fetishist, Freud tells us:

> Ja, das Weib hat im Psychischen dennoch einen Penis, aber dieser
> Penis ist nicht mehr dasselbe, das er früher war. Etwas anderes ist
> an seine Stelle getreten, ist sozusagen zu seinem Ersatz ernannt
> worden und ist nun der Erbe des Interesses, das sich dem
> früheren zugewendet hatte. (*GW* 14: 313)

> Yes, in his mind the woman *has* got a penis, in spite of everything;
> but this penis is no longer the same as it was before. Something
> else has taken its place, has been appointed its substitute, as it
> were, and now inherits the interest which was formerly directed
> to its predecessor. (*SE* 21: 154)

This passage illustrates the tension between the first scenario of the
fetish (substituting for the mother's penis) and the last depiction of the
fetish (taking the man's penis as prototype). Before the fetish, there is

the young boy's belief in the mother's penis; the fetish emerges as that belief is revised, and the fetish is both the substitute for and the new interpretation of this imaginary object. But why is the mother's penis not the prototype of the fetish?

The answer to this question lies in another aspect of the definition of prototype, the sense that it exhibits all the qualities typical of a thing, that it sets the standard. Making the man's penis the prototype establishes its qualities as the essential ones of a fetish. This makes the man's penis seem the natural or normal place to look for the substitute for the maternal phallus, thereby reinforcing the sense that the mother's body deviates from the masculine norm, but also reinforcing the idea that looking anywhere else than the man's penis in order to "correct" that deviation is perverse, unnatural. The penis is reaffirmed as the true guarantor of masculinity while the fetish is a sham, an imitator. But what are the qualities of a penis, especially in this text? The normative force of the prototype holds true only when we know what a penis is, or rather, more specifically if we overlook how this text destabilizes our certain knowledge. Indeed, the final paragraph's assertion that the fetish prototype is the man's penis seems like it would rouse the same disappointment that the earlier paragraph's assertion of the fetish as a penis-substitute does, insofar as each reiterates what is already known, rather than reveal to us something new about fetishism.

However, just as Freud muddled binary sexual difference in the final sentence, so does he confound priority in the passage cited just above, disrupting the seeming conclusiveness of his final sentence in yet another way. Claiming the man's penis as the fetish prototype implicitly puts knowledge of it prior to knowledge of the mother's penis, the substituted thing. Yet the whole scenario Freud concocts for the development of fetishism in fact models the fetish on the maternal phallus, not the man's penis. Both in the lecture on fetishism and in his description of the etiology of fetishism, what comes first is the mother's penis, not the man's. Thus, there are two priorities at stake here: textual priority—that is, which scenario is presented first to the reader—and theoretical priority—that is, which scenario happens first in the mind of the fetishist. In the development of a case of fetishism, the mother's penis seems to have come first, but the final revelation of the fetish prototype seems to lay claim to the true priority of the man's penis.

If we insist on a conservative interpretation of fetishism, that all it does is allow men to refuse to acknowledge fully sexual difference and still participate in heterosexuality, then the priority of the man's penis as fetish prototype will dominate our reading. If, however, we take seriously the instability of the penis in Freud's text, we are challenged to

affirm the priority of the mother's penis in both Freud's text and the
fetishist's fantasy. The man's penis has meaning only in the sense of being able to offer its seemingly incontestable realness in contrast to the
mother's imaginary penis. But even this offering is challenged in
Freud's text, through his rhetorical insistence that the woman's penis,
too, is real.

What this reading of priority reveals is that existence in "Fetishism" is hardly based on realness; rather it is the force of interpretation that brings something into existence, that makes it matter whether
it is real or imaginary. What counts is not whether something is real or
not, but the effect it has. This emphasis strategically erodes the boundary between reality and fantasy, underscoring the important role of interpretation, for that is what puts things in an order and creates
meaning. Freud himself indulges in a fantasmatic temporality in the un-
folding of his theory of fetishism. Only reality is subject to the linear ordering of time, while fantasy allows a more fluid relation to time,
enabling the subject to project forward (as Lacan's mirror-stage infant
does) or backwards (as Freud's fetishist does) through time.[16] The tension in Freud's prioritization of the penis, phallus, and fetish emphasizes the fantastic aspect of fetishism over any real basis. What this
gradual transformation over the course of Freud's essay from any
chance penis, to the mother's phallus, to the woman's penis, to the
man's penis elucidates is the mutability of temporality as well as sexuality (in the interrelated sense of gender distinctions and sexual activities) in fantasy life. By warping the priority of the prototype and the
substitute, Freud calls attention to the sense of time, framing the contrast between fantasy and reality through the question raised by the
very penis-phallus conundrum: in what symbolic order can a mother
have a phallus, or a man a penis?

This question raises the prospect that the fetish is the mechanism
by which we are able to maintain the distinction between the penis and
the phallus, precisely because it is the thing which substitutes for both.
The penis is a figure constructed through an interpretation of the real or
actual, while the phallus is a figure constituted through the symbolic.
The contradictory nature of the fetish asserts and draws upon both reality and fantasy simultaneously. Thus it can come after either the penis
or the phallus. Yet only in the act of substitution does the fetish put the
penis and phallus in a temporal sequence, which it anchors by being the
latest and last term. The symbolic figure in retrospect appears to be
modeled on the real one, but only because at last things can be put in an
order. The moment when priority makes a difference is also the moment when the penis is transformed into the phallus. The fetish creates

a new relation among these terms, going beyond either the symbolic or the real. In so doing, it simultaneously distinguishes the penis from the phallus and shows how they can be collapsed. Their collapse is possible because the whole operation actually works on the level of signification that is grounded in the fetish, not on some real existence such as a penis seems to offer. As Grosz reminds us, "The penis must already function as a signifier, an imaginary object, from the moment the boy attributes it to the mother" (44).

The fetish is thus not merely another term in the chain of substitutions, equivalent with either the penis or the phallus; it must be something different. In order to function as a substitute, the fetish must be understood as neither penis (in the ambiguous Freudian sense) nor phallus (in the symbolic Lacanian sense). The fetish falls short of "the real thing" even as it provides the paradigm for the excess of "the Thing." The fetish renders the difference between the penis and phallus visible, precisely because it is supposed to substitute. It is, after all, only around the naming of the mother's supplement that the terminology is unstable—is it a penis or a phallus that she has? Who can tell? Certainly not the fetishist, who cares more for the substitute, the fetish, than the thing being substituted, whether it's a penis or a phallus. The man in these texts, by contrast, is never attributed with a phallus, only a penis; what's more, this penis is an object of indifference, it never instigates any uncertainty or interest. Could we perceive the fetish as a new object which enables transformations and translations to take place precisely because it strategically destabilizes meanings? To do so would return us to the pre-Freudian meanings the notion of the fetish has had as the thing which can translate between two radically incommensurable cultures.

This exploration of fetishism's purported dependence on either the penis or the phallus raises the possibility that indeed the cart has been put before the horse. The question we should be asking is whether and how the penis and phallus are dependent on the fetish, to what extent they are particular, quite special fetishes? At the root, the problem of defining the penis and the question of its substitutability with the phallus raises questions about the intelligibility of sexual difference, the very questions that fetishism so strategically both troubles and plays out. It is to these questions that we must turn. Once we realize that if Freud is himself ambivalent about whether or not women have a "penis," to the point where he must specify the "man's penis" as the fetish prototype, then the issue of having or not having a penis turns out not to be the determining one for fetishism.

There are, thus, a number of rather different interpretations of the designation "penis." If by "penis" we understand Freud to mean the genital organ on which the child focuses attention during the phallic stage, then there may be no clear distinction between the sexes at the point where fetishism takes hold, and fetishism will be read as an attempt to make sexual and generational difference go away, as a way of refusing to separate fully from the mother. This is the interpretation Marcia Ian uses. In this version, which posits the etiology of fetishism on the basis of the child's understanding of his/her penis in relation to the mother's phallus, there would be no way based solely on anatomy to disallow women the position of fetishists. Men and women would be equally susceptible to the injunction against identifying with the mother, and would avail themselves of any number of strategies—among them, fetishism, masculinity, and femininity—in order to deal with separating from her.

However, if by "penis" we understand an anatomical member upon which sexual difference hinges through the interpretive process of castration—thus, as something one either has or lacks—then our understanding of fetishism would be limited to men only insofar as we could not comprehend sexual difference outside of the binary economy of presence and lack. But if we can understand that women might fear and refuse castration in the same way that men do, then this definition of "penis" could also render quite a productive notion of fetishism. In this scenario, there is sexual difference, although it need not be constrained by the heterosexual binary we are accustomed to. Rather, fetishism, like masculinity and femininity, would be a strategy for opening anatomical morphology to less deterministic conclusions about gender roles and possibilities. This is where Elizabeth Grosz's question of "Lesbian Fetishism?" is headed in its most productive moments, suggesting that gender is no obstacle to developing an anxious disavowal in the face of the threat of castration.[17] Yet at the same time as it may provide an opening into a more complex understanding of sexual difference, this second interpretation risks a certain sexual indifference analogous to that of the first interpretation above. Whereas the first makes the clitoris and the penis indistinguishable, the second renders fetishism, masculinity, or femininity indistinguishable as potential reactions to the threat of castration.

Finally, a third possibility presents itself, if we follow Grosz's suggestion to focus on the significance of the sexual difference between mother and son and understand that by "penis" we really mean "phallus." In this view, which may be the most perverse of the three, fetishism emerges when the dynamic of the mother-child dyad is affected by the child's realization that the most powerful one is not, indeed, so powerful, and that he stands a good chance of surpassing his mother's power. In this light, then, the phenomenon of fetishism might be read as a primitive and symbolic form of (male) feminism, where a child refuses to fully accept the constraints placed on women in patriarchy, and desires to maintain the fantasy of women's power. In this view, fetishism is a form of coping not only with sexual differences but, more broadly, with power differences, insofar as we can distinguish the two. Furthermore, this view could render fetishism as a productive phenomenon, since perceiving the limitations of someone once thought to be completely overpowering can provide the impetus for developing one's own sense of autonomy and responsibility while maintaining the desire for recognition from and connection to the other.

Freud's emphasis on the "quite special penis" as the mother's penis in the first part of "Fetishism" focuses on the maternal phallus not as an insignificant object of fantasy like the unicorn, but as a token of the power relation between mother and child expressed through the fantasy figure. Initially in the text, this is only hinted at through Freud's enigmatic "we know why" the little boy does not wish to let go of his belief in the maternal phallus. The explanation of this "we know why" in the next paragraph, through the perspective of the boy's thought process— "if a woman had been castrated, then his own possession of a penis was in danger"—is rendered analogous to the grown man's panic "when the cry goes up that Throne and Altar are in danger," thus underscoring the symbolic representation of power at stake here (*SE* 21: 153). Through his wording, Freud troubles the assumption that a boy necessarily has a penis: it is not the *penis* that is threatened, but the *possession* of the penis—"sein eigener Penis*besitz* bedroht" (*GW* 14: 312; emphasis added). This unsettles any claim that the penis in question serves merely as an anatomical appendage; what's at stake in castration is the right to ownership, not having the thing itself. That the issue is possession, and that the fetish-model shifts from that maternal penis to the man's penis by the end of "Fetishism," suggests that power is at the crux of the notion of fetishism, since it is no longer the mother but the man who can guarantee the potential significance of the penis.

The difference between the mother and the man is a difference of power, metaphorized through the process of castration. Freud notes that the fetish "remains a token of the triumph over the threat of castration and a protection against it" (*SE* 21: 154). In this light Freud's odd assertion that the fetish prototype is the man's penis, and not the maternal phallus or the woman's penis, begins to make more sense. The man's penis—not the boy's or the woman's—is the only one which clearly does survive the threat of castration. The boy's remains under that threat, while the woman's is interpreted as already having fallen to that threat. The man's penis, as the prototype of the fetish, is likewise a monument to the horror of powerlessness, providing reassurance as the remainder which has overcome that horror.

In all these cases, then, fetishism clearly emerges around the discovery of sexual difference. It is an ambivalent response, acknowledging and denying not only this difference but also its consequences, especially insofar as they reflect the power relations which structure the context of this discovery. Sexual difference is a difference already weighted with positive and negative values in its outcome. Overvaluation is possible only because the difference makes a difference in the larger scheme of things, in terms of who has the power to do what. Because sexual differences are fundamentally power differences, the question of power is what makes the overvaluation of the penis—even as a signifier, even as the phallus—so important for fetishism.[18] It is also, for instance, what distinguishes fetishism from hysteria, since the hysteric overvalues a part of her own body not valued by or symbolically charged for the rest of society. If the penis were insignificant, it would be easily and unproblematically substituted, and its service as the fetish-prototype would not be so strongly emphasized. Instead, the offense taken at the idea that the penis could be substituted—an offense which is indicated by the disparagement of fetishism—only underscores the implicit notion of the penis as both standard and special.

Because cultural forces pressure us to think of sexual differences as only and narrowly binary heterosexual differences, fetishism seems rooted in an interpretation of sexual difference too rigid to be productive. Yet we can use those roots to introduce a fuller form of fetishism that will undermine the assumptions about asymmetrical, binary sexual difference held in place by the constricted, fetishized fetishism. The classical understanding of sexual difference based on castration is strictly heterosexual in the sense that it is founded upon a narrow binary interpretation of what is kept and what is lost, and that the keeper and the loser are asymmetrically dependent on one another, and that there is an absolute, mutually exclusive difference between them. This binarism is the structure that Judith Butler calls the "heterosexual matrix": the reductive binary framework through which gender difference is compulsorily interpreted.[19] Ostensibly, we have no choice but to submit to one side or the other. Fetishism, however, provides a third option that is neither one nor the other.

In an economy of sexual differences where it is possible that the anatomical penis does not matter as a mark of difference—such as the case of the young boy whose phallus is his mother's, or, to evoke a different situation, in certain lesbian contexts—the instability and mobility of the penis or the phallus could become useful rather than threatening. To lose the penis or the phallus takes on a whole new meaning in such an economy because there is always the possibility of getting it back. Symbolic castration need not be irrevocable, much as real castration has recently been shown to be reversible (in certain cases). Castration, then, rather than being the gesture that fixes difference on one side or another of a binary power relation, would initiate the fluctuation of the phallus.

Fetishism might seem to be obsolete in this economy of phallic exchange, no longer necessary as a guard against loss, as a memorial to castration, or as a means of conservation. Yet, I would suggest, such an economy does not render fetishism meaningless. In fact it makes fetishism even more necessary, as the collateral to be held against the penis's return. In this alternative economy, the penis, as a signifier, becomes something that everyone has, if only as a matter of degree, and thus loses its power to mark sexual difference absolutely and heterosexually. It is precisely the exchangeability of the phallus or penis that— rather than contributing to sexual indifference, as if anyone could take it on and be the same—renders it a strategic means for marking sexual difference. Such an interpretation may seem impossible or utopic, but I suggest that a careful reading of Freud provides just such an understanding.

A Very Special Penis:
The Clitoris from *Three Essays* to the Later Works

Freud's analogy of the clitoris and the penis sustains a fetishistic structure by both claiming and denying difference. Freud's inherent ambivalence about the clitoris, caught up as it is in the matrix of sexual (in)difference at the end of "Fetishism" as both "penis" and mark of femininity/inferiority, invites me to interpret it as the "real" prototype of the fetish. The definition of the fetish as a "penis-substitute" reinforces this idea. The clitoris is the mother's unintelligible penis, which cannot be read as a phallus by the little boy precisely because he, unlike Freud, cannot read it as a penis. In calling our attention to the private knowledge of the fetish, Freud notes "The meaning of the fetish is not known to other people, so the fetish is not withheld from him: it is easily accessible and he can readily obtain the sexual gratification attached to it. What other men have to woo and make exertions for can be had by the fetishist with no trouble at all" (*SE* 21: 154). It is a secret that is concealed, like Poe's purloined letter, in clear sight, in the most obvious place.

Like the fetish, the clitoris's significance is not obvious to those outside of the hermeneutic circle, as the little boy would be. The clitoris is not overloaded with cultural meanings the way that the penis is; thus its significance is private, knowledge shared by insiders. In contrast, the penis is the model for public knowledge, what we are all expected to know. Once it is understood that the penis can only function as a public sign, however indeterminate that signification may be given the Freudian reading of "penis" as doubly a man's or a woman's, then it will not be surprising to suggest that the fetish prototype—or perhaps paradigm—is the clitoris. The "something else" which has taken over the mother's penis is the mother's clitoris, a sexual reality whose disavowal provides perhaps even more interesting implications than the disavowal of the mother's imagined phallus, because the clitoris has no function other than pleasure. Thus, the perhaps most unambiguously and singularly sexual part of the body provides the foundation for interpretive ambivalence.

As we move from Freud's text "Fetishism" to the place of fetishism in Freud's texts, we can take Freud's descriptions of the clitoris as a useful prototype to expand our understanding of the fetish. The clitoris is a problematic remainder for Freud's "feminine" woman. It performs the function of a supplement, in the specific sense of one of the most famous double figures from deconstruction. What Jacques Derrida calls "the logic of the supplement" is the irony of having it both ways: the supplement implies there is a lack in the whole, which it must shore up, while at the same time, the supplement, as a secondary appendage to an entirety, provides an element of excess.[20] The clitoris is central to fetishism's contradictory logic of having sexual difference both ways—acknowledging both lack and excess. On the one hand, the clitoris is a supplement to the castrated woman's lack, filling in for the missing penis. On the model of clitoral inferiority in comparison to the penis, this supplement is not enough of one; it falls short of completely filling the need. Yet, on the other hand, the clitoris is a supplement, in the sense of providing an extra part, to the vagina—which in normative feminine terms is really all a woman needs. The clitoris does not go away when she shifts her focus to the vagina; it merely "hands over" its primacy to the vagina, as if further confirming clitoral inferiority. The clitoris's function as an organ of inferiority is to preserve the loss that comes from accepting castration; it is supposed to be a reminder of woman's inadequacy. In this way too, the clitoris conforms to Freud's idea that the fetish object erects a memorial to the horror of castration (*SE* 21: 154).

Combining these qualities with Freud's persistent reading of the clitoris as a penis, we may begin to see how the development of fetishism lines up as curiously parallel to that of femininity. This becomes clearer if we put the penis = clitoris equation to work in the following passage: "In the world of psychical reality the woman still has a penis [clitoris] in spite of all, but this penis [clitoris] is no longer the same as it once was. Something else [the vagina] has taken its place, has been appointed its successor, so to speak, and now absorbs all the interest which formerly belonged to the penis [clitoris]." This passage comes from "Fetishism," yet it could fit in "Femininity" fairly smoothly, especially since Freud demonstrates there that femininity has less to do with physical morphology (having a clitoris instead of a penis) and more to do with psychical reality. The parallel resonates in the scheme detailed by Freud in "Femininity," where, "[w]ith the change to femininity, the clitoris should wholly or in part hand over its sensitivity, and at the same time, its importance, to the vagina" (SE 22: 118); the "penis" must be replaced by "something else." This parallel suggests that the "normal" course of development for a woman into femininity follows what might be a perverse development for a man into fetishism.

The gendering implicit in the distinction between these normal and perverse trajectories raises an interesting spectre: the denial of female fetishism seems to be rooted in the notion that it must be normal; a woman "should" in the face of the inadequacy of her "penis-equivalent" displace the value of her pleasure onto another zone. Yet, the course of attaining "normal" feminine development, Freud admits, is only one of three possible outcomes; the other two are the hysteric and the masculine woman. The difficulty of attaining femininity follows from the requirement of a double displacement, both in the castration complex (transfer of sexual aim) and at the Oedipal stage (transfer of sexual object). Freud repeatedly stresses the difficulty for women in achieving the feminine ideal. And indeed, he makes it clear that failing to achieve this ideal attaches no stigma. At the beginning of "Femininity" Freud makes exceptions of women analysts who may object to some "unfavorable" comparison of their sex. This strategy of imputing masculine traits to intelligent or exceptionally successful women, Freud tells us, avoids "impoliteness"; the lack of offense here implies that being more masculine than feminine on a particular point is no disgrace (SE 22: 116). Toward the end of this same lecture, he emphasizes the fragility of femininity, saying that "the development of femininity remains exposed to disturbance by the residual phenomena of the early masculine period" (SE 22: 131). In this light, it seems that femininity in women ought to be as rare as fetishism in men.

Given that both femininity and fetishism require a double displacement of sexual object and sexual aim from the original attachment to one's mother, and that both seem equally unlikely, yet unmistakably prevalent, what enables us to distinguish between the two? For Freud what distinguishes femininity from fetishism—and thus bars women from being fetishists—is the question of castration and its disavowal, especially in relation to an other. The wish for a penis for one's self is, as Freud notes, a wish that is *"par excellence* a feminine one" (*SE* 22: 129); however, the wish for a penis for one's mother is par excellence a fetishistic one. It makes sense, to Freud, that a woman would contest her own castration—he acknowledges that even "successfully" feminine women struggle for a long time with this knowledge. Yet for a woman or girl to deny her mother's castration is problematic for Freud. In his scenario of a girl's trajectory into femininity, she first recognizes her own castration as idiosyncratic, "an individual misfortune" (*SE* 22: 126), and only gradually begins to extend this sense to all women, arriving only in the end at her mother. The girl's acknowledgment of her mother's castration is the impetus which enables her to turn away from the mother as her primary love-object. Yet it is not clear why this break with the mother would necessarily be linked with femininity, since the girl turns away for the same reason as the little boy does, because each has discovered she is not the phallic mother. This turn away from the mother certainly does not push the little boy into femininity; in fact it facilitates his repudiation of femininity. Why does it not likewise facilitate a girl's repudiation of femininity? This question is not entertained, because for a woman to not be feminine can only be construed as failure, not as something she's strived to achieve. The break with the mother is a factor Freud insists upon but cannot adequately explain, and its intractability prompts him to propose his most notorious theory, penis-envy.

In Freud's account, the recognition of the mother's castration is necessary to catalyze the girl's hostility toward her mother. This hostility is crucial for Freud's understanding of feminine development and its double displacement of aim and object, since the girl must break with her attachment to her mother and turn to men as her love object. But the break does not lead her to repudiate femininity; rather, it facilitates her identification with it. For a girl to disavow her mother's castration is a logical impossibility for Freud, because it unhinges the psychical separation of mother and daughter and the motivation for the daughter's eventual transference of sexual object onto men. More importantly, for a woman to interpret, as Freud so often does, her clitoris as a penis(-equivalent)—to in effect, make her "wish" come true—regressively masculinizes her. Thus this wish may be feminine par excellence, but its fulfillment is not. The gap between the wish and its fulfillment holds apart masculinity and femininity as discrete categories rather than interconnected elements in a pastiche of sexual differences.

The ambivalence in Freud's text about the purpose of the clitoris makes the value of the clitoris oscillate between the poles of masculinity and femininity. The clitoris is supposed to essentially subtract its "masculine" pleasure from the sexual scene in order to make room for the "feminine" pleasure of the vagina (which Freud calls "the true female organ" ["Female Sexuality" 197]). But the clitoris remains a feminine organ in some respect, since in Freud's account the feminine woman has not completely lost her attachment to her clitoris, even though she has transferred the "leading zone" of her pleasure to her vagina. This ambivalence only further underscores the parallel between fetishism and femininity as forms of sexual difference that deviate from the masculine norm. The special penis of childhood is lost or demoted, yet that loss is preserved, a remnant remains of the feeling the clitoris offered as the girl's penis in the phallic phase. It is thus no less a memorial to castration than the fetish is.

By way of explanation, Freud proposes the scenario where the clitoris serves to spark sexual excitement "in the adjacent female sexual parts, just as—to use a simile—pine shavings can be kindled in order to set a log of harder wood on fire" (SE 7: 221). The fetish and clitoris thus both share the function of facilitating "normal" heterosexual intercourse, and to "save" the subject from a worse fate—either homosexuality (in the case of the male fetishist) or anaesthesia (in the case of the clitorally fixated woman).[21] Interestingly, there is not the explicit sense that the woman needs to be "saved" from homosexuality to parallel the apparition of the male homosexual in "Fetishism." Rather, the threat to sexuality in "Femininity" is the loss of sexual feeling altogether, not an "inappropriate" object-choice. Freud rather contradictorily suggests that "if the clitoral zone refuses to abandon its excitability" a woman may never make the transfer to her vagina and thus would remain "anaesthetic" (SE 7: 221). This anaesthesia—this purported lack of feeling—only results from refusing to let go of the clitoral excitability. This is an odd assertion, since such "excitability" is, if anything, a profusion of feeling. The difference between female anaesthesia and male homosexuality plays into stereotypes of hetero-normative gender ideals, suggesting that the greatest threat to masculinity is homosexuality while the greatest threat to femininity is asexuality or frigidity.[22] This difference does not alter the trait common to both the fetish and the clitoris: their useful function is counterbalanced by the potential threat they pose by diverting sexual interest from its normal aim.

Apart from their homologous development in their respective texts, fetishism and femininity crop up at either end of Freud's *Three Essays on Sexuality*, so examining this text may throw light on the parallel between fetishism or femininity as sexual differences. In the first section of his *Three Essays*, Freud discusses fetishism under the rubric of "Deviations of the Sexual Aim" within the context of "Sexual Aberrations." Yet he is far from settling the issue of where to locate a discussion of fetishism in the broader theory of sexuality. Freud defines the normal sexual aim as heterosexual copulation; the object is the partner with whom one achieves this aim. He acknowledges that "we should no doubt have done better to have mentioned this highly interesting group of aberrations of the sexual instinct among the deviations in respect of the sexual *object*" (*SE* 7: 153), but he argues that it is precisely fetishism's dependence on overvaluation, which is connected to the sexual *aim*, that makes it into a perversion. Fetishism, which perverts both the aim and object of sexual interest, thus confounds the normative basis of this distinction.

Freud's choice to discuss fetishism under the heading of aim rather than object reasserts that distinction and shifts the emphasis in the description of fetishism from the fetish object—which might seem to be the defining aspect of the perversion—to the function of that object in sexuality. This shift is crucial for the development of a broader understanding of fetishism as an epistemological function, as a strategy, because it directs our attention away from the thing to its employment. Instead of aligning fetishism with inversion, pedophilia, and bestiality—which are all sexual practices based on the identity of the practitioners and on that basis have been marked as beyond the pale of social acceptability—this move places fetishism alongside kissing and other widely accepted sexual activities that only become perverse if their engagement "stops short" of genital union—i.e., normative heterosexual union (*SE* 7: 150). This placement also aligns fetishism with activities such as anal eroticism, voyeurism, and sadomasochism, whose distinction is based not so much on the identity of the sexual partners, but on the practices themselves, since they may range across the categories of heterosexuality and homosexuality.

In this section, Freud points out that fetishism is indeed "habitually present in normal love" (*SE* 7: 154) as a "necessary condition attached to the sexual object," as an aspect of sexual attraction. This point is consistent with Freud's larger effort here to challenge the category of the "normal" not as a separate, pure category distinct from the marginal, abnormal, perverse, or neurotic, but in fact as one contaminated by those elements it seeks to exclude. I would extend this claim further to suggest that fetishism not only pervades "normal" sexuality, but also "normal" strategies of knowing and negotiating difference. According to Freud, when, through overvaluation, the fetish becomes displaced from its function of abetting the sexual aim to become either the entire sexual aim or the sexual object, it has crossed the line into perversion. Yet in describing this point where fetishism becomes a pathology, Freud reinforces a normative sense of sexuality and the deconstructive gesture that his use of the word "normal" signifies breaks down. There is the sense initially that fetishism is not only acceptable, but inescapable; however, if it subsequently takes over reproductive sexuality then it is pathological.

This extreme case pushes beyond even the distinction "normal" and "perverse," for Freud tells us, pausing to discuss fetishistic tendencies before introducing the full-blown version, that there exist "those cases of fetishism in which the sexual aim, whether normal or perverse, is entirely abandoned" (*SE* 7: 153). This distinction is rather odd, given that the binary choice between normal and perverse leaves no room for something to be neither; it would seem entirely reasonable to put fetishism on the side of "perverse," as a deviation of the sexual aim. It is not as if there is no sexual aim or object in the extreme forms of fetishism; given Freud's initial definition of sexual aim as "the act towards which the instinct tends" (*SE* 7: 136), these extreme cases still conform. This odd moment suggests that implicit in the definition of the sexual aim and the deconstructibility of the categories of normal and perverse is the idea that sex must be read either as reproductive or as a perverse but still recognizable imitation of reproductive sexuality. This necessary condition of recognizability narrowly conflates the sexual with the genital.[23] Once a deviation of the sexual aim veers into unrecognizability, no longer corresponding in any way to copulation, it threatens the very basis of sexual aim. Thus fetishism not only confounds the boundary delimiting the difference between sexual object and aim, but undermines the constitution of the notion of "aim." The emphasis on overvaluation impedes fetishism's recuperation into a recognizably sexual practice, and underscores the scant weight given to the qualities of pleasure or satisfaction in determining the sexual aim.

Sexual overvaluation, Freud notes in this earlier work, is what fetishism hinges upon. This understanding is the primary one that has seeped into nonpsychoanalytic understandings of the term, eliding entirely the questions of ambivalence and castration, as well as the sense of fetishism as a strategy for complying with compulsory heterosexuality by "making [women] tolerable as sexual objects."[24] Yet in the *Three Essays* overvaluation is also taken to be important to femininity. It comes up again in Freud's discussion in "Transformations of Puberty" near the end of *Three Essays*, where, in outlining the differences between men and women, and particularly the progress of a girl into a woman, he attempts to sketch out the "vicissitudes of this excitability of the clitoris" (*SE* 7: 220). In Freud's account, the girl undergoes a wave of sexual repression, which overtakes her clitoral and (as Freud judges it) childishly masculine sexuality and provides an "increase of sexual overvaluation which only emerges in full force in relation to a woman who holds herself back and who denies her sexuality" (*SE* 7: 221). Unlike men, however, in whom puberty's increase in the libido incites activity, women's pubertal increase in libido invokes the opposite reaction—that is, repression. Thus the overvaluation in the above passage has an oddly inverted sense; rather than overvaluing in the direction of the libido and thereby augmenting its force, the girl's overvaluation exerts itself against the force of the libido. Nonetheless, this overvaluation is what femininity, as well as virginity, hinges upon, as the context clearly implies.

The woman "who holds herself back" is not likely to do so forever. Freud continues his description of the trajectory of overvaluation by announcing that "When at last the sexual act is permitted, the clitoris itself becomes excited" (*SE* 7: 221). This phrasing makes it seem as if the last thing to become excited in the series of possible organs is the clitoris, and thus the release from repression only occurs at its instigation. Since this sentence begins immediately after asserting that the woman is in denial about her sexuality, the elision of the circumstances or agent who enables the sexual act to occur, who in effect lifts the ban of repression, is rather striking. And this produces in turn a sense in this paragraph of the old double standard now explained through psychoanalysis— boys will be boys and act on their libido as a matter of course, while girls will be girls and naturally repress their sexual urges until the proper moment, which will be externally introduced. At the same time, this elision of the subject in the sexual relation in favor of the personification of the clitoris as the catalytic object for sexual activity replicates the classical interpretation of the process of fetishism; the thing is what is sexual here, not the person.

In the *Three Essays* overvaluation provides the route for the fetishist to become perverse and the woman to become feminine. But women's overvaluation is not limited to femininity: either she overvalues by affirming the primacy of her clitoral zone and becomes masculine or anaesthetic, or she changes her leading erotogenic zone, repressing the clitoris, and overvalues her sexuality through denial. There is no escape for overvaluation for a woman, in this paradigm. Interestingly, when it comes to examining femininity head-on, Freud drops the explicit term of overvaluation—however convoluted it has become—in favor of the theory of "penis-envy" in "Femininity." Yet this is not so much a change in direction as it is merely a substitution; this "penis-envy" is itself a form of overvaluation. [25]

The notion of "penis-envy" fits quite smoothly into the matrix that concludes "Fetishism," especially once we learn there is an equivalence between penis-envy and the clitoris as a model for inferiority. Freud implicitly tells us this through apposition in "Some Consequences of the Anatomical Distinction between the Sexes": "There is yet another surprising effect of penis-envy, or of the discovery of the inferiority of the clitoris . . ." (SE 19: 255). As in the final sentence of "Fetishism," the term "Minderwertigkeit" is used, so that the notion of inferiority here conveys the sense of value or worth. We can use this equation to work through the peculiar transformations of the "clitoris" in Freud from Three Essays to "Femininity." In the later lecture, the little girl's compulsion to give up clitoral masturbation stems from the clitoris's inferiority to the boy's penis. "Her self-love is mortified by comparison with the boy's far-superior equipment and in consequence she renounces her masturbatory satisfaction from her clitoris" (SE 22: 126). The clitoris has changed radically from being an informative model for the little girl of "Transformations of Puberty," where Freud tells us that

> Frequent erections of that organ make it possible for girls to form a correct judgment, even without any instruction, of the sexual manifestations of the other sex: they merely transfer onto boys the sensations derived from their own sexual processes. (SE 7: 220)

In this passage, the clitoris is not yet the model for inferiority or shame; rather it is a model—and apparently quite an adequate model—for the penis. It is, in this case, an instrument of knowledge. This view of the clitoris is central to understanding how fetishism can serve as an epistemological model; the fetish establishes a relation between two seemingly incommensurable things (boys and girls, penis and phallus, etc.), and brings out a functional understanding of the two by providing a contingent standard by which to negotiate their differences.

What we have here, then, is Freud taking up in his textual development through the years the very trajectory of femininity that he outlines for women. It is the clitoris that provides the little girl—and Freud—with the basis for comparison of the two sexes; it is the clitoris that serves as the focus for the girl's phallic phase, which enables her to parallel the boy's development. This parallel is what makes it possible for Freud to abstract even further, from the anatomical realm to the psychical realm, announcing, towards the end of "Female Sexuality" that there is a definite conclusion about femininity as a whole which we cannot resist: the same libidinal forces, we have found, are at work in female and in male children, and we have been able to convince ourselves that for a certain period these forces take the same course and produce the same results. (208)

Even if the clitoris falls out of favor as a basis for common ground in the field of sexual differences, Freud still needs something to function as the clitoris did. It seems, therefore, that Freud does not wholly give up on the idea of clitoral homology with the penis, rather much as the feminine woman does not wholly give up clitoral sensation. Instead, he employs this partial repression to develop a theory of a common libido. By doing so, Freud maintains both a sense of sexual difference and a sense of sexual indifference throughout his work on gender and sexuality. One moment, a point of sexual indifference, the clitoris is masculine enough to be metaphorized as a penis; another moment, sexual difference intercedes to code the clitoris as feminine, put to the service of the "true female organ," the vagina, like kindling.

Thus, femininity and fetishism both set the stage for comparing the sexes, and the fulcrum of that comparison is the clitoris and penis. The difference is precisely a question of value. In the process of femininity, the child confronts difference only to arrive at a determination of her own inferiority through analogy to the other's genitalia. In contrast, fetishism's confrontation with difference establishes a refusal of the child's own inferiority in view of the other's genitalia by denying the mother's difference *and* insisting on oneself as the model. Here we see how the idea of women's fetishism operates in a blindspot. Femininity purportedly only comes about through identification with the mother, and with the presupposition that the child is already similar and that the child knows who the mother is. Fetishism comes about through identification with the mother that willfully revises who that mother is, making the mother like the child while also maintaining a sense of the mother's difference. If we have only a binary heterosexual view of sexual difference, then there is no possible way of perceiving the struggle of a girl's identification with her mother—her search for autonomy—as anything but rebellion against the imposition of her gender. This paradigm reinforces the sense of femininity as inferiority. If we understand fetishism to be a different strategy for interpreting sexual difference, we open up the possibility for better describing the girl's development of a sexual and autonomous self as something other than simply rebellion. A fetishistic girl, for example, might endow her mother with a penis in order to claim a strong femininity for herself, or she might use fetishism in order to set her mother up as a nonfeminine model to emulate.

With this fuller understanding of why women might come to be fetishists, we should return to the final sentence of "Fetishism" once more. The assimilative force of the analogy at the end of "Fetishism," draws our attention to the question, how does the little girl become ashamed? Shame and sexual difference are inextricable at this point, since it is through becoming ashamed that she becomes aware of difference. This correlation is underscored in the world beyond Freud's texts, where those whose desires and identities do not conform to the normative standard—gays, lesbians, and other queers—frequently experience shame as they become aware of their own sexual difference. [26] Fetishism provides a way out of the inevitability of shame; in lieu of inferiority it offers satisfaction. That is why the inadequacy of the fetishist's penis does not leap to our attention in the same way that the inferiority of the woman's penis does. The crucial difference between inferiority and fetishism hinges on the issue of what counts as an accurate perception of reality. The fetishist eschews complete accuracy for a more satisfying interpretation; the "shame-ist" eschews satisfaction for a more accurate interpretation of reality. Of course, an accurate interpretation is elusive and already shot through with cultural values. This point makes the fetishist's goal of satisfaction seem like a much better proposition. In the interrelation between shame, fetishism, and sexual difference we also see how subjectivity emerges. The child who opts for fetishism expresses dissatisfaction with the implications reality presents; the wish for a penis for one's mother is a claim for one's own capacity to interpret the world. The child who opts for shame takes on the interpretations the world presents as a means of individuating the self.

The fetishism at work in "Femininity" shows to what extent our shared cultural understandings of gender—masculinity and femininity—are infantile ideals, perhaps no more accurate than other infantile theories, for instance, that of anal birth. Yet the inaccuracy of these ideals does not undermine their instrumental efficacy in how we construct our identities, as the infant's projected sense of a whole self in Lacan's notion of the mirror stage attests. We are not limited to merely two gender ideals, masculine and feminine, which directly correlate to father and mother, precisely because inherent in infantile theory is the structural possibility of the inaccurate interpretation of reality and an openness to subsequent revision.

Freud's masculine woman, who is considered "regressed," may in fact be one who has not submitted to those infantile ideals by which psychoanalysis measures regression, but has rather opted for a more complex and impure interpretation of sexual difference. In this case the term "regression" has a curious irony to it, marking out the resistance not to maturity, but to immaturity. This irony gains credence when we observe how, in the Freudian text, the masculine woman is implicitly privileged, be she the analyst conducting the research on which Freud's "Femininity" lecture is based, or the exceptional woman in the audience of that lecture. In contrast, the sexually inhibited or neurotic woman is clearly out of the running. And though she may achieve the norm of femininity after much struggle, the feminine woman, according to Freud, fails to fully develop her superego and remains dependent, since "it [the superego] cannot attain the strength and independence which give it its cultural significance" (*SE* 22: 129).[27]

Indeed, like the (heterosexual male) fetishist, the feminine woman of Freud's text needs a little something to help her out in the world. If she overvalues men for that purpose, she is not perceived as a fetishist, but as a pragmatist in a patriarchal culture. She may even exhibit fetishistic ambivalence as she oscillates between acknowledging that she has no power in a man's world and exercising power nonetheless. Her incomplete superego requires a supplement, but since her dependence is both expected and figured on a subject—the heterosexual male considered to be her masculine complement—she is perceived as normal rather than perverse. Adhering to the norm, ironically, makes the feminine woman a failure as an autonomous subject; there is no sense in Freud's texts that a feminine woman could be strong and independent. On the other hand, the strength and independence of the masculine woman, who in her clitoral self-sufficiency may seem to be a full subject, only causes her to be construed as abnormal (if not perverse). The women who qualify fully as subjects in the texts of psychoanalysis are the ones who can be made exceptions, more masculine than feminine on certain points—ones who both succeed and fail. This combination of success and failure in developing sexual subjectivity recalls the fetishist's dependence on an object that makes him both a success and a failure. Insofar as he requires that object, he is a failure; however, since the significance of the object remains concealed, he "passes" for a successfully independent subject. If not just the feminine woman but also the masculine woman is some form of fetishist, succeeding and failing by overvaluing her clitoris as Freud describes, then it may seem inevitable for women to be fetishists if they are to be sexual or strongminded.

The supposed lack of fetishism in women thus correlates with an inability to perceive women as having the autonomy to desire; the development of subjectivity and desire go hand in hand. To be sexual is intimately connected to developing as fully functional a subjectivity as is possible within the stunting conditions of civilization. The figures of women's sexuality—neurosis, hysteria, repression, or objectification—all smack of an incompletely developed autonomy as a subject. Fetishism may represent a failed form of subjectivity, insofar as the fetishist remains dependent upon the fetish object to achieve "normal" sexual relations. Yet if we understand, as Freud strove to do through destabilizing the category of the "normal," that this achievement is a fantastic ideal and that failure is inevitable, we can understand fetishism as a pervasive strategy for constructing a sexual identity and subjectivity that only becomes more so as women develop a stronger sense of themselves and their desires.

At this point it is possible to see how fetishism can be a necessary strategy for developing an identity, an indispensable supplement for any of us failed subjects. After all, what is an identity if it is not taking a symbol to embody rather than represent, to reiterate Ian's definition of fetishism from the beginning of this chapter? The phallic mother, that ideal identity posited by the most restricted economy of fetishism, is no more—or less—real than the phallic father, the ideal identity that anchors patriarchy. The identities constructed through strategies like fetishism and femininity are inescapably failures, falling short of the ideal of gender paradigms or the myth of autonomy. But this failure is, in a Freudian paradigm, only one of a field of possible failures, since Freud maintains that no one can achieve the psychoanalytic ideal of an autonomous subject; all of us fail to reach that ideal on account of one trauma or another.

Given that pervasiveness of failure, given Freud's challenge to the centrality of the "norm," we must take fetishism seriously as a prevalent and important model for subjectivity. It is one path, like femininity or masculinity, toward developing a sexed identity and sexual knowledge. We cannot divorce femininity from fetishism, since fetishism is a theory of sexual difference, and femininity is a form of sexual difference. Rather, we must use their inextricability to understand each against and through the other. This is necessarily a double move, since fetishism has classically been a strategy for relating to femininity. Only if we turn the tables and use femininity as a strategy for viewing fetishism will the analysis be productive or rigorous. However, I would caution that, in returning to the question of the possibility of female fetishism, we not take up femininity as the sole form of female fetishism. After all, femininity is not a performance limited to women, just as women are not limited to femininity. In the next chapter, I will explore these intersections more fully, and elaborate how the failure of subjectivity known as fetishism could be employed as a feminist strategy.

The ambivalence one finds in Freud's determination and definition of sexual difference is fetishism par excellence. The problem of reading this fetishism is not due to the texts alone, but rather indicates the difficulty of challenging phallocentrism, the constraints placed upon our ability to perceive any sexual differences that are outside of a strict heterosexual binary. The inescapability of fetishism is a consequence of how narrowly sexual difference has been formulated in our culture. Freud's texts illuminate this difficulty, but they do not solve it because they do not—and perhaps cannot—confront it directly. There is a radicalism in Freud's gesture of making women parallel to men; by explicating the difficulty of achieving "normal femininity," Freud creates the space to pry apart the conflation of women and femininity.

The radical force of this gesture is held back by the normative drive of these essays and the underlying sexual indifference, two issues which remain difficulties for feminists as we persevere in the effort to change the social conditions for women's lives in the latter part of the twentieth century. It is now a cliché that as women have gained more and more freedom, they have had to conform more to masculine ideals, creating a tension between the drive for equality and the need to recognize difference. The effort to pry apart the equation of women and femininity has been put in the service of a continued repudiation of femininity; it has not provided perspective on how a strong femininity would take shape, or room to choose among forms of femininity or masculinity or a third difference, such as androgyny or transgenders. Fetishism as an epistemological strategy situated in a fluid interpretation of sexual differences proffers a possible resolution to the political problem of equality versus difference. As a third way to figure sexual difference, fetishism can strategically complicate a binary gender system, reinstating an excluded middle and foregrounding the narrow gender ideals which subtend claims both for oppression and for freedom.

But fetishism is more than a question of sexual difference, in its multiple senses of gender differences or differences in sexual practice and object-choice. Sexual differences constitute one system—albeit one basic and important system—in which a subject's drive to know and connect with the world can play itself out. Analyzing how fetishism functions as a strategy does help us see how this system's elements are defined, but the lesson does not end there. Fetishism illuminates not only the definitions of elements, but the dynamic interrelation of these elements, how subjects negotiate the world through objects, desire, and knowledge. Indeed, the most important thing about fetishism is not its complex arbitration of sexual differences, but more generally how it enables us to accommodate both desire and knowledge, even when the two conflict. The need to develop a sense of identity that does not constrict or prescribe, but does locate and leverage, is a need that reflects the intrication of knowledge and desire. To fulfill this need, an epistemological strategy with a foothold in the unconscious is required. Fetishism is the normal, pervasive prototype of such a strategy.

2

The Travesty of Clothes Fetishism

Just as Freud is widely credited with the formulation of the fetish as a substitute for the mother's penis, so too has he been blamed for restricting fetishism to men. Yet, contrary to common belief, Freud did describe a relation between women and fetishism. In 1909, Freud gave the lecture "On the Genesis of Fetishism" to the Vienna Psychoanalytic Society, in which he stated that "all women are clothes fetishists" (156).[1] This lecture was not included in the *Standard Edition*, since it has only recently been discovered in Otto Rank's minutes of the Society; its first publication was in 1988. Given this late appearance, it is interesting to note that in translating fetishism into a context of female sexual practice, feminist critics have also by and large focused consistently on clothing fetishism, dressing, and cross-dressing, at times even conflating the terms.

By examining the 1909 lecture and its tensions with Freud's more famous later formulation, and then analyzing the feminist theorists whose work repeats elements of this same thread, we can begin to elucidate what is at stake in the conjunction of female fetishism, clothes, and travesty. Initially this conjunction might seem to reinforce binary gender stereotypes, since attention to—not to mention strong investment in—clothing has long been a characteristic associated with vanity and femininity. Are clothes then simply "appropriate" fetish objects for women, or does the element of travesty—the sense that the identity constructed through the fetish debases or distorts what it imitates—offer a new way to think about not only fetishism, but the question of appropriateness and the rules of sexual difference? The previous chapter's argument about the problem of the "normal" and the questions about the prototype return here under the rubric of travesty and masquerade, the playful imitations of familiar categories of identity.

As we shift our attention from the later to the earlier model of fetishism, it is not so much to dispute the claim that the dominant model has had on our attention as to open up the lines of association that may emerge more clearly from the earlier model. Where the later model is too often narrowly understood as a process of resolving binary

heterosexual difference into sexual sameness, the earlier model can provide the leverage to pry loose the assumptions about sexual difference
and desire which subtend the interpretations of that later model. The
earlier model also more clearly emphasizes the epistemological ramifications of fetishism as a form of inventive interpretation, and this
emphasis challenges us to understand desire much less narrowly. Moreover, the intransigence of the subtheme of imitation and the proper relation to cultural norms in theories of fetishism, whether this persists in
claims about the fetish prototype or turns up in literary figurations
of female fetishism as travesty, suggests that the desire at work in
fetishism can inform us about reading, about producing a satisfying
meaning that has both private significance and public currency.

A Puzzling Thing

Freud begins his lecture on the origin of the phenomenon of
fetishism with a sketch of the existing literature, delineating the genesis of the notion of fetishism, how it originated and developed as a psychoanalytic concept. In this brief outline, fetishism is explicitly linked
with women, but only within a heterosexual framework in which the
men alone seem to have any desire or agency. Thus Freud initially falls
in line with the traditional focus on men as fetishists and women as either the objects or associated with the objects of their desire. Although
Freud concedes that Krafft-Ebing is one who offers the most complete
account, providing "everything essential in clear and honest descriptions" (151), none of the three authors Freud attends to offers a satisfactorily rigorous explanation of fetishism.

Freud cites Krafft-Ebing's description of fetishism as "the joining
of sexual pleasure to single parts of a woman's body or pieces of her
clothing" (151). Although he does not comment on Ebing's particular
gendering of the fetish, in the next paragraph Freud makes his own list
of examples of fetishes "to remind us of the facts": here he slides from
clothes, hair, and underclothing—all of which are ungendered in his
list—to announcing that "ultimately anything possible can become a
fetish, even those things whose connection to a person are not very obvious" (151). In this move, he lays the groundwork for us to consider
fetishism as something other than a form of heterosexual masculine desire, since the catalog of fetishes encompasses not only specific personal
items which could belong to either men or women, but "ultimately anything." That even tangentially related items could become fetishes suggests that gender—which is usually construed to be a central catalyst
for sexual attraction—may be incidental in fetishism.

The other author Freud devotes any sustained attention to, Iwan Bloch, likewise describes fetishism through a specifically gendered lens. Freud complains that Bloch "describes all of the woman's stimuli, breasts, hair, etc.—thus exactly the feminine stimuli—as fetishes, which contradicts the conception of fetishism" (152–53). Freud does not elaborate on how this is a contradiction—one presumes it is because Bloch's list has such a broad scope that discerning pathological from non-pathological attractions becomes impossible. Bloch's "confused notions" seem to serve merely as a contrast to Ebing's "clear and honest" descriptions; indeed, Freud describes each account twice, using "confused" and "clear and honest," respectively, both times.

In the end, however, even the originator of the term fetishism, Krafft-Ebing, has cast his net too wide, and thus includes under the category of fetishism both "1) Things which we can grasp and distinguish exactly, and 2) something puzzling" (153). Despite his apparent admiration for Ebing's clarity, Freud feels the focus is not sufficiently defined. Freud believes only the latter, the puzzling things, should qualify as fetishes; hence his "attempt [at] a clarification of these puzzling cases" (153). The notion of the puzzle accurately sums up the epistemological problem of the fetish in the everyday world. The fetish is an object we may all recognize as a puzzle, because we do not understand its power or know its secret—how it operates, why it works, how to "solve" it. Yet we nonetheless have a grasp of the fetish, a sense of how to interpret and use it. Freud briefly draws a comparison to the mechanism of hysteria, noting that many of the cases of fetishism in the literature "prove to be reminiscences along the model of the mechanism of hysteria" (153). Yet he distinguishes between fetishism and hysteria by pointing out that in the former case "it does not have to be unknown to him that it is so and that it does him no good if his attention is drawn to how it is so" (153). However puzzling fetishism may be to others, it is not a puzzle to the fetishist. The confident "we know why" which Freud asserts in the 1927 essay is not Freud's but the fetishist's in this 1909 account.

The notion of the puzzle provides Freud's motive for pressing us beyond the available interpretations of fetishism's origin. Freud is dissatisfied with Ebing's account because it presents yet another puzzle. Ebing seems satisfied with the idea that fetishism emerges through the random coincidence of an object and a person's attention to that object. But why would such coincidental juxtaposition make such a powerful impact? The only answer that logically presents itself is that there must be some pathological disposition in the person. Yet Freud is implicitly dissatisfied with this conclusion, determining that it only invites logical regression, which he points to by calling it "the rocks upon which the entire 'psychopathia sexualis' is built: upon the puzzling sexual constitution, thus upon the riddle of nervousness in general" (152). The substitution of one puzzle with another is not the path to knowledge.

Freud's dissatisfaction with the conclusion that fetishism arises from a person's own pathological disposition suggests that for Freud what is puzzling about fetishism is not its pathology. Indeed, he implicitly questions whether fetishism is inherently pathological. Rather, solving the puzzle of fetishism could prove instructive about more general mechanisms of sexual attraction and desire that operate within the realm of the "normal." I would add that this puzzle touches upon fundamental issues of how subjects relate to objects in a more general sense—the spark of attention that indicates sexual interest is not so far removed from the allure that leads to knowledge. How one chooses which intellectual problems to grapple with, or why one prefers one artist or author to another, or even what impels one to stick out a difficult line of inquiry when the going gets tough—these mechanisms of attraction work on us at a level we may not be consciously aware of, even if we can retroactively come up with reasons for our choice that make the selection seem less puzzling and more logically consistent, graspable.

The trajectory of Freud's ensuing discussion of a case of clothes fetishism in a man, takes us away from the fetish as "something puzzling" and back toward the fetish as a "thing we can grasp"; Freud is definitely focused on coming to know why by solving the puzzle. Under his analysis of this first case, fetishism proves to be not so puzzling after all, but rather simply and specifically a result of the *"repression of the desire to look"* (155). He subsequently revises this to a more general definition of the origin of the fetish in the partial repression of an instinctual pleasure, where the direct object of that pleasure becomes embodied in the fetish (157). Freud's account provides us with a handle on fetishism, that it involves partial repression and is not purely a reminiscence of early childhood activity. The thing we can now grasp or distinguish exactly is not the fetish object, or the memory which attached the subject's attention to that object, but the mechanism of repression which causes a split in the "original instinctual representative" (n. 9). By this account, Freud is trying to provide a better understanding of the connection between the fetish and the fetishist's interest in the object. For Freud, memories are not puzzling; undiscovered psychological mechanisms are.

To further remove us from the "puzzling," Freud adds that his exposition of fetishism as a partial repression is indeed not new. Availing himself of one of his standard moves, of making an analogy between individual history and cultural or social history, Freud remarks that this same form of splitting and repression took place in the Middle Ages with the idealization of the Virgin Mary and the simultaneous degradation of real women (155). (His reference to Catholicism here recalls Ebing's original motivation for choosing the label fetishism in order to make an explicit analogy between erotic and religious idolization.) Then, moving from historical practice to modern cultural practice and even further away from the case at hand, Freud makes a startling and sweeping announcement. "In the world of everyday experience, we can observe that half of humanity must be classed among the clothes fetishists. All women, that is, are clothes fetishists. Dress plays a puzzling role in them" (156). Once again, the word "puzzling" turns up, as a way of describing the undue attention paid to a thing. Yet, once again, it turns out that this puzzle is not so enigmatic, since the same drive to see is at work—only this time, Freud tells us, it is in its passive form of the desire to be seen. Clothes become idealized as fetishes precisely because they serve to repress this drive to be seen.

There is much to say about this digression, which not only interrupts and repeats but also foreshadows the course of Freud's exposition. Freud moves from the historical example of the cult of the Virgin, which provided an analogical illustration of the kind of splitting and repression he is discussing in the case history, to a separate paragraph wherein he sweepingly diagnoses a substantial portion of a population who have little to do with the case history at hand. In doing so, he, perhaps inadvertently, puts to rest any claim that he thought only men could be fetishists. But the claim that all women are clothes fetishists comes dangerously close to Bloch's sweeping description of "all the woman's stimuli" as fetishes, a description Freud has labeled confused and contradictory.

Both Bloch and Freud here seem to be equating fetishism with femininity; the only difference is Bloch sees this femininity as something that would hold a man's attention, whereas Freud is clearly making the trappings of femininity the object of a woman's attention. Is Freud's description likewise confused and contradictory? Or is it cogent, since it comes from the other direction—not the man fetishizing the woman, but the woman fetishizing herself or her objects? Certainly there is an implication that the woman's clothes fetishism is somehow not as erotic as the male fetishist's, since the objects are her own and thus familiar to her. Freud implicitly underscores this familiarity in how he leads into this claim about women's fetishism—by announcing that this account of fetishism is "no novelty" (155) and that it draws on the "world of everyday experience" (156). Is this difference enough to make his claim less sweeping than Bloch's? Perhaps it is the very familiarity of the clothes that makes a woman's fetishism of them puzzling, since fetishism as Bloch and Ebing construe it hinges on the thing's association with difference and otherness.

Freud does not explore this assumption that fetishism emerges purely as a strategy to negotiate difference, or the assumption that a woman would find no difference between herself and the clothes she is expected to wear. Instead, after announcing that all women are clothes fetishists and that this fetishism stems from a partial repression of a drive to be seen, Freud elaborates:

> Only now can we understand why even the most intelligent women behave defenselessly in the face of the demands of fashion. For them clothes take the place of parts of the body, and to wear the same clothes means only to be able to show what the others can show, means only that one can find in her everything one can expect from women, an assurance which women can give only in this form.

In other words, women wear clothes to guarantee that they have what any other woman has. But the only reason they wear the clothes to show this is because they already belong to the category of women— perfectly circular reasoning, unless we suspect that women might be able to be something other than women, and thus need to reassure men that they are not this other thing. Clothes, in this view, provide a guarantee of sameness among people in the same group. The role of clothes in this claim also buttresses the boundaries of the group, reinforcing the sense of the rightness of the division of humans into men (who might occasionally fetishize) and women (who always do). But toward the end of the paragraph the description takes an interesting turn:

> Otherwise, it would be incomprehensible why many women, following the demands of fashion, also want to wear, and do wear, pieces of clothing which do not show them to best advantage, which do not suit them. (156)

These two sentences present the paradoxical relation between the pressures imposed by gender norms and our inevitable failure to achieve these ideals. The perversity of some women to wear unsuitable clothes in the name of following fashion differentiates those women from the very group of women they are trying to prove they are like. Women's clothes fetishism names this queer phenomenon, which is construed as a failure of those perverse women to defend themselves against the demands of fashion, rather than a failure of fashion to design clothes that would suit women.

In this passage, two paradigms present themselves for individuals to pattern their gender performance after: those set by fashion and those which best suit the wearers, styles which are oddly implied to be outside the purview of fashion. Implicitly, however, what is at stake in these different strategies is the subject's relation to knowledge—in particular whether she knows what looks good on her, but also more broadly how well she knows the fashion field, the system of cultural signs that she is expected to participate in. Freud is struck by the fact that "even the most intelligent women" are plagued by this fetishism—in other words, even women who ought to know better. But this knowing better is very much a question of the context of knowledge, private or public. The slave to fashion may wear unsuitable clothes, but she knows what is fashionable; by wearing the latest fashions or top designers' clothes she demonstrates her command of the social vocabulary of style, through which she may gain cultural power or influence. Insofar as she wears something unsuitable, her knowledge lets slip an unsettling difference between herself and other women (or more accurately the ideally fashionable woman) but it also provides assurance that she will nonetheless live up to social expectations. In effect, her clothes fetishism guarantees that she will strive to uphold her gender ideal, which includes making herself the object of heterosexual masculine desire.

On the other hand, a woman who wears clothes that suit her may in fact know better who she is and what works for her—her knowledge is simply more effective than that of the unsuitably attired woman. This command of style is, after all, the image fashion magazines promote. Yet, this promotion takes place in a field of many competing styles—Chanel hardly projects the same image as Versace—and Freud fails to note that the "demands of fashion" are a diverse and even conflicting set of dictates. Along with this lack of differentiation of the field of fashion is an interesting slide from "all" women, who are clothes fetishists, to the "many" women who incomprehensibly fail to dress well, a difference which presumably leaves some women who do wear clothes that suit them. Such a woman, however, drops out of Freud's picture. Is her relation to dress also puzzling, or is it only the unflatteringly dressed women who seem so curious? Is this well-attired woman even a clothes fetishist, since her knowledge in itself provides her unambivalent assurance, giving her the confidence not to need anything else or worry about anyone else? Given that "all women are clothes fetishists," this woman can only be a spectre in the text, and not one who must be factored into the account of fetishism. Thus no woman, it seems, manages to have any defense against the social pressure to conform to the dictates of fashion, and the fetish of clothes does nothing to provide a protection. The idea of the fetish as a defense against threat thus seems to be a later addition.

The puzzle of clothes fetishism, for Freud, centers on why a woman *wants* to wear something fashionable but not flattering—in other words, why she might fail to build up a defense against fashion. Freud does not even begin to scratch the surface of this puzzling desire, however. Content to leave this perplexity unexplored, Freud posits that this form of fetishism derives from a partial repression of a desire to be seen—which is a passive construction of the man's case, where fetishism comes from partial repression of the drive to see. But in his insistence on bracketing femininity to the passive side of the active/passive binary, he fails to grasp what active drive may in fact be partially repressed here—one often metaphorized through the sense of vision. Clothes fetishism can be understood as a partial repression of an active drive to know, of what Freud himself will later call epistemophilia.

Here is how this partial repression might work. If even an intelligent woman knows very well that she looks terrible, but nonetheless she insists on wearing those clothes, it may be because she wants to demonstrate her knowledge of fashion, that she knows what commodities are hot. She may be, in fact, trying to express her mastery of knowledge in a realm that is acceptable, thus striking a compromise between her desire to be a knowing subject and the social pressures against women as knowledgeable agents. Clothes fetishism here emerges as desire tries to negotiate contradictions in knowledge, not only between private significances and public systems of meaning, but between private aspirations and public expectations.

This fetishistic desire, then, is puzzling only insofar as Freud fails to grasp the contradictory demands that women experience in negotiating gender identity. Women's devotion to fashion cannot be viewed except as part of the larger gendering apparatus; to be able to show what others can show is to strive for the ideal femininity. Yet if women were striving to achieve their gender ideal, they would wear clothes to show themselves "to best advantage," since part of the gender imperative for women is to look their best. If you look best in black, but pastels are in this year, you must decide between looking your best and fitting in. The dictates of fashion may be at odds with what suits a woman, yet in Freud's depiction these dictates prevail, even over common sense— or even over a woman's desire to deviate from fashionableness or the feminine ideal, possibilities that Freud does not consider here. The ef-

fect of the normative force of fashion is that instead of serving to differentiate women, clothes serve to render them the same. In this light,
what is perverse about women's clothes fetishism is that it contributes
to women's inability to differentiate themselves as individuals, to the
point where they put themselves at an aesthetic disadvantage rather
than claim a positive sense of self.

Freud has announced that "to wear the same clothes means only
to be able to show what the others can show, means only that one can
find in her everything one can expect from women." The insistent repetition of "means only" in this passage is slightly ironic: if this wearing
really does mean *only* one thing, why say it two ways? The answer is
that the meaning is defined from two perspectives—the fetishist's, who
is able to show, and her observer's, who wants to find his expectations
fulfilled. The repetition thus serves non-ironically as reassurance that
the two are on the same wavelength, just as the fetish-clothes confirm
for the woman and her observer that they are in accord.

This rhetorical repetition underscores how women are expected to
eliminate their outstanding qualities; by showing what others show, by
fulfilling expectations, one hides the truth of individual difference, distinction, or deviation. Moreover, this sameness is culturally and broadly
interpreted as a fundamental difference—*the* difference between the
sexes, which overwhelms and contains all others, ultimately limiting
women's ability to reach their full potential as subjects. Women's
fetishism unites rather than divides them, confines rather than enables
them. Freud masks the difference between men, who can be taken indi-
vidually and differentiated by whether they are fetishists or not (to say
nothing of the kinds of fetishists they may be), and women, all of whom
are undifferentiated clothes fetishists.

Freud's unwillingness to delve into the puzzle of women's clothes
fetishism—typified by his totalizing claim—puts women's perversions
squarely in the range of the norm. Freud is not interested in exploring
whether women's clothes fetishism covers up a lost instinctual pleasure, partly because of the form of his analysis—a generalized observation drawn from cultural history rather than the particular observations
of a case history. But this blind spot also suggests that in some way it is
"natural" or even warranted for women to fetishize clothes, that they
lose nothing by doing so, and indeed gain something—namely, a self
assimilated to the norms of femininity—through this fetishization.
Freud's description thus moves beyond confused to "contradict the
conception of fetishism" as an aberration or a perversion. If fetishism is
normal, it loses its status as a perversion. The move here is not the same
as Freud's earlier deconstruction of the categories of normal and per-

verse in *Three Essays on the Theory of Sexuality*; in fact, it is quite the opposite. Whereas in *Three Essays* Freud tells us something new about "normal" sexual relations by discussing fetishism, here he tells us nothing about fetishism by framing it as something all women do. The lack of differentiation here replicates the lack of differentiation Freud found fault with in Bloch.

Yet we can see how clothing fetishism in women, as Freud formulates it in this paragraph, does resonate with some of the classical characteristics of fetishism. The elements we recognize from the later conception of fetishism are present here in the specific case of the male patient and in the generalization Freud makes about women, although they differ in informative ways. First, and most obviously, there is the substitution of a body part with an object not from the body. Clothes, as signs of what others can show, stand in for anatomy, which remains a sort of basic, uninterpretable and unvarying (from case to case, woman to woman) morphology here.[2] In fact, women must use these non-body objects to guarantee a truth about their bodies. But, whereas for the male fetishist in the later essay the fetish guarantees a woman still has a penis in spite of it all, for the female fetishist in the earlier lecture the fetish guarantees that she doesn't. Nonetheless, this guarantee is put in implicitly positive terms, rather than negative: we can understand the phrase "everything that one can expect from women" to be a euphemistic description of her sexual sufficiency and the sense that she will be able to satisfy a lover's desire. Thus substitution of the fetish object leads to satisfaction, as it does in the later formulation. The difference is that here the satisfaction belongs not necessarily to the (female) fetishist, but to the (presumably male) lover of the fetishist.

This early version of fetishism resonates with the reassurance of sameness offered in the later version. Notably, however, fetishism in the early version serves to render women all the same as each other, whereas in the later version fetishism is understood to render women the same as the fetishist. For the women in this early formulation, the clothes provide assurance that everyone really is the same, that no one is lacking, that "one can find in her everything one can expect from women" (156). The assurance, strikingly, is an assurance of plenitude, not lack. The rhetoric of shame, inferiority, and lack that permeates so much of Freud's later work on sexual difference is missing here. Instead, not only are we reassured that we *will* find what we expect, but we are told it will be *everything*. Women's clothes fetishism provides the route to wholeness, without the undercutting implication of lack.

The digression's similarity to the later formulation of fetishism is foreshadowed in the parallel drawn between the general and specific instances of clothes fetishism. Just as the sartorially impaired female fetishist of this digression fails to achieve her gender ideal by sacrificing her own suitable style for fashion's dictates, the fetishist of Freud's later work fails to achieve his sexual ideal: he tries but is unable to be heterosexual. In the former case, fetishism proves to be a crutch for achieving one's ideal or normative gender, fashionable femininity, as women are induced to want to wear fashionable clothes, and yet find their exercise of good sense inhibited once they actually put fashion into practice. In the later case, the fetishism facilitates the fetishist's achievement of his ideal sexuality, heterosexual intercourse, as the penis substitute makes women palatable sexual partners. In both cases, the fetishists' reliance on the fetish makes them unsuitable, makes them fall short of the ideal.

The digression interrupts Freud's discussion of this particular case history of the male clothes fetishist. The sudden shift back to the first case history in the paragraph afterwards only underscores the tangential nature of the digression and Freud's refusal to engage with the possibilities his generalization presents. Freud leaves off accounting for women's sartorial errors, and without any more transition than a paragraph break, he resumes the case history: "The same patient exhibited yet a second perversion . . . [he] also had become a boot fetishist" (156). "The same patient," contrary to the rhetorical implication, had not been referred to for a paragraph and a half; the singular male serves in striking contrast to the plural females. The digression into women's clothing fetishism serves as a break between the case history of the clothes fetishist and the case of the boot fetishist, even though the two cases are actually the same patient. Nonetheless, this break is strategic, since Freud only treats two cases of fetishism in the lecture, yet stakes his claims about fetishism on this limited sample. The digression implants the illusion that a wider variety of examples are discussed.

Freud does acknowledge at the beginning of his lecture that his effort is weakened in "that it rests entirely on the observation of three instances divided among two persons" (154). This statement follows a much earlier declaration that the author would depart "from his principle not to formulate theory before it can be supported by observations" (150), and thus this theory of fetishism is presented "by way of exception" (150). This avowal comes at the same point where Freud dispenses with the need to survey the literature, since he will not be publishing these ideas soon; he determines that three authors—like three examples—will "suffice" to orient the reader to the matter. (We might read this as his own partial repression of the desire to look, since he gives us only a glimpse.) Initially, then, Freud proceeds with a warning that further clinical observation will be necessary to provide a firmer basis for this theory of fetishism. In the last paragraph of the talk, Freud determines that "five or six more similar observations of fetishism" will suffice to prove the theory (158). The digression into women's clothes fetishism, however, curiously undermines this sense of sufficiency. If women's clothes fetishism is, as the digression claims, the same thing as this patient's clothes fetishism, then certainly in the set of "all women" we could find the "five or six more" examples to justify the theory. On the other hand, these women may not prove to be "similar observations of fetishism," since they are the norm rather than the deviation from the norm that the male fetishists are.

In examining the "two" cases presented by the male patient, Freud finds that they have in common a lost instinctual pleasure that reemerges as a fetish. This, he announces, "is the novelty" (157). Moreover, later on the same page, Freud characterizes this theory as the "solution to fetishism." He uses a third case, of "hand fetishism," taken from the annals of Krafft-Ebing, to confirm this idea; he claims that "This case contains the solution to hand fetishism in its essentials" (157). It is striking that he begins his discussion from a point of dissatisfaction with Ebing's account, his refusal to delve into the puzzle, only to find that in the end one of Ebing's cases contains the solution.

But just at the moment when Freud's rhetoric shifts from the puzzle to the solution, his actual analysis tends in the opposite direction. His discussion of the Ebing case is so brief that one might miss the fact that the "essentials" presented by this case are different from those in the previous two cases, and indeed that the conclusions Freud draws from this case fail to support the claim about partial repression. Freud summarizes the case thus:

> The youth of the man is filled with immoderate mutual masturbation. At the age of twenty-one and a half he conceives a horror of masturbation, and from this time on he becomes a fetishist for female hands (partial repression and displacement from men onto women). The wish to have a woman stroke his penis was probably already present during the period of mutual masturbation. (157)

What is notable about this passage, to anyone familiar with Freud's later essay on fetishism, is that it centers on fetishism as a strategy to facilitate heterosexual activity. This case differs from the first because heterosexuality is here opposed to homosexuality. This opposition is implicit, since of course mutual masturbation may be a heterosexual or homosexual activity. But it is clear, from the parenthetical remark about displacement from men onto women, the adjective "immoderate," and the claim in the third sentence that the wish for a woman's touch was already present in the earlier period, that this "immoderate mutual masturbation" involves gay rather than straight sex. In the first patient, by contrast, Freud reveals that fetishism was a strategy to avoid incest. In that case, while the fetish still facilitates normal heterosexuality, it does so in contrast to incestuous heterosexuality, rather than in contrast to homosexuality. Freud, however, does not call attention to this incest-avoidance, beyond mentioning the first patient's "inclination toward his mother" (154); instead, he prefers to focus on defining the repressed drive as the desire to look.

What is truly striking about the passage cited above, however, is the projection inherent in the third sentence. Freud claims, without any substantiation, that the wish for the woman's stroke is present even in the context of mutual masturbation; it thus seems to be more Freud's wish than the patient's. This claim does not support Freud's argument that fetishism results from the instinctual drive being neither fully repressed or sublimated, but "hold[ing] a middle position between" the two (156), since the emergence of the hand fetish, if Freud is right about this wish, would bring out a previously repressed desire.

In fact, it would make more sense to understand the man's hand fetishism as a partial repression of his homosexual desire; he is still engaging in the same activity, only with a different category of person. Yet the patient has chosen to fix upon a part of the body that might not distinguish his new partners from his old—for, depending of course on the body type, the hand of a woman is not necessarily much different from the hand of a man. Indeed, the hand as a sexual instrument is no less likely to be gendered than is an object, and far less likely than an article of clothing. Thus the type of hand or object the fetishist chooses could reflect the importance of gender in his or her desire. If gender were important as a sexual difference, then the fetishist might opt for a small hand or a highly gendered piece of clothing, such as a lace undergarment; if gender were a matter of indifference, the fetishist might fix upon a hand or object whose characteristics would not tip it one way or the other toward masculinity or femininity. This patient's preference for having a woman stroke his penis is best read as a compromise that he struck between the pressure to be heterosexual and his own homosexual desires. The threat that induces his development of fetishism could be the threat of being discovered, and a horror of the loss of social status attendant on being gay at the turn of the century.

Thus, once again Freud fails to capitalize on what his insight about the origins of fetishism has suggested. His rewriting of homosex-

ual desire in this case of hand fetishism mirrors his reluctance to interrogate women's desire in his generalizing digression. Yet despite his
failure to pick up on several important points, there is something valuable in this early lecture on fetishism. Freud convincingly shows
fetishism not as an oscillation between poles of sexual difference
marked by masculine and feminine, but as a compromise between two
psychical processes, complete repression (which holds back the instinct)
and sublimation (which redirects it). Freed from this binary gendered
framework, we can more clearly see how the fetish is an effect of a subject's negotiation of contradictory demands. More importantly, we can
see how this negotiation emerges from desire's confrontation with
knowledge.

Dressing Up Fetishism in Feminist Clothes

Since Freud's 1909 lecture was lost to scholars until quite recently,
there must be some other reason to account for the persistent interpretation of fetishism through dressing and cross-dressing by feminist cultural theorists. One explanation for this may come from the specific
historical moment of fetishism's introduction into the discourse.
Fetishism emerged in Anglo-American feminist discussions in the early
1980s from two directions: film theory, with its focus on theories of
spectatorship and the psychoanalytic construction of the spectator, and
French poststructuralism and its feminist critiques, which were also influenced by psychoanalysis. I will focus on the latter because it brings
us most directly to the issues we have been following around clothing
fetishism and travesty.

Initially, the notion of the fetishist, drawn from the French tradition, served as an abstract metaphor rather than a practical description:
in a 1982 review article of texts by Luce Irigaray and Sarah Kofman,
Elizabeth Berg figured the "affirmative woman" of deconstruction as a
fetishist, a formulation derived from Kofman. This woman affirmed the
undecidability of castration, and hence of her own sexual difference as
either active or passive, masculine or feminine. Her affirmation thus is
ambivalent rather than, as we tend to think of affirmation as being,
straightforward. An even more influential conception of female fetishism by Naomi Schor in 1985 drew from Kofman as well, but Schor's argument hinged on forms of fetishism in the work of George Sand,
raising the possibility of female fetishism in the very title.[3] I will consider the promise of "Female Fetishism" more extensively in a moment,
but suffice it here to say that Schor is less interested in the generalized
notion of undecidability offered by Kofman's fetishism—which draws

on Derrida's work—than on locating and analyzing the specific inter- and intrasubjective relations that fetishism marks.

Yet while the female fetishist might be affirmative for deconstruc- tionists, other feminist theorists have been anything but affirmative of the idea of fetishism for women. Mary Ann Doane took such a position on female fetishism in a 1982 article, asserting that the "female . . . must find it extremely difficult, if not impossible, to assume the position of the fetishist" (23). Perhaps because of this sort of resistance, Schor sig- nals at the outset that her move is an act of appropriation, applying psy- choanalytic concepts "to ends for which they were not intended" (301). Such carefulness reflects not only the resistance many feminists have felt in claiming perversions for women, but also the intransigence of the hypothesis that fetishism is an exclusively male perversion.

This wary attitude has influenced even feminists writing ten years later. In the introduction to their recent book on female fetishism, Lor- raine Gamman and Merja Makinen address the question of why femi- nists should be concerned with fetishism, acknowledging that "perhaps caution is needed when claiming that fetishism is something that women might do" (2). But they are clearly starting from a very different vantage point than Schor or Doane. The very first sentence of their book professes their "surprise" that "the idea that women do not fetishize was still taken for granted," especially since they "found so much em- pirical evidence that shows [the female fetishist's] existence" (1). They further argue for the value of claiming perversions for women by as- serting that "the female fetishist breaches many of those [cultural] boundaries and 'binary oppositions' about sexual difference" (3).

Gamman and Makinen's book makes a major break away from viewing women's fetishism as only sartorial or transvestistic, though they do touch on those forms, and we might wonder what relation this difference has to their willingness to accept that women do fetishize in- stead of entertaining a skeptical attitude toward the possibility of fe- male fetishism and its application toward feminist ends. Indeed, they note that every feminist critic they examined "despite the best inten- tions, stumbled with Freud and Lacan in the same places" (7), a coinci- dence which they attribute to an underlying theoretical bias against considering women as active sexual agents.

When feminist critics have thought about women as active sexual agents, they have tended to do so around the related issue of masquer- ade. The fact that Schor's female fetishism article appeared at a time when masquerade was a hot topic for feminist thinking suggests that masquerade may have provided an important context for her develop- ment of fetishism through the notion of female travesty. Looking at masquerade does suggest some parallels with fetishism. Masquerade, especially in feminist theory, is formulated as a strategy to conceal lack; thus it seems to be parallel to, if not the same thing as, fetishism when it is understood as a disavowal of feminine lack. Ever since Joan Rivière's essay on womanliness, masquerade has been discussed as a compensatory effort by women to reassure men that nothing/no one is really out of place; it thus seems similar to fetishism's compensation as it is classically understood through the simple penis-substitution theory.[4]

From this vantage it seems that perhaps Freud's comment about women's clothes fetishism was directed more at their masquerade than their fetishism. If that is the case, then we need to unpack a bit more the connections between fetishism and masquerade. It is possible that masquerade is a more acceptable practice to claim for women (since it is not a perversion), or that the notion of "women's masquerade" has been a masquerade for their fetishism. After all, the notion of femininity as seductive packaging has a long history in Western culture, so claiming women's masquerade for feminist theory falls in line with assumptions that women's agency is appropriately relegated to manipulating appearances rather than things. Women's relation to clothes, then, would be understood as subordinated to their concern with appearance, and not as a relation to objects that would in themselves garner women's interest.

Performances of gender as masquerade are not far from what Schor has called "female travesty," which she associates with female fetishism, nor are they far from the clinical association of fetishism with transvestism. The reassurance that feminist theorists have suggested masquerade offers seems similar to the reassurance that psychologists have theorized in fetishistic transvestism, a diagnosis listed in the DSM-IV, the catalog of psychological disorders and their treatment. Robert Stoller, one of the best-known specialists on gender identity, describes the male transvestite as anchored in a male identity even as he is fully attired in women's clothes; he is reassured of his masculinity by his erect penis. As Marjorie Garber notes in her discussion of transvestism, Stoller's description is fully evident in transvestite literature, and she suggests that "[t]he Stoller scenario of reassurance as potency . . . is clearly indebted to the Freudian scenario of fetishistic display."[5] Yet however tempting it may be to conflate fetishism and masquerade, it is important to underscore here that fetishism offers reassurance to oneself, whereas masquerade offers reassurance to another. This is a critical distinction as we think through the feminist appropriation of fetishism, since the wariness around fetishism signals a certain hesitancy in embracing erotic reassurance or sexual satisfaction for women.

Notably, the question of women's agency, sexual or otherwise, drops out as the frame shifts from masquerade to transvestism; the clinical literature such as Garber describes has centered on men's cross-dressing. This makes Schor's choice of travesty particularly significant. In Schor's use of the term, travesty designates an imitation that is not politically charged as either conservatively reassuring or radically subversive.[6] It is also not inherently gendered. Although travesty and transvestism share a common root in the Latin *vestis*, meaning clothing or garment, they differ insofar as travesty retains a general connotation of parody through disguise, while transvestism specifically indicates cross-gender dressing. In the example Schor draws upon, travesty takes the form of cross-dressing within one gender; as other feminists have taken up Schor's work, the connections between travesty and fetishism have become more closely knit even as travesty itself is broadened to encompass a range of imitations.[7]

The fact that discussions of fetishism by both feminists and scientists specializing in gender identity repeatedly invoke strategies of gender or identity performance like masquerade, transvestism, and travesty is striking. This juxtaposition of masquerade, transvestism, travesty, and fetishism draws our attention to the prostheses with which we construct our identities, and to the rules we may both follow and violate in the process. But the choice of these prosthetic objects is not haphazard, and this is why we must read these theories of fetishism alongside Freud's claims about clothes fetishism. Freud's 1909 discussion of fetishism directs our attention to a different dimension of the clothes/fetishism conjuncture, suggesting that the partial repression of instinct involved might indicate something beyond a negotiation of the threat of castration and the subsequent assumption of one of two genders. The comparison of these two perspectives on fetishism suggests that desire might not only produce its object but also its subject through the interpretation and negotiation of the available categories of identity. We cannot so glibly disconnect sexuality from gender as if one or the other were a static category or stable baseline for the development of identity. For feminist analysis this means that we must dispense with voluntarist notions of identity, and especially of identities that have been cast as the workhorses for political change.

As with the orthodox interpretation of fetishism, both masquerade and transvestism have been cited as strategies that uphold a binary gender system whose options are defined through castration as either presence or absence, having or lacking. But more importantly, these strategies all offer a more hopeful, potentially progressive aspect, in that these three terms share a common inappropriateness, whether it is attributing a penis to one's mother, adopting feminine masquerade to cover one's own phallic transgressions, or taking on the characteristics of the "opposite" sex. The willingness to veer from the script, or to use norms to achieve one's own ends, is clearly what these strategies have in common; however, only masquerade has escaped disparagement as a perversion.

When feminists have directed their attention to fetishism instead of masquerade, they have focused on Freud's late work, specifically two essays, "Fetishism" (1927) and "The Splitting of the Ego in the Defensive Process" (1940). The dominant trait they have drawn on is thus the split ego. Parveen Adams exemplifies this attitude when she asserts that "what Freud made abundantly clear is that fetishism is crucially about a splitting of the ego" (254). Naomi Schor also relies on the *ichspaltung* as the salient feature of fetishism, the one that makes it thinkable for women: "for the little girl's ego can be split along the very same fault lines as the little boy's" (306). This juxtaposition opens up a clearly epistemological dimension of fetishism, emphasizing the contradictions of the fetishist's belief and knowledge in relation to the real. It also serves to rescue fetishism from the taint of sexual perversion, raising it to the higher cultural value of an intellectual phenomenon. More interestingly, this emphasis on splitting redirects attention to the less gender-bound aspects of fetishism, just as Freud's reading of the psychoanalytic literature shifts the terms from consideration of feminine articles to any possible thing, however tangentially related.

Despite the fact that Schor's explicit concern in appropriating fetishism focuses on the splitting of the ego, a characteristic of fetishism that need not be understood in gendered terms, her examples, all drawn from the work of George Sand, illustrate a range of aspects of fetishism beyond the *ichspaltung* and are expressly understood through gendered differences. The first examples Schor provides are recognizably fetishistic—as she says, each scene "so prophetically rehearses the gestures of what has come to be known as fetishism" (303). In two different Sand novels, *Valentine* and *Mauprat*, the female protagonist is wounded by her male suitor, who fetishizes the wound. While in *Mauprat*, the eroticized wound is on the heroine's arm, in *Valentine* it is on her foot, a classical fetish object. Though these scenes are undeniably examples of fetishism "before the letter," it is less clear that these are cases of *female* fetishism. In both of these cases, the male suitor is the fetishist and the heroine is "fetished" [Schor's word], or the object of fetishistic attention. Thus these examples replay the classic scene that troubles so many feminist critics who confront fetishism: the threat that women's desire and subjectivity are occluded by the fetishist's focus on the fetish object.

In making her case for these scenes as fetishism, Schor tells us that "If . . . the author of the scene were male, we could satisfy ourselves with the assumption that the male character somehow bodies forth male fantasies of wounding and reparation, male recognition and denial of women's castration" (305). Yet in making her case for these examples as female fetishism, Schor seems to be satisfied with the assumption that the female author somehow bodies forth female fantasies. Despite the fact that the fetishist in the text is male and the fetishism is recognizable because it replays the scene we have come to know through Freud, it is the gender of the author that has prevented these scenes from immediately being recognized as "a textbook case of" (male) fetishism, and it is the gender of the author that makes these scenes now recognizable as *female* fetishism. As Teresa de Lauretis notes in her reading of Schor, the appeal here is to authorial desire.[8] Undoubtedly, the tactic of arguing for authorial desire is one way of opening up space for women's subjectivity to reemerge. But the claim for female fetishism in this particular case hinges upon a sort of authorial cross-dressing; the female author becomes a recognizable fetishist through her male characters. That this example is recognized as female rather than male fetishism hinges on the author's having a particular body to guarantee or authenticate meaning.

Authorial desire would be a risky foundation for an argument positing female fetishism in the face of a psychoanalytic tradition that believes only in male fetishism, because it relies on the very same predetermined meaning of the body that led psychoanalysis to be blind to the existence of female fetishism in the first place. But this authorial desire is not the foundation for Schor's argument, only its threshold. Schor does not rest the weight of her argument only on these examples; as she continues on to other examples, however, her argument takes the shape of a one-way trajectory that moves away from the term "female fetishism" to "bisexuality" and ends at "female travesty." Examining this chain of terms will shed light on the interconnection between fetishism and travesty.

The strength of Schor's argument and the feasibility of these substitutions lie in the fact that there is more than just authorial desire at work in her formulation of female fetishism in Sand's two texts here, *pace* de Lauretis. Each shift in terms illuminates a new aspect of fetishism. Schor elicits two especially useful aspects of fetishism by considering female fetishism through a textual reading. First, she posits parenthetically that the wound is a particularly Sandian fetish, "for wounds *per se* are not generally fetishized by men" (304). She thus uses a strategy, typical of literary criticism, of attending to an author's singularities in order to characterize the phenomenon. This level of reading fetishism offers a path away from any guarantee the body might offer about the nature of the author's desire and instead posits fetishism as a literary strategy—thus as grounded in interpretation within a text rather than in the physical world or the relation between the author and text.

There is a second and more important argument, however, that shifts the emphasis entirely away from the less reliable authorial or intentional level and onto the purely textual level, where the evidence for the interpretation can be directly located. Schor argues that these forms of fetishism provide a "liminal space wherein the struggle between male desire and female sublimation is played out" (304). According to her reading of the scenarios, these scenes do not present an active male agent acting upon a passive female object in the fetishistic process of wounding and idealization; rather, both characters actively and fetishistically relate to the wounding. For Schor, this demonstrates that fetishism is intersubjective in nature.

With these examples providing a springboard into the appropriation of fetishism, Schor follows up this discussion with an analysis of how Freud does "go about masculinizing fetishism" (305). Both of these moves open up the space to view how female fetishism could take shape; the latter by showing the gaps in psychoanalytic assumptions (that anyone with an ego is subject to it being split, whether one is a boy or a girl), and the former by suggesting that fetishism in females may take a different form or object (wounds, for example, rather than shoes). We may not recognize forms of female fetishism by simply looking for the same objects males fetishize. This insight makes it clear that fetishism is determined by a particular *relation* to an object, not by the specific object.

What is striking about Schor's argument is that she's not content to let these two "textbook case[s] of fetishism" (305) suffice. Instead, she seizes on the notion of undecidability in fetishism as "what is pertinent to women" (306), and introduces the notion of "bisexuality" to describe this oscillation. She suggests that the scenes of wounding prior to sexual initiation serve as "a refusal firmly to anchor woman—but also man—on either side of the axis of castration," a refusal Schor labels "bisextuality" (307). This term "bisextuality" presents itself, at the moment of its introduction, as the linchpin of Schor's interpretation of Sand. In Sand, argues Schor, "this perverse oscillation takes the form of a breakdown of characterization which is quite possibly Sand's most radical gesture as a writer. . . . her occasional rejection of firm boundaries between characters subverts the fiction of individuation that is the bedrock of conventional realism" (307).

This bisextual oscillation may seem to be an extension of the notion of intersubjectivity underscored by the first examples of female fetishism, but in fact bisextual oscillation highlights an *intra*subjective vacillation. The shift between the intersubjective notion of fetishism in the first examples and the intrasubjective fetishistic oscillation that is introduced with the term "bisextuality" is unremarked, but perhaps best indicated by the choice of examples. Rather than return to the fetishism scenes already introduced and read the bisextuality there to illustrate her new term, Schor directs our attention to yet another of Sand's works, *Lélia*, where she argues Sand's bisextuality is most prominent (307). It is Lélia herself who teeters between being seen as a man and being known as a woman, who thus is not firmly anchored on either side of the axis of castration, according to Schor's reading. The lack of return to the initial examples is significant, since it constructs a double effect. On the one hand, Schor moves easily from "fetishism" in Sand's texts of 1832 and 1837, to "bisextuality" in one from 1833, as if the two terms represent different forms of the same thing, since they crop up in texts of the same time period. On the other hand, the lack of return leaves open the idea that "bisextuality" is not simply an extension or an elaboration of the idea found in the first scenarios presented and labeled "female fetishism"; it cannot be found in the fetishism texts, but it is present in *Lélia*, suggesting these two "perversions" might be mutually exclusive.

If the first set of examples illustrates a classical notion of fetishism that we have come to know from readings of Freud, the second set of examples illustrates the fetishistic oscillation in bisextuality. Yet bisextuality is not an end unto itself. At its most radical, what this bisextual breakdown of boundaries paves the way for is "female travesty," according to Schor. While "bisextuality" is explicitly described as an oscillation within the binary sexual difference between masculine and feminine, the examples Schor provides of female travesty do not hinge on this particular binarism. They also take us out of the realm of the purely *intra*subjective, replicating further the ambivalence about intra and intersubjectivity bisextuality produces. Schor notes that although there is a long history of "naturalized, intersexual travesty in fiction, drama, and opera, the exchange of *female* identities, the blurring of differences *within* difference remains a largely marginal and unfamiliar phenomenon" (308). In directing our attention from *Lélia* to *Indiana*, from bisextuality to female travesty, Schor takes us into a critical space in which sexual difference can be configured without recourse to a heterosexual binarism.

The radical potential of this critical space, however, remains untapped. The effect of moving from fetishism between male and female characters to bisextuality within a female character to the cross-identity play between female characters sets up this elaboration of fetishism as moving ever closer to the target female specificity, but one defined within a narrow set of gender binaries. The classical binaries of male and female are first modulated to masculine and feminine poles within "bisextuality" that either males or females may oscillate between, and then with the introduction of "female travesty" both men and masculinity are eliminated for a more diffuse play of differences within the category of women. Yet the characterization of this as "differences within difference" retains a claim on binary gender categories, effectively demonstrating the intransigence of a dualistic gender system.

The article's seemingly smooth progression along the chain of three terms, from "female fetishism" to "bisextuality" to "female travesty," covers over a gap between intersubjective and intrasubjective fetishism, and this blindspot plays a crucial role in reaffirming the hetero-binary underpinning this elaboration of fetishism. All of the forms of fetishism along this chain of terminological substitution remain constrained within an uncontested binary gender system, closing off the radical and disruptive potential her critical reading might unleash. This is most evident if we read her final example.

Schor closes with an example of female travesty from Sand's first novel, *Indiana*. She describes how Raymon, suitor to the heroine Indiana, had his love destroyed when he was confronted by Indiana holding "a luxuriant mass of hair" shorn from her drowned servant's head. In an earlier scene in the novel, the same servant had stood in—clad in Indiana's pelisse, as if a body double—as the object of Raymon's amorous advances. In his seduction, Raymon fantasized he was with Indiana when he made love to the servant, Noun. Schor uses this example to focus our attention on Raymon's response to Indiana—"You have inflicted a horrible wound on me"—and on the travesty of Indiana by her servant. The fetishism at work in the female travesty, in Schor's reading, is the oscillation around the two effects of the travesty, which both "causes male desire to misfire" and "perpetuates the myth of the exclusive masculinity of the libido" (308). Here fetishism is shown to be both intersubjective and intrasubjective. It is intersubjective insofar as Raymond reacts to Indiana's holding the hair, and his reaction builds upon his interpersonal relations to both Indiana and Noun. It is *intra*subjective insofar as the desire is read as one-way, both firing and misfiring within the male character's subjectivity.

But if we are interested in *female* fetishism, then the suitor's aim is not our concern. What might be our concern, however, is the fact that the hair—a paradigmatic fetish object, cut and conserved from a woman's head—is oddly omitted from Schor's commentary. Schor does not discuss what Indiana is doing with the servant's hair, other than to say she uses it to "entice" Raymon. This may be due to the fact that Sand is equally opaque on this point, since as feminist critics have pointed out, she does not clearly convey desiring female subjects in her writing. But reexamining the scene in the novel suggests that the disruption of Raymon's desire is not all that is going on in this scene; other fetishistic elements are also at work.

If we look at the scene from a perspective that accepts that women can be fetishists, we may interpret Indiana here as appropriating the role of a *coupeur des nattes*, a classic form of fetishism in which the fetishist clips a lock of hair from the fetishee. Perhaps this interpretation is not considered by Schor because in the scene the hair has the opposite effect of a fetish—rather than facilitate the suitor's sexual aim, it thwarts the aim outright (although Raymon does recover to pursue his object). But if it is the heroine's aim that counts, not the suitor's, then we may see how this scene of fetishism serves to facilitate the heroine's desire or enables her to sustain her ambivalence: the failure to consummate the seduction in this scene in fact enables the seduction to be prolonged, and Indiana's ambivalent desire is likewise drawn out.

In the primal fetish scene, Indiana, waiting in her room for a rendez-vous with Raymon, struggles with the recently imparted knowledge of his earlier seduction of her maid, which conflicts with her own desire for him. Suddenly, although we are not told why, Indiana has the idea to wrap her head in a kerchief and hold Noun's hair in her hands, as if she had sacrificed her own locks. This at first is what Raymon believes she has done, until he recognizes the hair as Noun's. This confrontation produces the effect of Raymon swooning and falling to the floor, effectively deferring the seduction. However, the confrontation does help Indiana achieve one of her aims, of confirming the suspicion behind her unease. This confirmation prolongs her struggle in the novel, for it fuels her love and makes her realize how debased she would be to give in to it. Fetishism here marks an ambivalence more about knowledge than desire.

At the same time, we should not too quickly presume that Indiana's desire is necessarily heterosexual in this scenario. Her seduction of Raymon could be read as having more to do with her relation to Noun, perhaps as an attempt to place herself in her dead maid's position or to recapture her connection with her foster sister by mimicking Noun's earlier association with Raymon (which is itself a mimicry of a fantasy relation between Indiana and Raymon). This may not stem so much from wanting to *be* Noun as wanting to know her again, or at least know what happened to her. In this light, Raymon is a mediator between Noun and Indiana, one without even the status of a fetish. The hair fetish thus enacts the relation between Indiana and Noun and its loss. But this reading diverts us from the way that fetishism serves to trouble the ostensibly heterosexual love narrative, although the two perspectives shed light on how fetishism disrupts an easy definition of sexual differences based on objects of desire, or an easy definition of desire based on sexual rather than epistemological drives.

If, as Freud will announce some seventy years later, lingering "on the path towards the final sexual aim" is perverse, then Indiana's use of the hair may be even more clearly fetishistic, since it adds an element of perversion.[9] The scene functions as part of the process of deferral that is central to the novel's development—if not also to the generic convention of heterosexual romance. It thus can be seen as part of an authorial fetishism—using undecidability as a device to facilitate the author's desire to tell an interesting story.

It is precisely because this travesty and particularly the hair fetish succeeds in disrupting the trajectory of the "normal" aim of seduction that it recommends itself as fetishism. A number of elements of fetishism are at work in this scenario, though they are not explicitly harnessed together. The opacity of Indiana's desire in the text focuses our attention on the object she wields, just as the opacity of the fetishist's desire does. The indeterminacy of whose head the locks were cut from underscores how the hair fetish both effaces the difference between the two women and affirms it. The hair also represents a monument to the loss of Noun, who was not only Indiana's servant but her best friend and childhood playmate; in this way it plays into the Freudian interpretation that emphasizes the fetish's role as preserving that which is lost. Most importantly, the hair fetish enables Indiana to resolve, if only momentarily, the painful conflict between belief—that Raymon loves her—and knowledge—that he has previously seduced Noun and thereby contributed to her suicide. The female travesty—the blurring of boundaries between Noun and Indiana—serves to facilitate this fetishism, as the hair becomes ambivalently situated, belonging to either Indiana or Noun. The travesty also hearkens back to Noun's scene of seduction, importing resonances from that scene into this one. The fetishistic oscillation, then, is not merely the intrasubjective struggle by Indiana through her appropriation of Noun's hair, but also between the earlier and later seduction scenarios.

Each scenario—the servant's and the mistress's—throws different aspects, different poles of ambivalence, into relief. The description of Indiana's fetishistic appropriation of Noun's hair hints at crossing racial boundaries instead of gendered ones. Noun's hair is described as "of an Ethiopian black, of an Indian texture" in contrast to the "silken tresses" of Indiana with their blue-black gleam (163). In Noun's seduction, however, class transgression is most significant.[10] We see its effects in Raymon's reflections on his affair with Noun: "The wife of a peer of France who should sacrifice herself so recklessly would be a priceless conquest; but a lady's maid! That which is heroism in the one becomes brazen-faced effrontery in the other" (30). Noun's class transgression of writing a love letter to Raymon seals the lid on her fate, destroying any chance she might have had for reconciliation. "Yet she had taken satin-finished paper from Madame Delmare's desk, and her style from her own heart. But the spelling! Do you know how much energy a syllable more or less adds to or detracts from the sentiments? Alas, the poor half-civilized girl from Ile Bourbon did not know even that there were rules for the use of language. She believed that she wrote and spoke as correctly as her mistress" (33). If Raymon had attributed to Noun characteristics that were not hers—in effect, through his fantasy of Noun as Indiana, fetishizing her by believing she had education when she did not—this letter brings home to him the reality of her lack. Noun's chances of successfully carrying off this class travesty were slim.[11] The satin paper and sentiments from her own heart—the manifestations of her own belief in her lack of lack—fail to supply the necessary satisfaction to Raymon, although she finds no fault with them. We need look no further than *Indiana* to find a text that, as Schor says, "rehearses the gestures of . . . fetishism"—only in order to find them we must shift our attention from sexual difference as the focus of the fetishistic ambivalence to racial, class, and other differences in identity. The textbook case of *Indiana* instructs us to broaden the scope of our understanding of fetishism's poles of oscillation.[12]

This version of fetishism provides an insight that the scenario from Freud's 1927 essay obscures in its focus on (hetero-)sexual difference: it reconfigures fetishism so that it need not hinge solely around such heterosexual difference. This reformulation blurs the distinctions we could make between female fetishism and male fetishism; no longer can they be separated merely on the basis of the object involved or the subject's interpretation of sexual difference through the threat of castration. Fetishism as female travesty in the end works against the stated trajectory of Schor's argument—to describe female fetishism—much as it makes Schor's argument possible. Schor's appropriation of fetishism is continually and insistently gendered, despite the fact that her initial grounds for introducing the possibility of fetishism for women are founded on the assertion that the splitting of the ego is not a gender-restricted phenomenon. Indeed, the ungendered aspects of fetishism are what Schor uses to appeal to a feminist transposition of fetishism, but that appeal is couched in explicitly gendered terms. Thus, Schor asserts that "what is pertinent *to women* in fetishism is the paradigm of undecidability that it offers" (306; emphasis added). There is of course no outside to our gender system; what is interesting about the move into seemingly ungendered space in order to make a claim for women is the way that it challenges the notion of fetishism, but leaves the binary framework of gender undisturbed.

This gendering of fetishism is consistently accompanied by a move to generalize fetishism. Schor's choice to privilege undecidability as the aspect feminists should steal from fetishism opens fetishism out into a larger economy of conceptual reasoning. She cites Elaine Showalter's discussion of women's writing "as an object-field problem in which we must keep two oscillating texts simultaneously in view" and E. H. Gombrich's famous illustration of the duck-rabbit (qtd. in Schor 307). Both of these examples offer an epistemological model for holding together contradictory ideas—the very same epistemological model as fetishism employs.

Yet fetishism is not merely ambivalence or undecidability, even if that may be its most useful aspect for women—or, as I would prefer to argue, for feminists. Perceiving both the duck and the rabbit does not operate fetishistically to enable one to simultaneously avow and disavow difference, to hold belief in contradictory tension with knowledge in order to gain something for oneself, precisely because the duck-rabbit problem is not a loaded question. Feminist criticism, on the other hand, is—particularly as it struggled to establish credibility.[13] Schor's stake in opening up fetishism to a more generalized epistemological economy demonstrates the extent to which fetishism already haunts feminist discourse.[14] But because this opening is so thoroughly concerned with binary sexual difference, we risk losing sight of an important point. What is pertinent to fetishism, what separates it from merely a generalized ambivalence, are the loaded consequences of the distinction between whose poles fetishism vacillates.

The process of gendering fetishism—distinguishing a female fetishism from a male fetishism—courts trouble by obscuring a productive interpretation of what is at work in both Sand's and Schor's texts. The very usefulness of fetishism as a strategy lies with how it (potentially productively) undermines the rigid matrix of binary sexual difference through indeterminacy. In fact, this is precisely why Schor values Sand's bisextuality; yet the very formulation of bisexuality remains within a binary gendered framework. To then reinscribe fetishism within that same matrix—defining a male or female fetishism—undercuts fetishism's strategic effectiveness. Perhaps this is why Schor herself moves on quickly to consider female travesty, rather than resting content with the notion of bisexuality as female fetishism. The "female" in female travesty functions differently than the "female" in female fetishism, since the notion of travesty foregrounds differences between the females, while the category of "female fetishism" implicitly emphasizes similarities.

Through this last example from *Indiana*, we can see how other elements of identity provide the occasion for fetishistic oscillation, although these other differences are not foregrounded in Schor's reading, because of her emphasis on gendering fetishism through a binary opposition of female/male. This persistent gendering leads Schor to conclude her article with a warning, rather than with optimism about fetishism's subversive potential. This warning comes in the form of an acknowledgment of her own nagging doubt that this "perversion theft" is "only the latest and most subtle form of 'penis-envy'" (309). Thus Schor does not unambivalently advocate female fetishism as a productive feminist strategy. Nor is she unequivocally against it. The necessary conditions, however, are rather utopian: "What we have here is an instance of 'paleonymy,' the use of an old word for a new concept. To forge a new word adequate to the notion of female fetishism, what we need now is what Barthes called a 'logothète,' an inventor of a new language" (309). In short, in order for female fetishism to present itself as a more hopeful or optimistic contribution to feminist thinking, we have to have a new or at least transformed order of the signifiers and associations that define our field of vision—and that includes the ordering of the signifiers of sexual difference and the assumptions that underpin that organization. It is not fetishism per se that requires the services of the logothète, but rather the idea that anyone could be a fetishist, that sex is not a constraint on who could have the special relation to an object that we call fetishism that requires inventive thinking.

This rethinking involves a new epistemological framework to guide our interpretation, for the organization of sign systems is backed by systems of knowledge. A more complex understanding of sexual difference(s) that embraces ambiguity or hybridity, such as one developed through an analysis of the very phenomenon of fetishism, may provide the first step for entering into a renovated epistemological field, since sexual difference is such a crucial, if unacknowledged, rubric for ordering knowledge. If what we know is no longer strictly separated from us as an external object, but can be acknowledged as a relation we are invested in as deeply as we are now understood to be invested in categories of identity, will we be able to sustain the same gendering of knowledge—the masculinization of objectivity and the feminization of subjectivity?

Reading Schor and Sand suggests that, *pace* Freud, there is more at stake in female fetishism than just an inappropriate preoccupation with clothes. Schor's elaboration of female fetishism as travesty pushes us beyond Freud's assertion that "all women are clothes fetishists" to foreground the mechanisms of identification and identity-construction that operate through and partially constitute sexual difference, and which also, like fetishism, involve the unconscious. The shift in analyzing fetishism through the notion of travesty in this chapter rather than the notion of prototype in the first chapter marks a change in emphasis from an object's relation to another object—the prototype to the finished product, the substitute for the thing substituted—to a subject's relation to other subjects through objects. Although all objects are imbued with meaning, some may be more public, such as those objects that designate cultural categories of identity (the way a high-heeled shoe embodies femininity), while others have more private meanings attached (the way Noun's hair functions in *Indiana*). Of all things clothes are most closely associated with our identities and particularly our gender—after all, the cliché is that the clothes make the man. The truism points to our need to have our things express some truth about ourselves, even if that truth is a message mixed between public and private meanings, or only a projection of an image we wish were our own. And, though they by no means are the only such items, clothes are the things which are most likely to be gendered in a way that seems natural; we have men's and women's shirts, for example, but not men's and women's garden tools. Freud was right about one aspect of women's purported clothes fetishism: clothes serve as some form of gender guarantee. Clothes provide reassurance about identity, and particularly about gender identity, that other mundane but less intimate objects cannot offer.

But most importantly, reading the examples from Sand through Schor lays the groundwork for us to see that the differences fetishism negotiates need not be restricted to a binary heterosexual form. From this perspective, reviewing Freud's assertion that all women are clothes fetishists provides a valuable insight about what is at stake in fetishism: fundamentally, fetishism is about the negotiation of the boundary of the self, the establishment of identity, of which sexual difference is only one aspect, albeit a fundamental one. Fetishism plays a key role in the process of identification and the construction of identity; fetish objects provide evidence for and sites of investment through which identification can work.[15] One can say one shares the same relation to a fetish object—for example, the claim to love a popular novel—that others have, and thereby solidify one's relations to other individuals or a group, even though these relations may be contradictory or one may feel ambivalent about claiming inclusion in the group. But, importantly, the process is not restricted to other subjects; the relation to fantasmatic ideals also comes into play. Fetishism is a response or strategy that reflects a failure to develop a fully autonomous subjectivity, but still recognizes the need to strive for that autonomous ideal. We need to find fetishes that suit us, because they are instrumental in helping us find satisfaction in the face of impossible or fantasmatic demands.

In light of the example of fetishism developing from the details of Indiana's relation to Noun, we can reframe the classic fetishistic scenario through the question of individual autonomy rather than sexual difference: how does one begin to differentiate oneself from one's intimate associates? The child looking up at the mother perceives difference only by assuming a common ground, a similar anatomy. Fetishism in the late Freudian scenario is a reaction to the process of differentiating oneself from one's mother, and sexual difference is, for the boy, the most obvious means.[16] In a context that emphasizes binary sexual difference, such as the one in which Freud formulated his investigations of sexuality and sexual difference at the turn of the century, the strategies for this differentiation are necessarily limited to three: the two poles of the binary and the third which refuses to choose. But in a cultural context where binary sexual difference is configured differently, the choices that fetishism helps the subject navigate are more numerous. In the 1830s in France, class difference was as significant as gender; now, in the late twentieth century, differences of race, political affiliation, or sexual practice are seen to operate similarly.

This returns us to the impetus for Schor's choice of texts. In setting out her argument, Schor emphasizes the fact that these scenes predate psychoanalysis's description of fetishism (302). For her this is important, given that psychoanalysis has elbowed female fetishism out of the picture to such an extent that it becomes a hazard even to reassert it, as Schor's closing doubt as to whether "female fetishism" is merely "the latest and most subtle form of 'penis-envy'" warns us (309). If a heterobinary sexual difference is *the* difference for our very understanding of fetishism, then perhaps we are too fixated upon this form of sexual difference. It would thus serve as a fetish itself, blocking our view of other differences, a monument to their loss, making them seem somehow less imperative.

If we were to de-fetishize our view of Schor's choice of texts and open up our examination to account for other differences, we might also be struck by the fact that these scenes predate Marx's notion of commodity fetishism and the development of modern department stores. Fetishism is tied not only to the emergence of modern Western interpretations of sexual difference, but also to the changes in the formation of class differences in the modern era. Schor's text only latently addresses this difference; Leslie Camhi's work on kleptomania in the nineteenth century helps draw this connection out further. We might see Camhi's concern as the chiasmatic opposite of Schor's—where the latter is focused on perversion theft, the former tackles the theft perversion.

In the urban environment of the nineteenth century, the classes mixed in unprecedented proximity. To negotiate the potential threat of cross-class contamination, the illusion of sameness had to be constructed to reassure the middle class. Department store clerks, as Camhi points out, had to project an image of bourgeois femininity in order to mediate between the store's goods and its clientele, yet they "were paid insufficiently to maintain the illusion themselves" (33). This mediation became all the more important as the introduction of the fixed price "suddenly made the commodity's aura its sole negotiable consideration" (32), and put further emphasis on image over substance. In such a context, Camhi argues, the department store kleptomania that emerged in the mid-nineteenth century was a sexual disorder, emphasizing the element of fantasy involved in the motive for theft.

Although she links kleptomania to hysteria and "a crisis of consuming identities" (33), she does not explicitly call the phenomenon fetishism. Yet here too certain boundaries of difference are threatened and transgressed, only it is class, not sexual difference, that is at stake:

The dangers of the urban crowd, in which classes promiscuously mingled, were reflected in the department store's hybrid displays of luxurious and inexpensive objects, disorienting the consumer by transgressing the boundaries of class identity. (33)

This boundarylessness is similar to Schor's notion of "bisextuality." The refusal to be anchored firmly on either side of the axis of sexual difference, however, is replaced by an oscillation of class difference, particularly in the person of the department store clerk, but also in the shopper's experience of the store's self-presentation. In this oscillation, objects provide an anchor for subjects' identities.

As she proceeds through her discussion of kleptomania, Camhi recalls Gatian de Gaëtan de Clérambault's case histories of "women's erotic passion for fabrics." This would seem to be a prime opportunity to connect kleptomania and fetishism. All of Clérambault's women were classified as kleptomaniacs, and all chose silk as their particular erotic object. Clérambault and Camhi both focus on the women's relation to the silk as a sexual autoeroticism: Camhi notes that it seems as if "the feminine aberrance were too formless to describe without recourse to its masculine counterpart." She quotes Clérambault, who characterized the women's reaction as "very variegated, subtle, complicated, innumerable for a fine epidermis" yet denigrated this same reaction as "schematic next to the complex of sensorial, aesthetic, and moral evocations which the fetish evokes in man" (qtd. in Camhi, 40). Clérambault's (hetero-) sexist insistence on the women's passivity in relation to their chosen object exemplifies the bias against women in the classical notion of fetishism. Yet clearly these women were relating to the objects themselves, and this relation can best be described as fetishistic.

The blindness toward fetishism in the reading of these cases underscores questions not only about how subjects are defined, but also about the object's definition. If these women's objects were more formless and fluid (as silk swatches, scarves, or clothes) than rigid and set (as, for example, shoes) this only challenges a narrow conception of appropriate fetish object, or indeed of how we think about objects in general. Fetish objects, for example, tend to be thought of as small or medium-sized objects. Yet cars, farm machinery, and other significantly larger objects have all been documented as fetish objects, proving that our fetishes may indeed be bigger than ourselves.

While Freud asserts that all women are clothes fetishists, Clérambault is at pains to differentiate these women's erotic attraction from fetishism. As Camhi summarizes it:

> The fetishist distinguishes between himself and the object of his fixation, and thus (according to Clérambault) participates in a properly "sexual" relation. The silk addict seems precisely to desire in fabric an absence of boundaries, a loss of distinction between the thing and herself. (41)

If Camhi's clarification reinforces Schor's description of female fetishism as an oscillation,[17] we can also see how it pushes Schor's reading further, giving us to understand how Noun's desire to be Indiana is also fetishistic. She appropriates her mistress's objects—namely her peignoir—to aid in her seduction with Raymon. But this focus on the sexual remains contained within the narrow hetero-binary of sexual difference, and the drive to interpret female fetishism as boundarylessness all too easily replicates clichés of femininity as unformed and oceanic.

If, however, we read the silk as an emblem of *class*, rather than a purely sexual or gendered object, we begin to understand how these women's attractions follow a more orthodox pattern of the fetish as a monument to the loss of a thing that was never there. Of course, things that were never there offer a much broader catalog of fetish possibilities than does a hetero-binary notion of sexual difference that restricts fetishism to the specificity of the penis.

The case of women as clothes fetishists is thus not as simplistic as Freud's blanket statement may have initially made it appear. Indeed, the feminist work on fetishism shows that we must consider sexual difference beyond the purely binary difference represented in the gender fundamentalism of male and female, to understand that the sexual difference fetishism negotiates may be a sexual difference of class or queerness. The solution to the puzzle of female fetishism is not simply to replace binary heterosexual difference with a more fluid oscillation between the poles of other elements of identity. However important it may be as a first step, this solution is only partially adequate; merely adding on additional forms, terms, or identities fails both to address the fundamental challenge to interpretation that fetishism raises and to account for the epistemological function of fetishism. As the first chapter of this work has shown, even the narrow definition of sexual difference predicated on the presence of the penis opens to a more multiple interpretation. While expanding the definition of the set of fetish objects to incorporate a broader range of things might seem to complicate fetishism overmuch, it is nonetheless necessary to consider what these different objects teach us about fetishism. Rather than render fetishism impossibly multiple, they show consistently that fetishes operate as a fundamental tool for subjects to interpret themselves and their world; moreover, this interpretation is strung between the realm of fantasy and a clear sense of reality. We have now looked at the alternative paradigms which challenge assumptions about the constitution of the fetish subject (as female rather than male) and the fetish object (as potentially fluid or formless rather than fixed). What we need to consider next is an alternative paradigm of desire within the dynamic of fetishism; in lieu of an assumption of heterosexuality, let us examine what feminist theorists have theorized about lesbian fetishism.

No Two Ways about It: What Lesbian Fetishism Can Do for You

After decades of feminist scholarship, it has now become a commonplace to assert that sexual difference itself has a history; it has not always been understood through binary heterosexual terms as a biological fact. Thomas Laqueur, for example, points out that male and female genitalia were long considered homologous, up until the eighteenth century, when the one-sex model of the Renaissance and classical Europe was succeeded by a two-sex model that emphasized women's difference from men. Laqueur asserts that "the problem . . . well into the seventeenth century was not finding the organic signs of sexual opposition but understanding heterosexual desire in a world of one sex" (106). He adds, furthermore, that "[t]he Renaissance shared this concern with Freud" (113), thus connecting Freud's ambivalence over sexual difference to the contingencies of a larger historical perspective.

Not only is the timelessness of the idea of binary sexual difference contested, but the very term "sexual difference" has come under critical examination. In one fairly well-known salvo with the seductive title "The Technology of Gender," Teresa de Lauretis challenged the conflation of sexual difference with gender difference as the basis for feminist thought. De Lauretis is intent on bringing to light differences among women rather than just the binary difference of women from men; similarly Valerie Traub argues that "the very term 'sexual difference' conflates two related but different trajectories of subjectivity—gender identification and erotic desire—which . . . results in an elision of erotic practice" (307). In short, what many theorists of sexuality in the late twentieth century emphasize is that sexual difference, which in Schor's reading is still a binary bodily difference, is less an absolute and binary bodily difference than a range of possible differences mapped out on the body through a matrix of desire and identification. As we move away from a binary, bodily definition of sexual differences, we focus more attention on two factors: the sense of oneself—who or what one identifies with, how one aligns oneself—and the object for which one reaches, what impels us to seek connection with an other.

Given that sexual differences are being rethought and given the way that fetishism complicates how sexual differences are organized, we would do well to reconsider the basis of fetishism in lack. If we are to regard fetishism as part of the construction of autonomous subjectivity, as one strategy for negotiating the difference between oneself and others, we will see fetishism primarily as an issue about loss. In a broad view, this is indeed what the castration theory of fetishism is based upon. Recent feminist work has chosen either to rewrite the meaning of castration (de Lauretis) or to challenge the dominance of castration as the only form of early loss (Gamman and Makinen, Apter). Yet the ambivalence inherent in fetishism signals that the phenomenon is not a simple reaction to loss, but rather circulates around two poles—fetishism is not only about processes of identification, as the emphasis on travesty illustrates, but also about desire, an aspect downplayed by the emphasis on fetishism as travesty. Fetishism is thus not about simply substituting an object for the lost object, but about developing a complex relation that engages both the subject's own sense of herself and her knowledge and fantasies about the object.

Six years after Schor's article posited the existence of female fetishism, Elizabeth Grosz raised the question of lesbian fetishism. Like Schor, Grosz sees her work as an appropriation of psychoanalytic terms for feminist goals. As in Schor's case, there is an explicit ambivalence about what is to be gained by claiming a female or lesbian fetishism; in Grosz's case, this ambivalence is foregrounded in the opening paragraphs and reasserted at the close. Unlike Schor, Grosz repeatedly thematizes this ambivalence as part of her own fetishistic desire: "Like the fetishist, I too want to have it both ways," she announces at the outset (39). At the end, announcing her attitude toward feminist appropriation of psychoanalysis, she reiterates: "I prefer to have it both ways" (52). She advocates neither a wholesale rejection nor acceptance of psychoanalysis's tenets, but rather urges feminists to consider "selecting a notion that is deemed impossible or foreclosed by the theory to show how it may not be as implausible as it seems, if the terms are stretched beyond their normal confines" (52). This "cultivated ambivalence" offers a pragmatic approach to psychoanalysis that enables theorists to move beyond psychoanalysis's limitations. These announcements serve not only as a warning, but more importantly by pushing ambivalence to the forefront, they work rhetorically to present Grosz herself as a fetishist, even as she questions whether lesbian fetishism is possible. Yet in the end Grosz fails to marshal the unsettling aspects of this ambivalence to effective ends; in contrast with Schor, whose title "Female Fetishism" is an almost pugnacious assertion, Grosz's title "Lesbian Fetishism?" remains a question that refrains from challenging assumptions about sexual difference. This question form raises the possibility that ultimately Grosz herself may not be convinced, and that this ambivalent stance is merely a glib rhetorical device rather than a trope with important theoretical consequences.

Working from Freud's and Lacan's theories of fetishism, and a case presented by Sandor Lorand, Grosz's point of departure is firmly established within psychoanalytic orthodoxy. Perhaps because of this more thoroughly psychoanalytical grounding, Grosz's treatment of fetishism in relation to castration is less concerned with the intersubjective processes such as wounding or travesty that mark Schor's reading of the phenomenon in literary texts and more concerned with intrasubjective psychical processes. For Grosz, the key to understanding female fetishism is recognizing the displacement of value at work in the process of disavowal (46). Indeed, Grosz believes that examining disavowal enables us to "understand why Freud considered it impossible for women to be fetishists, and yet to understand that lesbianism could be seen as a form of female fetishism" (47). Through a reading of narcissism, in which the feminine woman phallicizes her own body, Grosz develops an interpretation of lesbian fetishism for the woman "suffering [sic] from the masculinity complex" (51), who parallels the fetishist in disavowing women's castration and taking an external object as a substitute for the phallus. As in Schor's reading of female fetishism, Grosz draws our attention to the splitting of the ego. However, she links this splitting with feminist political engagement, "insofar as feminism, like any oppositional political movement, involves a disavowal of social reality so that change becomes conceivable and possible" (51). This form of splitting involves one's beliefs in relation to oneself within the impersonal social, in contrast to the Freudian model of splitting, which involves beliefs structuring the intimate, personal relation to another.

Such differences can help us see that while there seem to be a number of similarities between Schor and Grosz, in fact these congruities point toward more important differences. For example, although both theorists emphasize the value of ambivalence in fetishism as a means for having "both/and" rather than "either/or" and they each formulate this ambivalence through Freud's notion of the splitting of the ego, only Grosz's sense of splitting is directed outside of purely textual relations, toward the political aims of feminism in the world and more narrowly toward weighing the usefulness of psychoanalysis for feminist theory. Teresa de Lauretis, in her reading of Grosz, terms this shift a "displacement from the realm of the psychic to the realm of the social" (280). Schor's reading of ambivalence, in contrast, provides a strategy for interpreting the characters within a text; her concern is to mark Sand's literary skill in pushing the boundaries of characterization, the splitting of *their* egos. Thus, her concern remains focused not on the social but on the psychical, even though this psychic reality is purely a fictional reality.

As a second example of this pseudo-convergence, both theorists address fetishism in the masculine woman, yet they differ in regard to the relation between self-phallicization and that masculinity. Schor tells us that "Denial is not a male prerogative, as is proven by the behavior of those women who suffer from what Freud calls a 'masculinity complex,'" and she suggests that Sand's Lélia, in her masculine garb as a dandy, "is an eminently phallic figure" (306). In contrast, Grosz argues that the masculinized woman, in her disavowal of her own castration, takes on a phallicized object outside her own body, just as the fetishist does (51). This sexual object, however, is another woman, a narcissistically invested feminine woman who "displaces the value of the phallus onto her own body, taken as a whole." (48). In Grosz's view, the masculine woman thus manifests a fetishistic splitting of the ego, living in tension with having the phallus by having the feminine/femme woman and not having the phallus because of the reality of her castrated position in a phallocentric economy. This very economy furthermore pressures the masculine woman to give up her masculinity in order to be the phallus (or object of desire) for an [implicitly male] other who *can* "have" her. Schor's choice of Lélia, on the other hand, exemplifies bisextuality, rather than orthodox fetishism in a woman; her masculinity enables her to phallicize herself, rather than seek the fetish/phallus/object in someone else. Her bisextuality is more of an expression of gender identity than sexual desire—a desire, perhaps, to *be* rather than to *have*.

The most interesting contrast between the two is marked through their implicit epistemological models, the articulation of fetishistic ambivalence in a feminist framework. Just as Schor discerned three different models of female fetishism in Sand's text (author-centered desire represented through heterosexual fetishism scenes, Lélia's "bisextuality" or what today might be called "genderfuck," and the cross-dressing of female travesty), so too do three different models of fetishism emerge in Grosz's text. The familiar model of the Freudian fetishist appears, wanting to have it both ways—to avow woman's castration and to deny it. On a second model, Grosz's lesbian fetishist denies the social reality of her castration and thus desires the phallicized femme, while at the same time she avows her castration through having the phallicized femme. Meanwhile, the third model, Grosz's own rhetorical fetishism, vacillates between feminist theory in its rejection of psychoanalysis and psychoanalysis in its rejection of women's realities. This latter vacillation is particularly evident between the poles of the psychical and the social. When, as we noted above, de Lauretis characterizes the splitting in Grosz as a "displacement," it only underscores this third form of fetishism at work in Grosz's text, since it draws our attention to her authorial relation to her material.

These three forms of fetishism, whether implicit or explicit in this text, produce only two different consequences. The first consequence of the differences in the levels at which fetishism functions in Grosz's text is that a contradiction opens up between what the text says and what the text does. As we know, the Freudian scenario is classically construed to be a strategy for maintaining one's belief or knowledge both before and after the discovery of castration; it thus enables the fetishist to hold onto an outdated or superseded belief that is nonetheless reassuring. Insofar as Grosz's ambivalent reading likewise maintains a certain rigid division between psychoanalysis and feminist theory (which shows up psychoanalysis's castration, if you will, by demonstrating its shortcomings in theorizing women's experiences), it too functions like the classical interpretation of fetishism. Indeed, rather than acknowledge how a sizable corner of feminist theory is already steeped in psychoanalysis, Grosz's ambivalence holds the two apart, disavowing the roots of her own thinking, and reverting to a mythical past when each theory was uncontaminated by the other (for, although Freud has many shortcomings on the subject of women, he is not unaware of feminist thinking in his work, even if its influence does not always lead him to what we would now consider feminist conclusions).

Grosz's announcements about her own ambivalence only serve to foreground this fetishism, to claim herself as a fetishist while disavowing that lesbians can be fetishists. This renders the question in the title a rhetorical question, closed to analysis, a self-fulfilling prophecy: Lesbian fetishism? well, yes—here I am doing it. However, this "yes" is muddled because while Grosz will position herself as a fetishist, she does not ever claim to be lesbian. Unlike the fetishists, the lesbians in the text are all *in* the text—they are her examples, but they are not part of her rhetorical structure. What's interesting is that only fetishism works rhetorically here, not lesbianism. What's at stake in Grosz's willingness to claim fetishism, explicitly if however ambivalently, but not lesbianism? Perhaps here too, as in Freud's 1927 text, fetishism "saves the fetishist from becoming a homosexual" (*SE* 21: 154). Or it may be evidence that once we enter the realm of the fetishist, sexual distinctions such as those between heterosexuality and lesbianism break down.[18] Because this is an effect of the text, however, it cannot be explored directly in the argument, which does not consider the challenges fetishism mounts to our conceptions of sexual difference.

This is not the only contradiction in what the text says and does. The lesbian fetishist in Grosz's text also does something quite different from the classical fetishism Grosz exhibits in oscillating between feminism and psychoanalysis. In contrast to the Freudian scenario, where the fetishist reacts to the perception of another person's castration, the lesbian fetishist's ambivalence is centered on herself, not on another woman's castration. This ambivalence may be no less a perversion than the narcissism of the femme, who in phallicizing her body perversely extends her erotogenic zone "beyond the regions of the body that are designed for sexual union" (Freud, *SE* 7: 150). But if this is the case, why is this (femme's) narcissistic, perverse extension not viewed as fetish-ism? What difference is there between the femme's narcissistic phalli-cization (which is made possible by disavowing her own castration) and the lesbian fetishist's fetishistic appropriation of the phallicized femme? If the site of castration can shift from the mother to the self, why not also allow for a shift in the location from whence the fetish ob-ject is appropriated to defend against that perceived loss? Because she bases her model on the masculine woman and the desire for the phalli-cized [femme] partner, Grosz forecloses these questions, limiting what we can see about lesbian fetishism, and reducing the threatened loss to a question of phallic presence. There is no room in Grosz's paradigm of lesbian fetishism for the butch (or any lesbian who does not phallicize her whole body) to be the object of desire.

    If the masculine woman has been figured in psychoanalytical the-ory (both in general and in Grosz's text) as wanting a penis or phallus for herself, the desire of the feminine woman for the masculine woman, which might be similarly understood as a desire for another woman to have a penis or phallus, has not been accounted for, in either psycho-analysis in general or Grosz's text.[19] Not to recognize the difference be-tween wanting a penis for oneself—ironically, the feminine wish par excellence, according to Freud—and wanting one for one's mother (or, more importantly, for another woman)[20] replicates the classic blind spot toward female fetishism: it overlooks the possibility that a woman would want another woman to have the phallus, and closes down the possibility of femme fetishism in order to promote butch fetishism. Im-plicit in this move is the residual notion that only men can fetishize—the definition of men can at most be expanded to include men or the mascu-line women who act like them. We are snapped back to a grid of binary sexual difference, where masculine desire is a redundancy and feminine desire an oxymoron. This gives us little benefit for claiming fetishism for women. One of the strongest arguments for recognizing perversion in women posits that to perceive improper desire in women requires an ac-knowledgment of active desire in women. Grosz concedes this problem, wondering aloud "what is to be gained by describing this form of female homosexuality as fetishistic?" (51); this question, which with its implied negative answer suggests a sense of loss, is the seed that generates the rhetorical fetishism, the strategic ambivalence, of the essay. This rhetori-cal ambivalence between feminism and psychoanalysis seeks to guard against losing anything by using these theories. Yet much is lost in how the text plays itself out. If lesbian fetishism remains, ambivalently, a question, the possibility of femme fetishism—as an example of the dif-ferences within lesbian fetishism—cannot even be broached.

The second consequence of the different ways that fetishism works in this text is that we begin to see how usefully disruptive fetishism can be when it is interpreted as unsettling categories through its ambivalent transgression of boundaries rather than as reifying those same boundaries. Thus, the flip side of fetishistic fixity is the productive reinterpretation of reality. This reinterpretation is able to challenge the stultifying definitions that restrict and direct a subject's actions in the world. To consider the possibility of a femme fetishism brings out this latter aspect of fetishism, insofar as it makes us rethink assumptions about what sort of desire a feminine woman would have, or about what it means to have a penis. Where the phallus has served in psychoanalytic thinking to mark desire, the penis has served in the world of contemporary Western culture as the figure of pleasure, par excellence. These figures have provided normative models for enacting desire (without even blinking at the oxymoron) and blocked our conception of a more accurate picture of the diverse and creative forms of subjectivity. The possibility that a woman would seek pleasure with another woman's penis, or desire another woman's phallus, is unthinkable in our current cultural framework. I suggest this has less to do with its probability than with the paucity of interpretations of bodies and pleasure that our current cultural norms, predicated on a binary heterosexuality, offer us.

These considerations offer a picture of the disruptive potential of desire. The different fetishists in Grosz's article thus enable us to see two different epistemological aims for fetishism. One reinforces the status quo, rigidifying and reasserting difference as binary through its insistence on both/and; such conservative inflexibility does not recommend it as a useful strategy for progressive politics. However the other, a repetitive insistence on moving from one option to another, refuses to settle on one single interpretation and undermines naturalized claims to truth. This second strategy is pragmatic, attentive to the circumstances, and negotiates among conflicting impulses and factors to reach the interpretation that works best. It thus offers a potentially theoretically sophisticated approach to troubling political and philosophical issues, such as identity politics.

The rainbow flag offers one small example that shows how this kind of fetish might play out in—and perhaps change conceptions of—identity politics. A symbolic affirmation of gay rights, it easily may pass unremarked by many straight people, yet its significance registers with queer-identified (or even simply queer-savvy) people as a mark of gay visibility or presence. It is designed to be an inclusive symbol without being prescriptive about the identity categories that it represents.

Among gay friends we might note a rainbow flag on a car and say, "queer car"; we mean that someone else around here is like us, when in fact we know nothing of whether the person is, for example, a gay man or a lesbian, a fag or queen or sportsdyke or biker, a radical feminist or a misogynist, a queer, a bisexual, or a straight supporter. What does it mean, then, to identify with the person who has placed the rainbow flag on their car? While such a gesture is political, marking as visible a difference which our culture has strived to repudiate or repress, it is political only in terms of its backdrop, a time when gay political issues, such as the right to marry or to serve in the armed forces or to be protected from discrimination, have also achieved a certain visibility. The object becomes a fetish when it is imbued with such debates; it expresses a belief that there need not be negative consequences for being openly queer (such as oneself or one's car being harmed), but also acknowledges the reality of combating homophobia by taking a visible stance and not being cowed by the threat of violence or discrimination. It is ambivalently only a bumper sticker, a cheap gesture, and an indication of a deeper commitment, one that might inspire others to act.

While this example may seem trivial, that is in fact part of the nature of the fetish in its oscillation between the general and the specific. It is always in danger of seeming ridiculous or obvious to those outside of the special relation to the object. The example of the rainbow flag's opaque or uncertain referent elicits a question with regard to Grosz's text: if the conservative aspect is seen in the way that the rhetorical fetishism renders the title a rhetorical question, the productive vacillation that problematizes both the lesbian and fetishism in the title might get us somewhere—especially if we add, what kind of lesbian, and what kind of fetishism?

One theorist who is able to seize on this epistemological breakthrough to answer the question, "lesbian fetishism?" is Teresa de Lauretis. In her analysis of lesbian desire and fetishism, *The Practice of Love*, de Lauretis is critical of Grosz's central concerns, though she finds moments in the text useful for her own ends. De Lauretis only sees the negative fetishism at work in Grosz; in her view, Grosz's "argument remains mired in the paradox of sexual indifference" (280). Grosz's position upholds the paternal phallus through her division of lesbians into masculine and feminine according to whether they want to have or be the phallus. Thus, argues de Lauretis, Grosz maintains unquestioned a formulation of sexual difference based on the (paternal) phallus "and all it stands for in psychoanalysis and in the culture at large; consequently it colludes with the heterosexual and patriarchal purposes for which psychoanalytic orthodoxy was and is intended, and most immediately the foreclosure of lesbian sexuality" (281–82). From this reading, we can see that the question in Grosz's title, "Lesbian fetishism?" is as much a question about the possibility of the lesbian's desire as about the nature of the fetishism. De Lauretis, whose theoretical stance seeks not only to articulate lesbian desire and sexuality, but also to claim fetishism as a grounding model for that lesbian desire, hones in on this question, transforming it from a question to a founding tenet of her theory.

De Lauretis is also critical of Schor, and it is through this critique that we can best see the key to her critical depiction of Grosz's shortcomings. De Lauretis asserts that "the argument for female fetishism must rest on the meaning of castration" (268). She is dissatisfied with the influence of Sarah Kofman's generalized and Derridean notion of fetishism on Schor's thinking. As in her complaint about Grosz, here too the fault lies with the fact that the interpretation of fetishism "does not allow her to go very far either in the subverting of the Freudian orthodoxy or in the specification of a female fetishism" (268). For de Lauretis, the oscillation between masculine and feminine poles that bisextuality offers is not enough. The refusal to be anchored "does not call into question the fulcrum of that 'axis of castration' on which is balanced the seesaw of such a subjectivity" (269). For want of a thorough disruption of the privileged position of the phallus, Schor must end on such a skeptical, if not pessimistic, note.

The answer for getting beyond the limits of either Grosz's or Schor's adaptations of fetishism, according to de Lauretis, is more—not less—castration. This means that the paternal phallus can no longer be the only thing threatened with loss. Instead, its privilege must be disrupted, and some other phallus or fetish must take its place and provide a different anchor for meaning. We can see a parallel to this necessary shift in the second epistemological aim of fetishism in Grosz's text, with its emphasis on a dynamic of exchange, of repetitive movement between options. We can also see intimations of this shift in Schor's closing warning or instruction that female fetishism would require a new order of language. If, following Lacan, we understand that language and the symbolic order is grounded on the phallus, and that in such a symbolic order female—much less lesbian—fetishism is deemed impossible, then the conditions of possibility for this fetishism to become visible would be not a different relation to the phallus, but a different sort of "phallus" altogether. It is but a short step to suggest that female fetishism would be the symptom of a different linguistic/symbolic order, grounded on the fetish rather than the phallus.

This is the value of de Lauretis's breakthrough: her exposition of the place of the fetish in lesbian desire offers precisely this new grounding for conceptualizing this new symbolic order. As her predecessors do, de Lauretis takes up the model of the masculine woman in developing her theory of how a female fetishism would operate. Like Schor, she draws upon literary texts—only de Lauretis uses twentieth-century characters, such as Stephen Gordon, of Radclyffe Hall's *The Well of Loneliness*, and Marisa in Cherríe Moraga's play, *Giving Up the Ghost*. But her consideration of masculine women does not lead to understanding their masculinization in terms of a drive either to be or to have the phallus; rather, she views their adoption of masculine signs as a semiotic strategy to signify the desire for a woman, since "in a cultural tradition pervasively homophobic, masculinity alone carries a strong connotation of sexual desire for the female body" (243). Here masculinity is less a gender identity than a sign of sexual orientation. Against the psychoanalytic tradition of reading the masculine woman as suffering from penis-envy and as refusing to acknowledge her own castration, de Lauretis reads the masculine woman as one who does not simply disavow her own castration through her fetishistic display of masculine signs but, paradoxically, may also acknowledge it.

This reworking gives us a new perspective on the masculine woman: rather than viewing her as inappropriate and transgressive, which implies a normative feminine standard for women to conform to, this depiction of the masculine woman opens the possibility of understanding her in completely different terms, as struggling to assert her own identity according to a standard other than femininity. This more complex framework can help us understand how subjects come to achieve their own identity in a way analogous to how the classical fetishist finds sexual satisfaction: by negotiating conflicting interpretations and directives to arrive ultimately at an interpretation they are comfortable with. This interpretation may be unusual, creative, or deviant, but it provides a position that alleviates a subject's sense of dissonance in the world, even if this position is one that generates systemic paradoxes, relocating the sense of dissonance away from the subject and onto socially shared systems of meaning. Here we may also be reminded of the puzzle that women's clothes fetishism presented to Freud, only perhaps now we can see it as resolved from the point of view of the female fetishist: what seems to be an inexplicable fixation on clothes serves to alleviate the tension between conformity to a culturally imposed standard and its conflicts with a sense of what is suitable for one's self. However, this is not exactly the scenario de Lauretis offers.

The reinterpretation of the masculine woman, like that of fetishism, hinges upon the meaning of castration. Traditionally, the threat of castration has required no more explanation than the meaning of the penis or the significance of the fetish. Castration was understood to be based on the presence or absence of the phallus, with a variety of consequences depending on one's anatomical sex. While the consequences could be interrogated—that is, we could ask why a particular woman develops a masculinity complex or a certain man becomes a fetishist—the nature of the loss was unquestionably phallic. However, de Lauretis convincingly argues that castration can be viewed as the originary loss of the female body: "In lesbian subjectivity the ultimate meaning of castration as narcissistic wound is not the lack of the penis but the loss of the female body; and consequently the *threat* of castration threatens a lack of being in the subject's body-ego" (275). In such a scenario, the subject seeks to resolve this loss by taking a woman as her object of desire, rather than by seeking the phallus or penis-substitute, as the classical fetishist does.

The point on which the credibility of this theory pivots is the point of bodily dispossession, the idea that one might lose one's body only to incessantly refind it through another along the trajectory of a perverse desire. In de Lauretis's model of lesbian fetishism, "disavowal produces the ambivalent or contradictory perception of having and yet not having a body; having a body designated as female, and yet not having a female body that can be narcissistically and libidinally invested" (288). In this view, masculinity seems to serve as the necessary default, as what one is left with once femininity (the narcissistically invested female body) is lost. With this assertion, de Lauretis makes an important acknowledgment of the contradictions some masculine women experience in relation to their own bodies, their having to negotiate between their difference from other women which they know to be true and the refusal of a binary gender system to countenance that difference, shunting them under the heading of "female." But she rules out the possibility that some masculine women may experience a slightly different contradiction, namely between having a body that is libidinally invested *as masculine* but which is socially marked as female. Because de Lauretis reinterprets a woman's masculinity as a sexual sign, as specifically a signal of her desire for another woman, rather than as a gender identity, she emphasizes the woman at the expense of the masculinity. Yet not all masculine women give equal weight to these two terms.

Thus despite the likelihood that the designation "female" is socially imposed on this masculine woman, the question remains open as to how designating this body as female works. Such a designation is hardly simple, especially in context of an argument that does more than attend to representational or cultural constructions of gender, sex, and the body, but focuses so acutely on the libidinal and unconscious investments in a particularly gendered and sexual body. To what extent does a masculine woman accept the designation of her body as female? Her interpretation of her body may indeed be grounded in ambivalence and disavowal, but her ambivalence may not necessarily be anchored in a perception of her body as female. She might vacillate between seeing her body as masculine/not masculine, or male/not-male, or androgynous/monstrous.[21] It all depends on how she manages to libidinally or narcissistically invest in her body; this does not correlate to an expression of femininity.

This problem of investment is perhaps most evident in de Lauretis's central concept, the reformulation of the notion of castration. For de Lauretis, it makes no sense for the girl child to fear penile castration. She argues that "the phallus—as representative of the penis—is not an essential component of the female subject's body image; what is essential is what the mother desires" (241). She adds that psychoanalysis had blindly presumed that only the phallus would be the object of the mother's desire. Thus, she deflects a potentially damaging objection: if what is essential is what the mother desires, and the mother desires the phallus, then the phallus *is* an essential component of the female subject's body image. This, indeed, is Freud's assumption all along. The assertion that the mother might desire something other than the phallus is a deft move for de Lauretis; in proposing the female body as an object wished for by the mother, she plays into psychoanalysis's extant theories of feminine narcissism. Castration is thus shown to hinge upon what the mother wants. If the daughter senses "the mother's narcissistic wish for a feminine body (in the daughter as in herself)," and feels that she cannot live up to this feminine ideal, then she produces a fantasy of castration, "refiguring a lack of penis as what was first and foremost a lack of a lovable body" (242).

But the mother's wished-for object is not the only thing at stake here. A certain experiential knowledge is absolutely critical for de Lauretis, which is why the threat of penile castration is a less satisfying account in the first place. In her view,

> what is disavowed must be the loss of something of which her body has knowledge, pain, and pleasure; something toward which she has instinctual aims. That something is not, cannot be, a penis but is most likely to be her body itself (body image and body-ego) although the symbolic structure of castration rewrites that loss as lack of a penis. (288)

This assertion is quite striking. It seems absolutely accurate and thus compelling. Who could refute that bodily knowledge is essential to the threat of castration? That this knowledge is constituted in terms of pain and pleasure targets our very epistemological and phenomenological foundation.

Yet this claim elides the issue of interpretation, that even seemingly self-evident affects of pain and pleasure are shot through with meaning. It is precisely the meaning of these affects that enables knowledge to be constituted or derived from them. When de Lauretis asserts that "that something is not, cannot be a penis," her persuasiveness breaks down. Her insistence shifts us out of the interpretive realm of analysis, in which de Lauretis had so patiently explicated the mechanism of castration, and into the reductive realm of anatomical evidence. But this sidestepping raises the following questions: Why could that something not be a penis? Why must it be "her body itself"? Neither of these terms are absolutes or givens. What her body has knowledge of is precisely what is at stake here. Thus, despite the appeal to a form of anatomical essentialism, we shift through the back door into the hermeneutical realm with the acknowledgment that the body is translated into a penis.

The obvious answer—which is part of why this assertion seems so compelling—is that lesbian fetishist does not know what a penis is because she does not have one. But perhaps this answer is not so obvious. Freud tells us that "Frequent erections of [the clitoris] make it possible for girls to form a correct judgment, even without any instruction, of the sexual manifestations of the other sex: they merely transfer onto boys the sensations derived from their own sexual processes" (SE 7: 220). Could we not conceive, as Freud so often does, of the clitoris as a penis, at least in this case?

We not only could but should think through this possible interpretation of the clitoris, for it calls attention to the most important aspect of the theory of fetishism: that it models how knowledge—of our bodies, of our world—is shaped and directed by desire. We are libidinally invested in both our bodies and our objects, and this investment structures our experience of the world. Knowledge is anchored by a subject's libidinal investments (which help construct the subject's identity) and directed by the subject's negotiation of loss and partiality. For Freud, the girl's knowledge of her body helps her understand other objects in the world; he illustrates how we use our bodies instrumentally in order to know other things in the world. A masculine woman, who knows her body as having a penis, might employ fetishism as she negotiates the conflict between her interpretation of her body and the one imposed from the outside; she illustrates how we do not need to adhere to dominant norms in order to achieve a meaningful identity and to function in the world. Whether it emerges through loss of belief in the mother's phallus or in possession of one's own body, fetishism provides an epistemological model for a passionate connection to particular objects in the world.

This Freudian inference about penises (which is really an inference about clitorises) illuminates another trouble spot in de Lauretis's formulation: why would the girl necessarily take her whole body as this object, rather than, as the boy supposedly does, some particular part? We cannot assume, especially for subjects of perverse desire, that a subject's understanding of her body—the phenomenological picture of the body's image—necessarily conforms to the cultural norms. As Judith Butler notes in *Bodies that Matter*, "if there is a law that must compel a feminine identification with a position of castration, it appears this law 'knows' that identification could function differently" (104). If there were no position for a feminine identification other than being castrated, there would be no need to compel; all feminine people would merely take up their position without hesitation. The threat of castration would no longer work—for either feminine or masculine subjects. The very possibility of failure—that a masculine subject could become feminine, or vice-versa—is built in. The fact that castration's threat exists does not mean that there is only one interpretation for succumbing to it, just as there is more than one interpretive strategy for overcoming it (e.g., masculinity, masquerade as compensatory femininity, fetishism).

De Lauretis's argument for understanding differently the object threatened with loss through castration offers one such difference. But Judith Butler's notion of the lesbian phallus, which like de Lauretis's work draws upon Freud's notion of the bodily ego and Lacan's "projective idealization of the body" (90), suggests a significantly different conclusion about how a body has knowledge, pain, and pleasure of itself. Butler, for example, suggests that "'having' the phallus can be symbolized by an arm, a tongue, a hand (or two), a knee, a thigh, a pelvic bone, an array of instrumentalized body-like things" (88). Arguably, the phallic interpretation of such items may not be available to the young girl in de Lauretis's scenario; these are things that we learn only later to recognize as "having a phallus." However, Butler's point is to call attention to the imaginary constitution of bodily morphology. Her point also serves here to complicate the appeal to the body—and the assumptions concomitant with it being specifically a *lesbian* body— in de Lauretis's text. There is no real, directly accessible anatomy; rather, the subject constitutes her sense of her body through the imaginary. In this realm, the objection that the girl has no penis carries little weight.[22] Even if we introduce the notion of the symbolic into the equation, where the child's imaginary body image is mediated through the shared meanings of the symbolic, there may be little difference in the subject's self-understanding, because there's no accounting for how the subject interprets the symbolic's decrees about the significance of body parts that she has such a strong imaginary investment in. In fact, here a form of self-fetishism makes even more sense, as the subject disavows her own lack of a penis.

Behind this paradigm of the masculine woman remains the vestiges of a gender fundamentalism that constrains de Lauretis's discourse in a peculiar way: we are always returned to the lesbian body, which is always a female body, even if it is dressed with masculine signifiers. Like Freud's clothes fetishist, de Lauretis's masculine woman seems to use fetishes to guarantee to her partner that she has what any woman has. A normative model is, of course, inescapable; de Lauretis points this out herself from the first chapter. Her elucidation of a perverse theory of sexuality in Freud's work, as one that provides a negative foundation or "clinical underground" (23), recalls this very inseparability. At issue, however, is the extent to which interpretation can reach. Is the body fully interpretable by individual subjects, even if they have little or no conscious control over the direction of that interpretation? Or is there a bedrock of sexual difference that is located in the body, an asymptote beyond which change through interpretation cannot reach? These questions can be germanely framed not only in terms of travesty or transvestism (dressing as a sex other than the one assigned at birth), but in terms of transsexualism (being a sex other than the one assigned at birth), and especially transgenderism (identifying as a sex other than the one assigned at birth, which may be an intermediary gender rather than a purely masculine or feminine one). Can we draw a line to distinguish who is the real lesbian—a butch "transgendered woman," or a male-to-female transsexual who seeks lesbian partners, or a female-bodied femme who seeks a partner in other femmes, male- or female-bodied? These possibilities all raise the question of what is it to know what a lesbian is, or to know who is lesbian?

This question has been used in damaging ways in lesbian communities, to police who does and does not belong, according to gender identity, sexual practice, and body morphology. But it can also be used productively; indeed, it is the question every lesbian initially confronts as she comes to terms with her sexuality, be it at fourteen or forty. Being lesbian is thus necessarily being a knowing subject. By not interrogating the designation of a female body, de Lauretis presumes the lesbian is not only a knowable object but a prescription for how to inhabit one's body. While this is partly a necessary assumption for her project, it obscures two important points: that the body is no guarantee of knowledge (a masculine woman may not know her body as female), nor necessarily a limit to knowing (a girl may know about penises through analogy with her clitoris). As we build on de Lauretis's insights, it is thus crucial not to confuse what is knowable with how knowledge becomes normative. We should push the question of knowing who is a lesbian to its limits, and call into question the idea of knowing how to possess a lesbian body—for possession is nine-tenths of the law of fetishism.

Thus, de Lauretis's focus on bodily dispossession has a double edge. On the one hand, it offers a breakthrough paradigm for rethinking the function and meaning of castration in relation to lesbian desire, while on the other hand, it snaps us back to the grid of a particular and expected interpretation of the body, for which normative sexual difference offers the only standard. If we can discuss bodily dispossession, then there must be some standard of bodily possession. But the more important question is how, in what ways, can the body be possessed? To feel the threat of bodily dispossession is already a way of possessing one's body. Because de Lauretis situates her analysis within an explicitly lesbian framework that presumes a certain knowledge of what a lesbian is, the body that the subject is to possess is always a particular interpretation of a female body that is inevitably, if not directly, referred to a feminine standard. The strength of de Lauretis's reworking of the notion of fetishism is its effectiveness in challenging the normative account of sexual difference. The weakness is that the same acuity does not as incisively examine how—just as desire can elude the heterosexual imperative—gender identity can reinterpret the body against the normative injunction that particular genitals lead to particular knowledge and identity.

As a result, we end up with a sexually indifferent model of lesbian fetishism. As in Grosz's account, there is no room for the femme fetishist, or the daddy-and-his-boy relations (among other role-playing possibilities) that some lesbians engage in, or lesbian sadomasochism such as Gamman and Makinen discuss. These configurations of desire perhaps more clearly suggest that not everyone possesses their body (or seeks to possess their lover's body) according to normative standards. While de Lauretis would certainly agree that deviation exists, her account only allows for a singular kind of loss—the dispossession of the proper. The femme fetishist or the dyke daddy, however, emerge from the dispossession of the improper; they use fetishism to recover as their own what they could never have (the phallic woman, the child), not what they were expected to have (the female body libidinally invested

as feminine). The exclusion of such forms of lesbian desire as these—
and they are by no means the only ones—may explain why de Lauretis
loses sight of an important lesson from Freud's theory of fetishism: that
the loss can be of something that never was, and which, because of cultural limitations, never could be. The gift of fetishism is that it enables
us to imagine something outside the bounds of the cultural script.[23]

Insofar as she focuses on the perverse, lesbian fetishism from the
perspective of de Lauretis's text seems not only inevitable, but in line
with the creative solution the fetish represents in Freud's 1927 text. The
fetish signals desire in a specific relation *between* two women, who
translate cultural ideals from the social to the personal or intimate
sphere; the fetish-signs are immanent, rather than transcendent. The
process of translation inevitably generates new meanings, including a
belief in "what was never there." Where Grosz's reading of lesbian
fetishism viewed it as shifting signs of desire from the intimate scene to
the larger social scene, this trajectory of fetishism moves in the opposite
direction, away from the social into the realm of the intimate and in-
terpsychical. This move certainly opens up a creative realm with richer
potential, since private or intimate meanings are negotiated with fewer
people and thus can diverge radically from interpretive norms. But de
Lauretis constrains the creative scope of that interpretation by foreclos-
ing the range of things that could be dispossessed. She skirts the possibility of dispossession from the improper when she elaborates that her
notion of castration entails not only loss but prohibition: "[T]he threat
[the fetish] holds at bay is not the loss of the penis in women, but the
loss of the female body *and the prohibition of access to it*" (243; emphasis
added). It is precisely because of this reinscription of the operation of
the perverse into anatomical norms that de Lauretis seems blocked
when it comes to thinking through a paradigm of lesbian fetishism
based on the loss of the improper and impossible, despite the fact that
she acknowledges the essential role in lesbian fetishism of "prohibition,
difference, and desire," of which the fetish is the sign (232).

Despite this limitation, there remain valuable aspects to de Lauretis's theory of fetishism. Foremost is how her focus on intersubjectivity resonates with Schor's initial reading of female fetishism as
authorial desire played out between two (male and female) subjects,
as well as with my reading of Schor's formulation of female fetishism as
female travesty, in which the cross-identification of Indiana and Noun
was played out heterosexually in their respective relations to Raymon.
In Schor, the question of identity performance becomes inextricable
from modes of cross-dressing. In a similar vein, de Lauretis takes up the
issue of identity performance in her consideration of fetishism in its re-

lation to masquerade. Both critics thus ascribe an important degree of agency in how subjects act upon their desires. But the intersubjectivity in de Lauretis's model of fetishism is different from Schor's in a crucial way: the emphasis on perverse desire. By the time Schor has articulated the notion of female travesty, women's desire is no longer in focus. Partly this is due to her material, as she acknowledges that Sand does not clearly depict women's desire; her example of female travesty in *Indiana*, as we saw earlier, focused on the "misfiring of male desire," not female desire. It is de Lauretis's emphasis on perverse desire that makes her account of fetishism much different from those which have come before, particularly those that confound fetishism and transvestism or forms of cross-dressing.

To view de Lauretis's theory of fetishism as transvestism or masquerade because it hinges on the masculine woman would indeed be a travesty. Although de Lauretis uses the term masquerade to indicate both feminine masquerade and masculine travesty, and thus may seem to court confusion, in fact this move enables her to set up a useful schema that will distinguish fetishism from masquerade.[24] This distinction is the strong side of her shift of the masculine woman from an expression of gender identity to that of sexual desire, although it is still hampered by the same binary that underpins her rewriting of castration. Within masquerade, as de Lauretis describes it, there are different forms of libidinal aims: either to the fantasmatic female body or to the phallus. There are also different audiences: women or men, or women/men; and different modes: masculine, feminine. These form a matrix where the crucial difference is not what gender is performed—as would be expected from the perspective of traditional binary sexual difference—but rather what the libidinal aim is. Such a schema takes seriously Freud's categorizing of fetishism as a deviation of aim, not object, and suggests that masquerade might also fall under that heading.[25] In de Lauretis's matrix, the difference in aim is still binary, but it is a difference between the phallus and the fantasmatic female body. This difference is consistent with her reinterpretation of the threat of castration as the loss of the originary female body rather than the loss of the penis/phallus. With the phallus, as a stand-in for the penis, and the fetish, as a stand-in for the female body, the point that becomes clear through this masquerade matrix is that the phallus signals one form of desire—perhaps the nonperverse form—and the fetish another.

By taking us from travesty to fetishism, in a sense along the reverse of Schor's path, de Lauretis propels us out of a purely representational economy and into an epistemological one. Performance is important, but neither the crucial nor the only point. With the shift to an epistemological economy, the free-will adaptation of travesty, taking on whatever identity seems appealing, ends, and an interested, motivated, knowledgeable, yet inextricably unconscious selection takes its place. This is consistent with de Lauretis's focus on the subject as she relates to another rather than on the question of how the subject constitutes herself. Fetishism remains a strategy to achieve a sort of satisfaction, as it is in the Freudian text of 1927, but because of de Lauretis's focus on the perverse model of desire—which in its "repeated process of displacement and reinvestment" directs itself towards an impossible object (266)— fetishism is simultaneously an acknowledgment that such satisfaction can never be achieved.

Although de Lauretis does not mention this, her conception of the masculine woman follows Octave Mannoni's paradigm of a fetishist perhaps more closely than Freud's. Mannoni's discussion of fetishism is summarized by its title—"Je sais bien, mais quand même . . ." ("I know very well, but nonetheless . . ."). Mannoni provides an interesting intersection with de Lauretis when he writes: "La croyance s'explique par le désir" "belief is explained by desire" (22), and, more explicitly, "La Verleugnung (par laquelle la croyance se continue après repudiation) s'explique par la persistence du désir" "Disavowal (by which belief continues after repudiation) is explained by the persistence of desire" (22). This notion of persistence resonates with de Lauretis's appropriation of Leo Bersani and Ulysse Dutoit's reading of fetishism, emphasizing the mobility of desire, and her concern with "the figure of loss and dispossession that yet sustains subjectivity and desire" in the texts she discusses (253). Knowledge and desire, on these models, are inextricably intertwined, dynamic, mobile.

We might see this contradiction between knowledge and belief as the grounds for sustaining desire in the basic scenario of butch-femme lesbian desire, but in which the masculine woman is desired by one who knows very well she is not a man, but nonetheless insists on masculinity; the fetishes of masculinity mark this. Here knowledge only seems to be in contradiction to belief; the desiring subject does at some level know what she desires, even if it is knowing that her desire is contradictory. This view helps us account for the problematic vestiges of normativity that subtly work in de Lauretis's text, the focus on the dispossession of the proper rather than improper body. There is a troubling sense lurking in de Lauretis's argument that the reinterpretation of the masculine woman does not take us very far away from the psychoanalytic reading of her condition as something she "suffers" (Schor's and Grosz's word) and wants to change.

We see this perhaps most clearly in the following passage: "The fantasmatic object represented by lesbian object-choice is not the mother,

I maintain, but the subject's own body, the denied and wished-for female body which castration threatens with non-existence, and disavowal makes attainable by a compromise fantasy" (288). This statement may well ring true for some, especially those who are more androgynous than masculine. But the claim presumes an identification with one's body as feminine or at least female at some early point. It also underscores the question whether a desire for women by a female-embodied person is necessarily a lesbian desire. This question takes seriously the complications that de Lauretis's analysis of fetishism has raised about the meaning of castration, or that our discussion has raised about the interpretation of sexual differences and embodiment. If the lesbian object-choice is no longer to be construed as the mother, why must it necessarily be limited to the subject's own "lost" body? Why can't a female-bodied object choice be perceived as sexually different or other for the female-bodied subject who makes that choice, especially once the meaning of castration has been loosed from the phallus? Such a perception would have to concede that morphologically similar subjects may possess or be dispossessed of their bodies in radically different ways. De Lauretis makes this difference partially perceptible, but it can be pushed further. The wished-for female body is not always an "appropriate" female body, someone of whom your mother would approve.

The two literary figures that illustrate de Lauretis's reworking of castration as the fantasy of dispossession may help us see the limits of the theory. Framing the theory of fetishism in the fifth chapter are readings of Stephen Gordon from the *Well of Loneliness* and Marisa/Corky from *Giving Up the Ghost*. Although de Lauretis is careful to emphasize the cultural and historical differences that inform these characterizations, she argues that both experience a dispossession of their own female bodies through a failure of narcissism. Each also heals her narcissistic wound through fetishism. Marisa's fetish is "her activist-writer self image, the openly transgressive, politicized image of the Chicana butch" (246). De Lauretis argues that "By assuming or identifying with this image [fetish] Marisa establishes a new libidinal relationship with her body image" (245). Marisa's fetish thus functions along the lines that Grosz discusses, providing a bridge between social and psychical reality, and emphasizing identification. Stephen's narcissistic failure came from a very different crisis, since she was explicitly rejected by her mother for being so phallic, for failing to live up to the feminine ideal. Stephen's fetish is more traditional, more concrete—the masculine clothes to which she is irresistibly drawn (242).

De Lauretis structures a parallel between these two through the psychoanalytic figure of the mirror stage. She defines this stage as the moment where one libidinally invests in one's body image and "constitutes the fictional matrix or first outline of the ego" (240). Because of the differences in the two texts, she must interpret the mirror stage broadly in order to draw a parallel. In her reading of Moraga, de Lauretis creates a metaphorical mirror stage for Marisa, arguing that her address to the audience, listed among the cast as THE PEOPLE, "functions as a performative enactment of the mirror stage" (245). However, she finds a scene literally before a mirror to draw upon from book 2 of the *Well*. In this scene, Stephen confronts the image of her naked body in the mirror; despite her attraction to masculine clothes, Stephen rejects her masculine body, as de Lauretis tells us, "precisely because it is masculine" (237).[26] These literary examples effectively flesh out the theoretical reinterpretation of castration and the mechanism of perverse desire, although neither fully arrives at an illustration of fetishism. The self-image and the masculine clothes only approximate the role of a fetish in de Lauretis's reading. Taking a look at another, very different example of the masculine woman and lesbian fetishism in a scene before a mirror brings out a fuller picture of fetishism.

In Leslie Feinberg's novel, *Stone Butch Blues*, the young protagonist, Jess, sneaks into her parents' bedroom while they are away in order to cross-dress in her father's clothes. Clad in a starched shirt, suit coat, and tie, Jess looks at her image in the mirror:

> A sound came from my throat, sort of a gasp. I liked the little girl looking back at me.
>
> Something was still missing: the ring. I opened my mother's jewelry box. The ring was huge. The silver and turquoise formed a dancing figure. I couldn't tell if the figure was a man or a woman. . . .
>
> I stared in the big mirror over my mother's dresser, trying to see far in the future when the clothing would fit, to catch a glimpse of the woman I would become. . . . I had never seen any adult women who looked like I thought I would when I grew up. There were no women on television like the small woman reflected in this mirror, none on the streets. (20–21)

In this passage we catch a glimpse of how the dispossession of the improper body would work. Jess does not realize her loss of a role model until she sees herself in the mirror, but when she does, she is immediately aware of its loss. The image in the mirror is a new thing that could only come into being through Jess's growing up and taking on that image; it is not one culturally prescribed for her. Note that she cannot, however, perceive this image until the outfit is complete, until the fetish is in place. As in Lacan's mirror stage, the subject before the mirror projects an image of wholeness. That fetish, the thing that was still missing and which was necessary to achieve satisfaction or completeness, is the ring. The indecipherable gender of the figure on the ring represents a possibility for being that Jess cannot see reflected in the culture around her. She cannot tell if the figure is a man or a woman, but she can read the figure in its indeterminacy, and know the loss of such an improper body in a world that insists upon determinate, properly gendered bodies.

De Lauretis does acknowledge that lesbian fetishes are not necessarily masculine (263), but her model leaves little room for the desire of a lesbian who fetishizes something other than masculine things.[27] In Jess's case the fetish object is not the masculine clothes but the ring with the figure of indeterminate gender. The ring, interestingly enough, comes from Jess's earliest days, when she was partially adopted by a Dineh (Navajo) family across the hall from her parents. When Jess was four, her parents forbade her to visit the neighbors. "Before they left, though, the grandmother gave my mother a ring and said it would help protect me in life. The ring threatened my parents, but they figured all that turquoise and silver must be worth something so they took it" (14–15). Thus, the ring is a fetish in the classical *anthropological* sense—as a token of exchange between two cultures, with purportedly apotropaïc effects—as well as in the psychoanalytic sense of a memorial to inevitable loss. Here it is not the female body that is lost to Jess, but the warmth and acceptance of family, and the sense of having a secure place in the larger social arena.

This idea is borne out when the ring appears again in the novel. After her incarceration in a mental institution and a failed bout of charm school, Jess remembers the ring again, and steals it from her mother. "During the day at school I hid in a bathroom stall and looked at it, wondering about its power. When would it protect me?" (23–24). The things Jess needs protection from are social, not psychological. In this instance the ring reassures Jess that she can resist the pressures of institutionalization and schooling; her expectations, though, are that it will do more, that it will radically change her world rather than simply enable her to survive it. Nonetheless, with the ring she finds marginal spaces—a bathroom stall—to hide in and recharge. There is, of course, a certain irony in Jess's finding refuge in the most gendered space of the school, but that was the only space that also afforded privacy, a refuge from the eyes of others.

Because of such isolation, Jess's search in the novel is primarily a search for community, acceptance, and belonging; because she is a

butch lesbian in the rabidly homophobic society of Buffalo, New York
in the 1950s and '60s, this search is necessarily also about sexuality. The
loss that threatens her is a loss of her being, living under the constant
threat of annihilation. This is a very different loss than what de Lauretis
describes in Stephen Gordon's mirror scene, and that difference is significantly affected by class. For Stephen, her reaction to her mother's rejection is a fantasy of bodily (not material) dispossession; as her father's
favorite and to the manor born, she is not about to be out on the street.
What Jess faces in *Stone Butch Blues* is a not a fantasy but a reality of
bodily dispossession, not only physically in the form of rape, battery,
and threats of death, but also semiotically, because of the lack of images
or knowledge about people like herself who inhabit neither side of the
binary gender categories our culture offers. For her, the tokens of masculinity are not fetishes, but her claims on the right to exist. On the other
hand, her fetish, the indeterminately gendered ring, functions as a guarantee that she has a right to make that claim, to broaden the categories
beyond binary heterosexual difference; as a transcultural token of acceptance, it marks the early loss of social acceptance, the other world of
the Dineh, where a nonbinary gender system allowed for people who
were neither purely masculine nor purely feminine to flourish. Her desire springs from that loss, and is a desire for social connection more so
than intimate connection. It is a desire to be known and acknowledged
for who she is, on her own terms.

The transcultural nature of the fetish promises Jess that her situation is contingent, even if it is too often overwhelming. In this respect it
is like the psychoanalytic interpretation of the sexual fetish, which
posits the contingency of interpretations of sexual difference. When Jess
is arrested and raped by cops, her transgression is not that she exchanges femininity for masculinity, but that she exists as an indeterminately sexed person, refusing to be contained by binary parameters,
and instead creatively interpreting a body that others read as decidedly
one sex. In this crisis she undergoes a splitting, oscillating between being conscious of herself brutalized in the police station in Buffalo, and
herself standing alone out on the desert. The scene of splitting is importantly not about oscillating between a "real" body and an "imaginary"
setting outside the body, but between two different interpretations of
that real body, in the intersection of differing symbolic and imaginary
relations to that body:

> I looked at the light on the ceiling, a large yellow bulb burning
> behind a metal mesh. The light reminded me of the endless stream
> of television westerns I saw after we moved up north. Whenever

anyone was lost in the desert the only image shown was a glaring sun—all the beauty of the desert reduced to that one impression. Staring at that jail light rescued me from watching my own degradation: I just went away.

I found myself standing in the desert. The sky was streaked with color. Every shift of light cast a different hue across the wilderness: salmon, rose, lavender. The scent of sage was overwhelming. Even before I saw the golden eagle gliding in the updraft above me, I heard it scream, as clearly as if it had come from my own throat. I longed to soar in flight with the eagle, but I felt rooted to the earth. (62–63)

It is clear from the text that the vision of the desert is Jess's splitting from her painful ordeal of rape at the hands of the police, which, because this is a literary text constructed through Jess's eyes, becomes a splitting for the reader as well. The appeals to the senses of sight, smell, hearing, and feeling are all quite different from the sensations Jess would have experienced in the police-station reality. The emphasis on the senses in the description makes the point that this is a reality as important as the objective reality of her brutalization in the police station. The fact that the alternative to the police station is the desert is important, for the desert is the Dineh counterpoint to cold, cruel Buffalo; it is the lost place of her childhood, the acceptance and social position symbolized in her androgynous ring. Jess's oscillation is thus between a body in which she can exist and a body through which she is annihilated.

The oscillation between the two realities underscores the fact that every relation we have to reality is mediated by fantasy. This fantasy is often an enabling and necessary tool. The cops' brutalization of Jess stems from their fantasy that she could be different than she is—that she could be a typically feminine, heterosexual woman—and their refusal to accept the truth of her identity. Jess's vision stems from her fantasy that the world could be different than it is, that it could accommodate people who do not fit its currently dominant, narrow gender roles. To emphasize the mediation of fantasy here is not to lapse into a complete subjectivism by saying that fantasy and reality are the same, or that all we need is a stronger fantasy life in order to escape reality. Rather, the oscillation foregrounds the fact that our experience of the real, of the facts, is inescapably subjective, mediated by imaginary relations that we will strive, often at great costs, to make real. This is no less the case for the cops' violent fantasy about Jess than it is for Jess's hopeful fantasy about herself. The vibrant imagery of the desert ties in with Jess's fetishistic belief that the world can be different than she knows it is. The ring represents this, even after it is lost to her. The ring becomes a leitmotif, a sort of literary fetish marking Jess's belief in a better, different world. This fetishistic belief, far from being incidental, is absolutely essential to Jess's survival.

At the end of the novel, the ring reappears in Jess's dream. There, she has a vision of entering a small, round hut. "There were people who were different like me inside. We could all see our reflections in the faces of those who sat in the circle. . . . Their faces radiated a different kind of beauty than I'd grown up seeing celebrated on television or in magazines. . . . One of the oldest in the circle caught my eyes. I didn't know if she was a man or a woman at birth. She held up an object. . . . It was the ring that the Dineh women gifted me with as an infant" (300). As with the initial mirror scene, the reflected images come from social mirrors rather than psychical ones—the television, magazines, and the faces of others in the group.

The fetish in *Stone Butch Blues* is a sexual fetish, insofar as gender identity and sexual desire are inextricable, but it is primarily a social fetish. It offers a very different model than de Lauretis's fetishism, though no less perverse a one (if only in the sense of a stubborn refusal to assimilate to social and sexual norms). The comparison of the two demonstrates the need for an account of fetishism that accommodates the intrapsychic, interpsychic, and social spheres. Jess's ring is much closer to Grosz's notion of lesbian fetishism, as an oscillation between psychical reality and social reality. Yet it differs from Grosz's model as well, in that it does not signify the phallus at all. What each of these feminist thinkers has foregrounded in their consideration of fetishism is precisely the interactive constitution of subjectivity, both within a subject's mind and in terms of that subject's relation to others—be it through identification, as in Schor's reading, or desire, as in de Lauretis's.

The common thread that binds all of these examples together— the literary, critical, psychoanalytical—is the model of the masculine woman. Indiana provides the only exception to this rule, if indeed one construes her as a fetishist (and Schor does not). Even my own choice of literary example follows this pattern, although I hope that my following this pattern shows up the deviation in my aim more clearly—repetition with a difference. Schor, Grosz, and de Lauretis all figure the masculine woman's gender oscillation as being between masculine and feminine poles; yet Feinberg provides a text wherein the masculine woman's oscillation can be figured between the poles of androgyny and masculinity, even if each of these poles function more as asymptotes than a real grounding. Through this paradigm of the masculine woman, we can return to other kinds of women, questioning more closely assumptions about how subjects know and inhabit their bodies, and from there how they know and inhabit the world.

It is therefore important not to let the model of the masculine woman as fetishist, who at some deep level wants to be affirmed as feminine, settle into being the only truth; while de Lauretis's model may well be true for many women, it does not offer a complete account. This contestation goes hand-in-hand with the effort to complicate and move away from the travesty/transvestistic model of fetishism, because the masculine woman seems to present such an obvious case of clothes fetishism. (Indeed, who are the women Freud speaks of as wearing clothes that are fashionable but not suitable, if not masculine women struggling to conform to a feminine standard?) De Lauretis's discussion of fetishism contributes perhaps the clearest sense that fetishism is a strategy. A catalog of fetishes, or a too-easy conflation of travesty and fetishism, will fail to adequately account for the phenomenon. The travesty angle at its best accentuates the mechanism of identification at work in fetishism, but it illustrates rather than accounts for the phenomenon. Freud's assertion that all women are clothes fetishists invites almost a visceral objection; however, we should counter not with the refusal that women could be fetishists, but with the argument that some women may be other kinds of fetishists.

At this point the necessity for an expanded model of fetishism as a strategy should be evident. In her survey of other theorists' use of fetishism, de Lauretis is skeptical of generalized fetishism. Yet, at the risk of running afoul of de Lauretis's criticism in once again generalizing fetishism, I believe there is something more general that can be applied here. Fetishism should be unhinged from bipolar gender models and compared to other paradigms of identification, representation, subject/object relations and intersubjective practice—but not without losing sight of the unconscious drives that structure it. De Lauretis rightly criticizes Emily Apter for extending her definition of fetishism to include any form of female loss (as an oft-cited example, Mary Kelly's figuring of maternal fetishism in the conservation of items from her children's infancy). Such criticism is not unlike Freud's criticism of Bloch, that the latter's definition resulted in all things feminine being fetishes. All loss does not lead to fetishism; what constitutes fetishism are neither the things we know nor the things we have lost, but the puzzling things that reflect the impulses of the unconscious in our processes of identification, knowledge, and desire.

The implications of expanding our understanding of fetishism need not be so broad as to eclipse the significance or specificity of the sexual difference that fetishism makes. In this extension we need not lose sight of Elizabeth Grosz's point that the fetish will mediate between the social and the psychical, not just, as de Lauretis has it, between two subjects as the mediating term, the signifier of desire (289). Nor should we throw out Schor's emphasis on intersubjectivity and cross-identification through differences other than binary gender difference. Still, we can learn from de Lauretis's criticism of earlier models of fetishism. Fetishism is not merely a subject/object relation, nor is it merely a play of theoretical indeterminacy that leads us into sexual indifference. Rather, fetishism offers interpretive challenges to fundamental assumptions about the identity of subjects and their distinction from objects, opening out a wider range of meanings to choose from, beyond simplistic dualisms that tend to organize our categories of race, class, and sexual differences. What fetishism offers, paradigmatically, is a bridge between social reality, built on material existence and subdivided according to the philosophical subject-object distinction, and fantasy or psychic reality, which offers more fluid interpretations of the constitution of subjects and objects. As subjects, we do not exist in isolation either from other subjects nor from objects; our relation to objects is as regulated as our relation to subjects, since the two are often interwoven. We use objects to relate to subjects and subjects to relate to objects; fetishism thus permeates our everyday lives. More importantly, fetishism enables us to imaginatively reconfigure the boundaries of our selves through the processes of identification and desire. Fetishes help us carve out a sense of self in the face of threats to our being; they remind us of who we are, and what we could become.

3

The Language of Loss

In our reading of fetishism thus far, first in Freud's work and then in feminist appropriations of Freud, the focus has been directed not, as might be expected, toward fetish objects, but toward the uses of those objects by fetish subjects. Indeed, the alignment of fetishism with strategies of gender identity, whether "serious" ones like femininity, or "playful" ones like travesty, suggests that there are no fetish objects, only fetish subjects who appropriate objects fetishistically. In this light, fetishism emerges as a useful strategy for the construction of subjectivity. What's more, as the reading of de Lauretis's and Feinberg's work brings out, the fetish can supplant the phallus as a subject's anchor in the world, and thus subjects need not be constituted in relation to the same singular standard.

Reading fetishism through feminist theories of the fetish elucidates the interplay between individual desire as it conforms to or deviates from normative injunctions and intersubjective relations in the formation of identity. The fetish serves as a mediator for this complex negotiation. For the fetish to ground the subject provides a resolution to the conundrum of postmodern, decentered subjectivity by allowing us to have it both ways: the fetish makes it possible to have a theory of subjectivity and simultaneously account for radical differences between subjects. Where the fetish provides a different version of the phallus in the individual's development as the thing through which all meaning is mediated, it opens up new possible directions for sexually diverse subjects to emerge and grow. Yet it does so without rendering the subject as a boundaryless and disoriented entity altogether, which is the spectre that narrowly binary logic posits as the result of doing away with a singular, transcendent signifier. In other words, we should reverse our thinking about the relation between the fetish and the phallus; no longer should we view the fetish as a phallus substitute, but rather the phallus as a fetish substitute, whose centering services are now more hurtful than helpful. Reconceiving the phallus as the fetish decenters and disperses the dominance of sexual difference culturally associated with the phallus, allowing individuals to negotiate their differences based on particular and local interests rather than as mediated through an ahistorical, atemporal standard. Since the hallmark of postmodernism is the loss of a center which can arbitrate meaning, fetishism, which has played a significant role in modern conceptions of the subject, becomes in its reinterpretation even more important in postmodern subjectivity.

But the issues fetishism raises are not just about reexamining the nature of subjectivity; fetishism also calls into question the very binarisms that make possible the forms of subjectivity that have emerged in Western cultures. The most obvious example is sexual difference. When we began by looking at Freud's notion of fetishism, it became apparent that binary notions of sexual difference—as, for instance, masculine/feminine, perverse/normal, or heterosexual/homosexual—were each deconstructed by the third term of fetishism. Furthermore, each of the above pairs of sexual differences is situated in relation to other seemingly binary sexual differences, thus reinforcing the illusion of duality. (Thus perverse/normal implicitly dovetails with homosexual/heterosexual, for example.) Fetishism is the monkey wrench thrown in this matrix of sexual differences that can potentially and productively bring its machinations to a halt by indicating how the binaries obscure the more complex interrelations of elements. Furthermore, in tracing out these threads we have seen that sexual differences are not the only ones fetishism sabotages; it also disrupts ontological differences—namely, the mutual exclusion between subject and object. Thus, sexual difference provides a point of departure for tracing out the ramifications of the analysis of fetishism.

Fetishism cannot be understood without recourse to the subject-object distinction. Thus far, the constitution of subject-object relations in modernity has lain tacitly in the background of our analysis. As we begin to take a wider-angled view of fetishism, this emphasis will necessarily change. The modern world view is founded on the split between subject and object, with the object subordinate to the subject's command; consequently, this subject views the world as a resource reserved solely for his appropriation. This conception supports a hierarchical view of the world, where only those at the top are deemed to be fully individual—and presumed masculine—subjects; all others are seen as objects having no relation to each other, only a subordinated relation to the fully empowered subjects. This formulation has been central for Western philosophy since the Enlightenment, and is integral to how Westerners used fetishism to disparage outside cultures in the modern age. For example, what was wrong with African fetish worship, in colonial eyes, was the overvaluation of a thing, the failure to acknowledge that a thing was not the same as a person and should not be treated as if it has the same power as a person. In short, fetishism was characterized by Westerners as a failure of rationality. It served as an epistemological reassurance of the superiority of Western thinking and reinforced the binary split between the purportedly savage or primitive non-Western culture and the civilized West. As Anne McClintock points out, this projection of failure in fact created the illusory boundary between the European self and the colonized other, a difference against which the West's notion of progress could be measured—fetishism was "the recurring paradigm for what the Enlightenment was not" (187).

Caught up thus in the web between subject and object, fetishism brings up epistemological as well as ontological issues. Epistemology provides the framework for how we organize our knowledge, what assumptions we make, and what logic we use to attain understanding; through epistemological norms we valorize reason over passion, separating out relations to objects that are rational from relations that are not. This framework underpins our relation to objects insofar as we strive to know them. The subject-object split raises the classical philosophical problem of how we can come to know the object if it is radically different from the subject. Fetishism violates this epistemological rule by positing that subjects and objects might not be so radically different; fetishism inappropriately bridges the gap between subjects and objects by disregarding the injunction that relations to objects should be rational and unclouded by emotion while only relations to subjects can be passionate or loving. Fetishism as a subject-object relation raises questions about the purity of reason, since fetishism contaminates knowledge with belief, dispassion with desire, defiling philosophy's epistemological ideals. Thus, just as Freud finds normal sexual practices incorporating perversions, so too do we find normal epistemic practices tainted by perverse knowledges like fetishism. In this light, fetishism is more than a deviant form of desire—it is a deviant form of knowledge. But because the mutual exclusion of subjects and objects is so crucial to Western thinking, fetishism appears inappropriate or threatening, whether as a sexual practice or an epistemic one.

In this chapter, our attention will begin to shift away from the fetish subject to bring the fetish relation into view. This change will help us make the move from sexuality to epistemology, from desire to knowledge. At the same time, it will help us reorient the direction of our interpretation from what has been—that is, how fetishism has been understood historically as an essentially modern "problem"—to what could come, an exploration of the possibilities for a postmodern fetishism. The focus on the fetish relation raises the issue of the constitution not only of the subject but also of the object, especially since we are shifting from psychoanalytic to philosophical discourse. Psychoanalysis's notion of the object is subject-based; the term "object" designates the thing toward which the subject's desire or attention is directed, and this focus is more often another subject or part of a subject than it is a thing. In philosophy, however, there is a bit more slippage in the notion of the object. An object could be, as in psychoanalysis, the focus of a subject's attention—this is particularly the case in epistemology, which speaks of the object of knowledge. But an object also designates an ontological category, the set of inanimate things. What I hope to do is suspend acceptance of the subject-object distinction as a given in order to examine how certain subject-object relations violate the assumption that subjects and objects are constituted as mutually independent of each other.

This chapter begins on a psychoanalytic note, comparing fetishism to melancholia, since both are object-relations that produce subjects and both are strategies subjects use to negotiate loss. While the aim of this chapter will be to lead us toward more philosophical approaches to questions of being and knowing, it remains with one foot in psychoanalysis so as not to abandon the discourse of desire and identification for some supposedly improved discussion of being. Broaching those philosophical discussions of being and knowing is important insofar as philosophical distinctions underpin psychoanalytic categories (as, for example, Luce Irigaray has demonstrated).[1] But more significantly, opening out the scope of analysis will help us examine other models for how subjects become who they are through their relation to certain, quite special objects, of which we have taken fetishism to be the paradigmatic strategy.

Two Kinds of Object Relations: Melancholia and Fetishism

Those who study the phenomenon would concur that fetishism originates in loss; indeed, this is a founding tenet of theories of fetishism. The origin of fetishism, as Freud has famously noted, is the loss of what the boy had believed was there—namely, the mother's phallus. Or, as we saw in the 1909 lecture, the loss that generates fetishism is the loss of an instinctual pleasure (157), whose original object remains preserved in the fetish. The recognition of loss as the root of fetishism is acknowledged in a different way by Lorraine Gamman and Merja Makinen in their study of female fetishism. They draw on object-relations theory to posit that fetishism's origins can be "moved back from phallic castration anxiety to an early stage of ego development" (112), namely, the separation from the mother in weaning. In their view, then, fetishism is not a strategy to negotiate the loss of wholeness resulting from the knowledge of sexual difference, but is still a strategy of disavowing loss—specifically the loss felt through individuation (123). Loss is also resonant in de Lauretis's view of fetishism, where the loss was the experience of female bodily dispossession by a masculine woman.[2]

In working from psychoanalytic theory, however, it is easy to fixate on the figure of the phallus and to slide into viewing the psychical loss of the penis as a generalized lack. Freud's text, in fact, slips between loss and lack as if they are equivalent. There is, however, a significant difference between loss and lack, and one should not be too hasty in discarding loss in favor of lack. The simplest difference is that loss indicates a singular sense of being without something one once had (or at least believed in), whereas lack implies a normative standard of plenitude against which one comes up short; it may also suggest a sense that one never had the thing to begin with. For the purposes of this study, however, there are more important ramifications. One is the reformulation of how we conceptualize gender in and through fetishism. Although Lacan's focus on the Phallus made it possible to understand how all subjects are castrated and lacking—that is, separated from the plenitude represented by the Phallus—his notion of lack does not challenge so much as describe bipolar and asymmetric gender divisions. This emphasis on sexual difference as having or not having the phallus occludes the epistemological aspects of fetishism, the conflict between belief and knowledge that is the fundamental mechanism of the fetishist's ambivalence.

The epistemological dimension, however, is the most interesting and significant aspect of fetishism, and my move to view fetishism as a negotiation of loss aims to make this epistemological dimension clearer. Loss of the maternal penis, or loss of the maternal body, or loss of the accepted, loved self—all these forms of fetishism from our previous chapters entail a belief in the existence of these lost objects, a belief which is contradicted by the knowledge of their loss. These losses all raise interesting questions about what it means to know, and the degree to which knowledge is inflected by desire and interpretation. In this light, ambivalence emerges as the most important element of fetishism.

Freud himself emphasizes this aspect of fetishism, focusing on ambivalence rather than only disavowal in "Fetishism": what saves the fetishist from psychosis is the thinking that in fact does align with reality, in addition to the current of thought that denies reality by asserting another belief. While many have taken disavowal to be a central mechanism in fetishism, a refusal to confront reality is not the only process at work. Disavowal is part of the larger mechanism of ambivalence in fetishism, and it is the combination of attitudes in the fetishist—both disavowal and recognition—that makes it possible for fetishism to be construed as potentially productive. By seeing both reality and its fantasmatic interpretation, the fetishist can move beyond paralysis in the face of the threat of loss in order to negotiate a more satisfying understanding of the situation. When one fixates on a thing, be it material or immaterial, in order to maintain a belief in opposition to one's knowledge, ambivalently choosing neither one nor the other, one is a fetishist. Both the fetish object and the fetish subject are constituted through this ambivalent relation to the thing and the loss—of either belief or knowledge—that it staves off.

An example of the usefulness of this sort of fetishism can be found in Toni Morrison's novel *Beloved*. The protagonist, Sethe, has a pair of crystal earrings that were given to her as a wedding gift by her former mistress; these earrings function as a fetish, helping her to negotiate conflicting beliefs about her social reality.

> She knotted the earrings into her underskirt to take along, not so much to wear but to hold. Earrings that made her believe she could discriminate among [white people]. That for every schoolteacher there would be an Amy; that for every pupil there was a Gardner, or a Bodwin, or even a sheriff, whose touch at her elbow was gentle, and who looked away when she nursed. (188)

The earrings are marked as special, to be held rather than worn; they are secreted away in her underskirt, becoming private things. The ambivalence inhering in this fetish is the oscillation between perceiving white people as good, helpful, or trustworthy, and white people as evil, violent, and humiliating to her. This discrimination is an important theme of the book, since as an ex-slave Sethe certainly encounters plenty of evidence for the untrustworthiness of white people. To survive, Sethe needs the ambivalent knowledge that white people are not all evil; she needs to be able to see the differences—between, for example, the Schoolteacher slave owner who allows her to be whipped when she's pregnant, and the Bodwins, abolitionist activists who provide a house to her and her mother-in-law in Ohio. The effectiveness of this fetish is borne out by how, after she is imprisoned and the white jailer requires her to give up the earrings, Sethe comes to believe her mother-in-law's opinion that "there's no bad luck but white people." She needs this complex belief/knowledge not only in a practical sense—for certainly the African American community has strategies for caring for their own independently of white society—but also in the sense that we need now as readers of the book: to move beyond identity politics, whether ill- or well-intentioned, to be able to read for multiple differences within categories, and make evaluations based on action.

If we expand our thinking about fetishism beyond the parameters of sexual differences to the category of strategies for dealing with loss, we find fetishism has different neighbors than travesty and transvestism—namely, mourning and melancholia. Both of these are clearly, if not most obviously, strategies for dealing with loss; mourning is the normal process of grieving and coming to terms with a loss, while melancholia is viewed as a pathological fixation on a loss. They are also both strategies for becoming a subject, since both practices produce subjectivity. Indeed, the parallels and interrelations between the perversions fetishism and melancholia may be even closer and more persistent that those between fetishism and travesty. Yet aligning fetishism with melancholia rather than travesty will not eliminate concern with sexual difference; it will simply underscore the interconnection between sexual differences and the subject-object split or the tensions between desire and knowledge. In this section I want first to outline what fetishism and melancholia share, and then suggest through their comparison why fetishism provides a better model for subject-building, insofar as it turns loss or the threat of loss into an opportunity for interpretive openness, and enables the negotiation of multiple differences. I will integrate examples from *Beloved* along the way, as the novel illustrates the difference between melancholia's and fetishism's effectiveness as a guide for understanding who we are, what we desire, and what we know.

The shift from lack to loss which brings fetishism into view with melancholia also puts pressure on the binary interpretation of gender, which is premised on both heterosexuality and the literal presence or absence of a penis and is thus intimately associated with lack. This framework serves to deny the possibility of women being fetishists, since it is their purported lack of a penis that provides the very reason for women's exclusion from fetishism. Shifting the grounds of fetishism to loss would seem to render fetishism accessible to all humans without regard to gender, since we all have experienced primordial loss in individuating from our mothers. But the move to loss does not so easily remove the obstacles posed by our system of gender, for loss is not recognized in the same way for everyone (remember that for Freud, the daughter's separation from her mother was so puzzling he had to invent the tenuous phenomenon of penis-envy to account for it).[3] While the move from lack to loss may have seemed to facilitate a move to a less gender-constrained way of thinking, it will not move us into a utopian, gender-free space. Even though we may have more room to maneuver in basing fetishism in loss rather than lack, the system of binary sexual differences will still impinge upon our options; the aim, however, is to have that room so that newer, multiple, and productive interpretations of gender can emerge.

Our binary-gendered culture fails to recognize the various strategies individuals use to cope with or react to loss. If we look at the history of depressive illnesses like melancholia, we will see that historically women have been invisible as melancholics, as Juliana Schiesari's study of melancholia makes clear. Indeed, just as women's "lack" was taken to be a given in patriarchal views of human subjectivity, so, as Schiesari notes, is women's loss presumed to be a given rather than exceptional.

More significant than their mutual exclusion of women, which in a phallocentric culture is hardly compelling grounds for comparison, is the fact that both fetishism and melancholia owe their contemporary interpretations to Freud's presentation of them. According to him, both phenomena construct a memorial to loss—only in fetishism Freud thinks he knows what the loss is. Certainly the fetishist seems to tolerate the loss better by replacing it with a satisfying substitute rather than disconsolately clinging to the lost object by trying to become it. Comparison of the two gains some momentum when we observe that Freud begins his discussion of "Mourning and Melancholia" on nearly the same note as he ends his discussion of fetishism: in terms of the normal prototype ("Normalvorbild") and the structure of an analogy. In the first sentence of "Mourning and Melancholia," Freud writes:

Nachdem uns der Traum als Normalvorbild der narzißtischen Seelenstörungen gedient hat, wollen wir den Versuch machen, das Wesen der Melancholie durch ihre Vergleichung mit dem Normalaffekt der Trauer zu erhellen. (*GW* 10: 428)

Dreams having served as a prototype in normal life of narcissistic mental disorders, we will now try to throw some light on the nature of melancholia by comparing it with the normal affect of mourning. (*SE* 14: 243)

Strachey's translation loses some of the resonances that make this passage seem so similar to the one at the end of "Fetishism," which reads: "In conclusion we may say that the normal prototype of fetishes is a man's penis, just as the normal prototype of inferior organs is a woman's real small penis, the clitoris" (*SE* 21: 157). We might translate the sentence about melancholia more closely as "When dreams have served us as the normal prototype of narcissistic mental disorders, we want to try to clarify the nature of melancholia through its comparison with the normal affect of mourning." Once again, this takes the form of an analogy, comparing the normal prototype with an implicitly pathological imitation: dreams are to narcissistic mental disorders as mourning is to melancholia.

Unlike in the analogy at the end of "Fetishism," however, there is no explicit gendering of the terms at the beginning of "Mourning and Melancholia." Yet, as Schiesari notes, the terms are gendered: mourning is culturally encoded as women's ritual function, while melancholia is culturally associated with men's creative genius (12). "If such a gender dichotomy obtains between (female) mourning and (male) melancholia, then the mimetic relation Freud describes wherein melancholia imitates the trappings of mourning points to something considerably less innocent . . ." (12). I share Schiesari's wariness of the apparent simplicity of the comparison. Thus while the explicit gendering of "Fetishism's" final analogy is lacking here, the larger cultural situation of mourning and melancholia, as well as Freud's further elaborations, implicitly genders the elements of the analogy.

What is more interesting to consider, however, is that Schiesari's characterization of the relation between mourning and melancholia in Freud's text as mimetic and imitative recalls our concern with the discourses of travesty and fetishism in the previous chapter. Her use of the word "trappings" serves to underscore this similarity; melancholia is a drag version of mourning. This imitative relation makes the analogy to fetishism more interesting, because in the classical Freudian sense of the fetish as penis-substitute, fetishism becomes puzzling precisely because the fetish does *not* necessarily imitate or mimic the penis externally or explicitly. However, Freud is convinced that the fetish does function mimetically on a hermeneutic or symbolic level, within the imaginary relations the fetishist inhabits.

The coincidences between melancholia and fetishism, however, go beyond just the first and last sentences of their respective texts, their analogical comparison to a "Normalvorbild" against which they emerge as pathological, yet curiously constrained by imitation. By examining "Mourning and Melancholia" point by point with "Fetishism" (taking neither as the normal prototype of the other) we can bring these resonances to light. At a number of points, Freud's description of melancholia parallels descriptions of fetishism. Perhaps the first thing we note is that Freud characterizes melancholia as a splitting, a struggle with reality and eventual turning away from it. Second, both fetishism and melancholia involve a loss of a loved object (possibly only at the level of the unconscious), a memorialization of the loss, an ambivalence about knowing that loss, and a lack of shame in one's conduct in re-solving that loss. The characteristics of ambivalence, memorialization, and lack of shame recall key aspects of fetishism as Freud, and the fem-inists in the previous chapter, have theorized it. While lack of shame is less explicit in Freud's description of fetishism than of melancholia, it is nonetheless evident from the contrast between fetishism and the feel-ings of inferiority inspired by the clitoris, the shame of femininity.

Freud characterizes the loss marked by melancholia in two ways. The first describes melancholia which is a reaction to the actual loss of a loved object; this loss, however, may only be an ideal or abstract loss, one where the subject no longer can have the object as before, even though the object itself remains physically unchanged. Freud asserts: "Das Objekt ist nicht etwa real gestorben, aber es ist als Liebesobjekt verlorengegangen" (GW 431). [The object has not perhaps actually died, but has been lost as an object of love] (*SE* 14: 245).[4] This kind of loss has an example in *Beloved*, where Paul D, Sethe's suitor, loses his love for Sethe upon learning of her murder of her child; he leaves her home to camp out in the church basement and drink. Sethe remains un-changed—it is Paul's relation to her that changes.

The second form of loss in melancholia has a less clear object. Such a case develops "where one feels justified in maintaining the belief that a loss of this kind has occurred, but one cannot clearly see what has been lost" (*SE* 14: 245). In mourning, Freud notes, there is nothing un-conscious about the loss; however, the loss may be largely unconscious in either form of melancholia, precisely because the lost object is an ideal (SE 14: 245). The second form of melancholia is even closer to the loss experienced by the fetishist, for the phallic mother too is not real but an ideal. Insofar as the mother's phallus never existed, but rather is the product of an unconscious desire, fetishism parallels the second cat-egory of melancholic loss; in this case those who are outside the experi-ence cannot clearly perceive the loss the subject feels and reacts to.

Both melancholia and fetishism thus present a mysterious relation to an object, a relation that cannot be accounted for rationally. In the work of mourning, Freud says, it is clear why the ego becomes inhibited and turns away from the outside world; this is part of the normal process, a stage that will be overcome. In melancholia, Freud terms this same turning away from the world "puzzling" (*rätselhaften*), "because we cannot see what it is that is absorbing him so entirely" (*SE* 14: 246).

Freud also characterized fetishism as "puzzling"; however, in fetishism the puzzle was not *what* was absorbing the fetishist's attention, rather it was *why*. Melancholia, then, seems to differ from fetishism's apparently obvious object because its object is not always clear or known, particularly in the second form. Yet I suggest that in fact neither the fetish object nor the melancholic object offers an epistemological edge over the other, particularly from the perspective of one outside the object-relation. The fetish object may not be detected by outsiders as anything extraordinary, and thus "passes" as a normal object to anyone but the fetishist. Sethe's earrings provide a case in point; although as a wedding gift they may be more likely to be recognized as special, nonetheless the reason why they are special as a fetish remains concealed. An object becomes a fetish because it is special to the fetishist, and not because it offers objective qualities that make it clearly more valuable than other objects. Similarly, the melancholic object may not be lost to anyone but the melancholic; its particularity likewise derives from the subjective relation rather than objective values. However, for melancholics, the particularity of the object is overwhelmed by the relation to the object. As Schiesari notes, "the reason the loss in the melancholic is not clear (is opaque to consciousness) is that it is the condition of loss *as* loss that is privileged, and not the loss of any particular object" (43). It is the particularity of the relation to the object that makes both fetishism and melancholia puzzling, but in fetishism the special relation to the object does not become so significant as to elide any sense of object itself.

In light of this point, it may seem reasonable to object that fetish objects and melancholic objects are different. This objection, however, presents an obstacle to our comparison only if we lose sight of the subject and end up focusing on the object that is lost. But neither for fetishism nor for melancholia is the object alone at issue; what makes fetishism and melancholia comparable is the unusual psychical investment in the relation to the object. This is evident even in the narrow Freudian explanation of fetishism, where the crucial element is the substitution of the penis/phallus and not the particular object chosen for that fetishistic substitution. But, *pace* Freud, it is not the phallus that is central to fetishism—although a fetish may indeed be based on the phallus. Rather, the importance lies in the complicated satisfaction the fetish offers, the use of ambivalence to resolve strategically uncomfortable contradictions and to negotiate loss.[5] Thus, a singular fixation, whether on melancholic loss or fetishistic satisfaction, provides the specific, clear point of reference according to which a range of different meanings can be interpreted, enabling the fetishist or the melancholic to impose order on her world. The motive for fetishistic substitution thereby parallels the motive of recalling loss for its own sake, which is how Schiesari defines melancholic incorporation. On this view, melancholia and fetishism are similar because each would be induced by a particular, determined thing—either the loss as loss, or the loss of what Freud calls "a particular and quite special penis" (*SE* 21: 152). It is the gesture (incorporation or substitution) and not the object that produces the phenomenon. This is important, because it highlights the fact that it is through the gesture that one becomes either a melancholic or a fetishist; the two phenomena are thus similar in that each is determined through the relation to the object.

What holds these two phenomena apart—why we can't just collapse melancholia and fetishism together and treat them as the same thing, despite their strong parallels—has to do with what these strategies have to offer subjects. While both are subject-creating, interpretive strategies that develop in the face of loss and involve an irrational and highly individual relation to an object, subjects take these strategies to different ends. To see this, we must comprehend not just *that* fetishism is crucial for subject-building, but *how* it is. By downplaying the gesture of substitution of the particular special penis in fetishism, we emphasize instead the nature of the compensation for loss—be it the threat of castration or of bodily dispossession—as being the constitutive element of fetishism. While the melancholic counters loss of an object with a retreat from the object to focus on the loss, the fetishist substitutes the loss with something that can provide satisfaction or resolution, thus moving past the lost object. The fetishist's substitution can take place through a variety of interpretations, in contrast to the melancholic, who is stuck with the singular interpretation of a fixation on loss.

What we learn from this view of fetishism, then, is that the loss is neither as opaque nor as reducible to a generalized loss as it is in melancholia; instead, the nature of the loss shapes the fetish relation. Fetishism is thus more adaptable than melancholia. The form of lesbian fetishism that de Lauretis outlines, for example, maps out a very different return on loss than the fetishistic negotiation of sexual difference in *Stone Butch Blues*, or than Gamman and Makinen discuss in positing bulimia as a form of food fetishism. Such fetish-forms would no longer be limited to penis-fixation, no longer analogous to the melancholic's fixation on loss for loss's sake, a display that serves to align oneself in the long tradition of melancholic geniuses. Instead, fetishism produces or disperses new and different forms of subjectivities, breaking with traditional molds. Thus while melancholia might beget sameness by reducing everything down to loss, fetishism would beget difference insofar as fetishes illustrate different kinds of losses.

We can see this contrast in the passage from *Beloved* cited above, in Sethe's negotiation of loss. Before they are taken from her, Sethe's earrings function as a fetish enabling her to discriminate among white people, to acknowledge, for example, the help Amy Denver gives her when she's on the run from the Sweet Home plantation and giving birth to her second daughter, Denver, or even the ambiguous courtesy of the sheriff who looks away while she nurses the baby Denver, in the face of the knowledge of continual abasement heaped upon her and her loved ones by racist whites. She loses not only this fetish but any sense of fetishism as the narrative progresses, becoming so melancholically attached to her boarder, Beloved, that she loses touch with reality altogether. Because of this melancholia, Sethe cannot distinguish the difference between the arrival of a white man at her house in the narrative's present and another white man's arrival twenty years before; she tries to stab her white landlord—a white abolitionist who has tried to help Sethe and her family, in this instance by coming to pick up Sethe's daughter to employ her— whom she cannot distinguish from the hated, slavemaster Schoolteacher who had come to take her and her children back into slavery.

In light of the parallel we have been pursuing between fetishism and melancholia, we can now not only distinguish the two but prefer fetishism to melancholia as an alternative epistemological model because it offers a flexible, effective, and creative strategy for negotiating loss. But it is not only in negotiating loss that fetishism offers a more productive and instructive edge. The way that both of these concepts help subjects negotiate reality and fantasy is also crucial here. Indeed, before we began drawing our parallel, perhaps the most obvious difference between melancholia and fetishism seemed to be that while fetishism is noted for providing or sustaining satisfaction (none of Freud's fetishists came to him complaining of the disorder), melancholia seems significant for its dissatisfaction: "dissatisfaction with the ego on moral grounds is the most outstanding feature" (*SE* 14: 248). However, this contrast is misleading, since melancholia contains its own satisfaction in "the idealization of loss as loss" (Schiesari 52), or from that very dissatisfaction, which as Freud notes provides the grounds for an "enjoyable" self-torment (*SE* 14: 251). These satisfactions that fetishism and melancholia share are significant because they both mark the subject's turn away from a full confrontation with reality. This contrasts with their analogical counterparts, mourning and the man's penis (as a symbol of surviving the threat of castration), which are privileged by their grounding in reality.[6]

But we should not rest complacent with the ease of distinguishing between the pathological and nonpathological pairs on the basis of which one survives reality-testing. The separation between reality and the imaginary or psychic world is not so clear-cut (although I would not go so far as to suggest it does not exist or influence our thinking). This is in fact what is so important about melancholia and fetishism, since they both contaminate a subject's confrontation with reality, and thus the constitution of that subject through the fantasmatic, the social, and the material. In Schiesari's reading of Freud, an important distinction between mourning and melancholia hinges not on the reality of the loss, but on the "excess of the affect" (39), so that even in the case of an objectively real loss, as in the death of a loved one, melancholia rather than mourning might take place.[7] This excess of affect, however, is specifically tied to narcissism, a central component to melancholia but not mourning; the elucidation of this distinction is what Schiesari most values about Freud's essay.

The ambivalence exhibited by melancholia derives from this narcissistic investment. Freud notes that melancholics exhibit an impoverishment of the ego, what Schiesari characterizes as "a loss in addition to the loss of the object" (43). Freud explains that in melancholia "an object loss was transformed into an ego-loss and the conflict between the ego and the loved person into a cleavage between the critical activity of the ego and the ego as altered by identification" (*SE* 14: 249). The narcissistic identification with the lost object becomes an introjection or incorporation of the object as part of the self, through a splitting of the ego. In this splitting, curiously, Freud finds the melancholic's satisfaction: "The self-tormenting in melancholia, which is without a doubt enjoyable, signifies . . . a satisfaction of the trends of sadism and hate which relate to an object" (*SE* 14: 251). This splitting provides strong common ground between melancholia and fetishism. Through the process of incorporation, the melancholic comes to identify with the lost object, and thus to both avow and disavow the object's loss; this process mirrors how the fetishist uses a substitute to avow and disavow castration of the mother, or in the case of recent lesbian revisions, castration of the self. Both the fetish substitute and the melancholic incorporation are strategies for negotiating a survivable relation to the reality of a loss, even if that loss is not objectively or physically real.

What is thus notable about melancholic satisfaction is that, like the satisfaction of fetishism, it arises out of a splitting that severs the subject from a full confrontation with reality. Just as a certain standard of realness marks the difference between the fetish and its prototype, the man's penis (which has verifiably escaped castration), the quality of realness marks the difference that separates melancholia from mourning (where the object is verifiably lost). Here too, threat plays a role—the potential loss in fetishism through castration echoes the cases where melancholia "proceeds precisely from those experiences that involved the threat of losing the object" (*SE* 14: 257). Indeed, it is precisely because melancholia derives from an imaginary loss that it loses the certainty of mourning. The melancholic subject, after incorporating the lost object as part of the self, vacillates between treating herself as a subject and as an/the object. On this view, it seems that the difference between fetishism and melancholia in the classical Freudian paradigm comes down to the poles of oscillation: whether one vacillates between being the subject and being the object, or between the object's masculinity and femininity. But with the analysis fresh in our memory of how fetishism breaks down the polarity of masculinity and femininity, we will find this parallel instructive only insofar as it points to the possibility of a similar deconstruction of the subject-object binarism.

Thus, while the distinction between melancholia and fetishism on the basis of what defines the poles of oscillation might seem to serve us well, we must not allow it to return us to a more restricted interpretation of the Freudian text, blinding us to the fact that fetishism is as much about the distinction between subject and object as melancholia is about sexual difference. For as much as fetishism is about the negotiation of differences, sexual or cultural, it is also about the negotiation of identity, through the oscillation between autonomy and connectedness, distance and proximity. In this regard, melancholia offers a particularly compelling parallel to fetishism, since the melancholic achieves a limited autonomy by separating himself from the incorporated object, yet he cannot, as Freud notes, give up the love for the object, even if he gives up the object (*SE* 14: 251). In fetishism the relation to the object is just as important for giving the fetishist autonomy through identification. As we noted in the first chapter, even in the strictly Freudian paradigm, where the little boy disavows his mother's castration, some degree of identification with the mother is necessary for fetishism to arise. In an expanded notion of fetishism, as we saw in chapter 2, identification with the object remains important, whether it is Indiana's cross-identification with Noun or Jess's identification with the androgynous ideal structured into Dineh culture. The persistence of identification in fetishism is crucial for the expanded notion we are developing here, but it is not the only mechanism in fetishism.[8] Identification facilitates the fetishist's attention to the fetish object, but it does not exhaust the possible ways the fetishist relates to the object. Rather, identification provides the setting in which the subject establishes her relation to the object, and this relation becomes understood as fetishism. This empathetic bridge that identification provides will gain importance as we move from understanding fetishism as a form of desire to fetishism as a form of knowledge.

Both fetishism and melancholia involve the contradiction between knowledge and belief, insofar as they both emerge from an ambivalent relation to reality that is manifested in the splitting of the ego. However, the epistemological status of the phenomena differ because of the disparity in their social currency. As we move toward emphasizing the epistemological dimension of these phenomena, we must take into account not only their Freudian interpretation, but also the larger sphere of their cultural history. Melancholia and fetishism, like many key psychoanalytic concepts, arrive in our hands through Freud's discourse as if they were ahistorical and acultural. They seem to be purely interior psychical phenomena rather than social formations subject to the dynamic of political challenge and change. But fetishism, at least, is not purely internal, or psychical, since it always entails an external object that exists in the world and that has some social meaning. It thus already violates the boundary between the psychical and the social, as well as that between subject and object. As we noted in the first chapter, the general history of the notion of fetishism places the phenomenon squarely in the social sphere, in the exchange between cultures, or between individuals in the marketplace. Indeed, in light of its sociable history, Freud's notion of fetishism is really quite odd. Not only does he translate an intersocial phenomenon into an intrapsychical realm, but he does it so persuasively that fetishism becomes a metaphor for a solipsistic relation to objects that excludes any other subjects. This "isolation," as it were, only further facilitates the comparison of fetishism to melancholia, since the melancholic—paradigmatically represented by Hamlet, though we can also see it in Sethe in the second half of *Beloved*—is a figure of social alienation.

Schiesari's work demonstrates that melancholia, like fetishism, has a social history. She locates Freud's reading of melancholia squarely within the classed and rationalized tradition: "Freud's essay can be shown to possess more than a casual complicity with the Renaissance discourse on melancholia." In fact, it "falls within a venerable cultural tradition that has, in fact, historically legitimated loss in terms of melancholia for men" (5). In Schiesari's account, melancholia's modern incarnation emerged in the fifteenth century, when "depression became translated into a virtue for the attrabilious man of letters" through the work of the Florentine philosopher Marsilio Ficino (7). It is transformed from its ancient and medieval meanings as a disease characterized by an excess of black bile, into a "specific representational form for male creativity, one whose practice converted the feeling of disempowerment into a privileged artifact" (8).

In its history, then, melancholia differs significantly from fetishism, since it is not radically altered when it is taken up by Freud or interpreted within the Freudian tradition. This divergence can be accounted for by the fact that melancholia is central to the Western tradition, not only entangled with its roots in Greek and Roman cultures, but pivotal in the Western conceptions of the artist or man of genius. In contrast, fetishism was introduced into Western discourse from the outside, as already a hybrid mediation between African and European cultures even in its earliest introduction, as William Pietz's study of fetishism shows. According to Pietz, although the Latin word *facticius* and its medieval permutation into *feitiço* touched on quasi-fetishistic phenomena (from commercial to theological discourse), these terms did not deal with the basic components of what we now recognize as the fetish, even though they provide the linguistic roots. It was not until the fifteenth century, when the Portuguese began to trade with West Africans, that the term *feitiço* emerged as distinct from idolatry or artificiality, accruing the meaning of an object that can be substituted across cultures through "its status as a value-bearing material object" (Pietz, II: 40). Thus, the meaning we now recognize for fetishism was grafted onto the root about the same time as melancholia took on its new significance as a marker of distinction. This distinction was twofold, marked by both class and gender. Melancholia was a special quality that not only elevated a man above the vulgar masses, but also separated out the man of genius from the common woman whose grief came to be coded as her natural role rather than as a culturally valuable expression. Note that at the time of this emergence, fetishism was the nongendered term while melancholia was specifically gendered as masculine.

In examining the parallels between fetishism and melancholia, we cannot overlook how Schiesari's project corresponds with feminist analyses and recuperations of fetishism. Just as the latter have had to justify (re)claiming perversion for women, Schiesari argues that "One task of the feminist analysis of melancholia is precisely to redeem the cause of depression, to give the depression of women the value and dignity traditionally bestowed on the melancholia of men" (93). Unfortunately, Schiesari neglects to remind us that not all men's melancholia was equally acknowledged; only those who had the privilege of being recognized as special could set themselves or their melancholia off from the common man's grief (Hamlet, not Rosencrantz or Guildenstern, is the melancholic; similarly, in *Beloved*, Paul D's melancholic withdrawal from Sethe and the community is not marked as either pathological or an indication of genius, but seems instead a reasonable response to be-

ing overwhelmed by having to take in one more horror). Still, her point
is well-taken; substitute "sexuality" for "depression" in the quote above
and "fetishism" or "perversion" for "melancholia," and you have a recognizable feminist argument for female subjectivity and desire.

Yet what that glib substitution reveals, especially when one arrives
at the last phrase "to give the sexuality of women the value and dignity
traditionally bestowed on the fetishism/perversion of men," is that
while melancholia may have been a privileged disease, and the concomitant lack of recognition accorded women's melancholia actually
deprives them of something, namely cultural power, fetishism and perversion are still disparaged, and the objection that women have lost
nothing by being excluded from these categories remains strong. In
bringing these two terms closer and closer together, I want not only to
call attention to the distinct valuations accorded suffering and satisfaction in our culture but to recognize that these values are themselves
problematic, and not merely because of their gendered implications. As
Schiesari' s study shows, the banality of women's suffering impedes cultural expression of their grief or depression, just as the banality of men's
satisfaction privileges the melancholic's expression as special or pro-
found. This is not to say that all men are satisfied, while all women suffer; rather, as Schiesari emphasizes, the focus is on the discursive
construction of these values, "how and in whom loss is not dismissed
but taken seriously" (29). Melancholia is taken seriously as a form of creativity, even a necessary step toward creation. Indeed, creativity is precisely another significant common thread between melancholia and
fetishism. Yet, however socially privileged and creative melancholia
may be, it remains a form of suffering, even when the clinical melancholic moves into the manic phase (which might seem to provide relief).
In contrast, foremost among fetishism's virtues is the fact that it is about
not suffering, but satisfaction, without regard to social convention. Thus,
while both melancholia and fetishism contain features that could prove
useful for understanding how subjects come into being and action, in the
end, fetishism proves to be the more useful strategy to embrace.

The emphasis on satisfaction, the range of interpretations of loss,
and the negotiation of subjective reality are not the only reasons
fetishism proves more suitable or appealing as a strategy of subject-
formation and object relating. Despite the fact that it may involve a mis-
recognition of the other (e.g., the mother as "castrated"), fetishism
retains a strong sense of the self, if not of the threat to the self, and an
equally strong grip on the significance of the lost object. In contrast,
melancholia misrecognizes the self as the other, retaining only a strong
sense of loss that underscores the relation to the object, not the object it-

self. This difference in the status of the object renders fetishism more epistemologically valuable than melancholia. The object in fetishism remains essential and external, though not necessarily subordinate, to the self, while the melancholic, because of incorporation, dissolves the very boundary between the object and the subject, to the point where the object no longer matters.[9] And, unlike fetishism's vacillation between masculine and feminine poles which provides the opening for a third sexual difference outside the hetero-binary, melancholia does not complicate the binary by offering a third option. Rather, it collapses into the indeterminate oscillation between one or two incorporated into one, dominated by the motif of loss.

Since loss is an inevitable part of human life, we do need to acknowledge the strategies individuals use to negotiate loss. We also need to pay attention to the values placed on those strategies according to who employs them, or who gets recognition for employing them. To this end, Schiesari is keen to argue that "loss must be rethought in terms of modes of mourning and depression, which differ from the melancholic tradition" (96). Here I diverge from her, because while I believe that it is important to understand all object relations as susceptible to—if not constituted by—loss, I want to underscore that loss need not be saddening; loss is not always something to mourn. Therefore, we need not limit our understanding of loss to forms of mourning, pathological or not. The similarities between fetishism and melancholia help us understand how we deal with loss, but more importantly their differences illustrate how we use loss to become subjects and objects with a meaningful existence. Indeed, we need a more fetishistic and less melancholic view of loss, a view that entertains the possibility of multiple and satisfying negotiations of loss rather than reductively lumps all losses indiscriminately into one totalizing loss.

It is this totalizing loss that undoes Sethe. The beginning of *Beloved* is all about losses—about the death of Sethe's mother-in-law, the flight of her sons from the haunted house at 124 Bluestone, and the loss twenty years before of her baby girl. Through the course of the narrative we learn that this last loss was at Sethe's own hands, and that cutting her baby daughter's throat in order to prevent her and her children being taken back into slavery caused other losses—loss of her place in the African American community, loss of her own freedom by incarceration, loss of a chance for a normal life because of the haunting of her house by the dead baby's ghost.

Before she acknowledged her guest Beloved as the return of the toddler she killed, Sethe seemed to be distinguishing among these losses fairly well, even started to have hope for a normal life when Paul

D, whom she had known as a slave, turned up and exorcised the baby's ghost. The loss of the toddler is substituted by the haunted house, and the loss of the haunted house is substituted by the presence of Paul D. That Sethe is returning to a more hopeful, normal life, with a full range of emotions and people to share them with, seems illustrated by her taking in a guest/boarder, Beloved.

Yet this accommodation becomes her undoing. Sethe comes to realize that Beloved is her returned dead daughter, and she becomes caught up in an intensely melancholic relation to her, in order to stave off the threat of Beloved's leaving. Whereas before Beloved's appearance, Sethe had bravely refused to explain or account for her murder to anyone, after Beloved arrives Sethe focuses on making Beloved understand what it meant, what it took to kill her daughter in order to save her from the ultimate loss—the devastation imposed by slavery and racism. As Morrison writes, these losses are "that anybody white could take your whole self for anything that came to mind. Not just to work, kill, or maim you, but dirty you. Dirty you so bad you couldn't like yourself any more. Dirty you so bad you forgot who you were and couldn't think it up" (251). In trying to persuade Beloved, Sethe loses her own sense of self in a melancholic attachment to the lost object of her dead daughter.

There is a hint of hope, a potential of moving out of melancholia and into fetishism at the end of the novel. Paul D tries to bring Sethe back to her senses after Beloved has been cast out; he tells Sethe "you your best thing, Sethe. You are" (273). In telling her this, he is offering the substitute of herself for the lost Beloved, whom Sethe was mourning as her best thing (272). But he is also offering himself—Morrison says "he wants to put his story next to hers"—and hope for a future— "we need some kind of tomorrow" (273). There are thus a number of things presented for Sethe to grab onto, and all of these are ambivalent things, fetish things—whether it is the combination of feeling righteous and feeling shame Paul offers through his story and Sethe no doubt experiences in hers, or the very mixed possibilities that any future lays before us between hope and fear. The end of the novel thus can be seen as a rejection of melancholia in favor of fetishism as a strategy for resolving adversity and loss.

But the fact that the end does not offer a clear rejection of melancholia suggests a more important lesson, one with an ethical thrust. For the narrative to have had a happy ending—the promise that Sethe could have a normal life after all she had gone through—would be to suggest that any loss can be overcome, with a little help from a strong enough will (or a fetish, for the less strong subjects). Such a conclusion would not only remain subject-oriented (recalling the ideology of individualism in the triumph of the hero) but it would also render the readers in an oddly melancholic position, focused on Sethe's loss as loss, but unable to distinguish among kinds and degrees of losses. Thus, Sethe's failure at fetishism is precisely what may enable the fetishism in reading the novel. The losses that fetishism negotiates are losses that a subject can survive, even if that subject is transformed. It is essential to be able to distinguish between losses that can be survived from those that cannot, especially for those at a remove from the threat of loss, as readers are.[10]

I offer this cursory reading of *Beloved* as a mini-object lesson in using melancholia and fetishism as models of interpretive process. What the fetishistic model enables us to see is the strength of Morrison's novel in leaving the question of who Beloved really is open to different possible interpretations. That undecidability is one of the things that draws us into the novel, the epistemophilic drive to know who she is. But in trying to assess who she is—a question that for some readers may be posed in simply reading the title, as they wonder "who is this Beloved?"—we find that this subject-centered epistemophilia necessarily breaks down. More important than "who is Beloved?" is the question of how Sethe and Paul and the others relate to her, what they learn from her, and what we learn from them. The form of the novel, which is not a straightforward linear narrative but a dense knot that only gradually unravels, underscores that relational emphasis. Through the fetishism in the novel we settle, in the end, on an interpretation which is neither completely open or closed, but which allows for the coexistence of multiple possibilities that resonate with each other. Such a reading underscores what the fetish of Sethe's earrings memorialized for her—that while it is easy to recognize categorical definitions, the world, except in its most extremes like absolute evil, does not work so simply, and a more nuanced interpretive attention is required. Being able to discriminate among white people is only a part of this nuanced reading strategy for Sethe, but it is an important one, for "whitepeople" as well as "coloredpeople" help her to survive. In learning from Sethe, we need to allow room for ambivalence and the loss of certainty, and be brave enough to sustain an interpretive openness in the face of unsettled and unsettling questions.

The Persistence of Parody

Not only do we want to avoid an undifferentiated sense of loss, we also want to avoid an undifferentiated view of melancholia. The lessons of comparing fetishism and melancholia indicate that in rethinking fetishism we need to take into account the subject as embedded in a system of relations, some of which will be to objects. For a take on melancholia that moves us in this direction of understanding the subject's constitution through discourse, I want to examine the work of Judith Butler, particularly her influential book, *Gender Trouble: Feminism and the Subversion of Identity*. *Gender Trouble* might not be at the top of anyone's list for texts on melancholia, because the most well-known—and, not coincidentally, the most reductive—readings of *Gender Trouble* have focused on Butler's model of gender parody. If all gender is parody, the casual interpretation of Butler's text suggests, then we can all be whatever gender we want to be, indulge in a sort of "shopping for gender" in a free-market free-for-all. Such a reading seizes on the commonly held assumption that parody is a willful, intentional act.

But this casual reading is not the best interpretation of Butler's work, because it conjures a consciously choosing subject. This is exactly the opposite of what Butler's argument aims for, since one of the most important issues she tackles is a critique of volition, of the notion of the freely willing subject. Not only does a free-will or conscious notion of parody run counter to Butler's main concern in *Gender Trouble*, but more importantly such an emphasis pushes aside the most fruitful aspects of her thought—namely, her consideration of melancholia as a prototype for how subjects come into being through incorporation. Melancholia is central to *Gender Trouble*, not only because its discussion is physically located in the center of the book, but also because it provides a crucial model of the mechanism for gender identity in Butler's analysis. The notion of incorporation, rather than impersonation, serves as the grounding for Butler's theory of gender parody. This distinction is crucial for understanding her reinterpretation of the term parody.

The notion of parody, resonating with ideas of performance, of copying or imitating, seems to invoke consciousness in a way that neither melancholia nor fetishism do. We might therefore initially perceive parody to be on the opposite side of the epistemological fence from fetishism and melancholia, which while frequently construed as imitations or mimetic activities, tend to be seen as manifestations of unconscious impulses. But if we turn to the example of the drag queen—which appears well into the book (137), and at the point in the text where references to parody also begin to proliferate—we see that what makes the notions of gender performativity and parody effective and interesting as illustrations of Butler's point is precisely their similarity to melancholia.

It is likely that the figure of the drag queen, as the most vivid illustration of gender parody, contributed to the clothes-horse reading of *Gender Trouble*. Yet, the allure of a drag queen, who might seem to be the best example of a conscious selection of sexual/gender identity, only covers over the anxious question of to what extent one can actually *choose* to be a drag queen, the threatening possibility that it is not a consciously motivated choice but more a conscious manifestation of an unconscious drive. In this light we can see drag as model melancholia—and not in the clichéd sense of the drag queen who is tragically unable to become the woman she longs to be. Butler asserts that "drag fully subverts the distinction between inner and outer psychic space and effectively mocks the expressive model of a true gender identity" (137). The inner/outer subversion here is markedly reminiscent of a melancholic's inability to distinguish between what is internal and what is external.

Butler capitalizes on this dissolution to argue that there is no lost identity or truth to mourn; at best, there is a melancholic dissolution of the subject and object of identification, an imitation that simultaneously incorporates and dispels the ideal of (in the case of a drag queen) true femininity. If drag as an example of gender parody is important for understanding the performative nature of identity, for how identity comes into existence through action and assertion, it is also crucial for demonstrating how melancholia is central to the construction of identity and the constraints placed on our agency.[11] Melancholia models how the assertion of identity is not haphazard or willfully chosen, but is rather produced through subjects out of the systems of meaning in which they find themselves, and produced through unconscious connections, associations, and fixations. The model of melancholic gender parody helps us move away from the depth model of subjectivity, the belief in an inner and an outer self.

At this point, we might also recall Schiesari's characterization of melancholia as wearing the "trappings" of mourning, a metaphor which plays into Freud's analogy of melancholia as a perverse imitation of mourning. It is striking how both Schiesari and Butler raise the spectre of drag to illustrate how subjects strategically appropriate objects in order to construct a gendered identity, whether it is the melancholic genius or the drag queen. Butler's critique of the depth model of subjectivity has interesting implications for Schiesari's reading of mourning and melancholia, especially if melancholia is a drag version of mourning; where Schiesari still maintains the category of normal, Butler's critique destabilizes this category, insofar as her analysis undermines the ability to distinguish true loss from other forms (such as imaginary and fantasmatic loss), as the emphasis shifts from the object of loss to its effects. Thus, just as the drag queen can no longer be perceived as a [false] imitation of a [true] woman, mourning is no longer a *Normalvorbild*, or normal prototype, for melancholia. Butler goes beyond Schiesari in that she posits melancholia not as opposed to mourning, but singularly as a necessary and central strategy for the ego's survival; it "may be the only way in which the ego can survive the loss of its essential emotional ties to others" (58). Through this loss, which instigates the process of identification, we internalize gender identities, becoming the parent whom we cannot desire.[12] Through the mechanism of melancholia, Butler provides an important insight on the interconnection between desire and (gender) identity.

However much attention the drag queen example may garner in *Gender Trouble*, it is not drag that provides the paradigm for gender melancholia, but heterosexual masculinity. Butler may thus seem in line with Schiesari's analysis, since both seem to work from the same prototype. While the two critics acknowledge a role for melancholia in subject-formation, Butler's treatment of melancholia differs significantly from Schiesari's. Where Schiesari uses melancholia to describe a type of largely masculine autonomy and privilege which serves as the basis for our culture's ideal of the man of genius or of superior subjectivity, Butler uses the term to describe the illusion of fixity bestowed upon all gender identities and sexual practices so that we no longer see genders as fluid and contingent. This fixity reinforces the belief that heterosexuality is both unchanging and natural, according to Butler. This view of melancholia seems further from Schiesari's melancholia and closer to the classical understanding of fetishism as a fixation on static gender identities in order to stave off fluidity and reinforce heterosexuality. Butler further argues that this form of melancholia underpins philosophical categories that rely on fixity and sameness—in particular categories of identity, and the very notion of identity itself, especially insofar as it is viewed as an expression of an internal truth. This too is an important contribution her analysis of melancholia makes, and one which works well with our epistemological view of fetishism, as we shall see in a moment.

What is most important about Butler's reading of melancholia as the basis through which gender performatively constitutes itself, and what makes it most relevant to understanding a postmodern fetishism, is the insight such a reading brings to the plasticity, the interpretive mutability, of the body. We touched on this briefly at the end of the previous chapter in the critique of de Lauretis's treatment of the masculine woman. This mutability is something that even the strictest Freudian fetishist already understood as he imposed his interpretation of the phallic mother onto the body of his female lover, endowing her with a penis to render her an "appropriate" object. But it is an important insight for non-Freudian fetishists and nonfetishists alike. Butler's melancholic parody integrates the notion of incorporation, the process of becoming embodied, with the equally important elements of repetition, interpretation, and performance, to illustrate how we constantly reshape and reassert our identities, materially as well as socially and fantasmatically. If the body takes shape through repeated actions of a subject who aims to become something she can only imagine—whether that is a parodic aim or a cultural ideal or a taboo parent—then perhaps the body is not some dumb source locked outside of meaning but a material, not unlike a text, already embedded in meaning and signification, molded by pain and pleasure.

This view of the body and the identity of subjects raises serious questions for anyone concerned with fetishism, since fetishism too is an interpretive process that repetitively uses materiality to embody imaginary aims. Incorporation, with its emphasis on becoming embodied, integrates the material world with the psychical or imaginary one more than identification does; as a primary mechanism in melancholia, it has not been associated with fetishism. Yet fetishism's attention to the thing, its inappropriate emphasis on an object, similarly transgresses the boundaries of identity and enables the subject to become or do something she otherwise could not by materializing certain desires through the body. The bodily effect of the relation to the fetish object suggests that incorporation is important for fetishistic subjects as well as melancholic ones. Fetish objects, as the chapter on travesty shows, are quite often things that are close to the body, things that are instrumental in if not essential to the subject's construction of identity and process of identification. If, like the fetish object, the body is an instrument of and for interpretation, what distinguishes bodies from objects? Can we distinguish between the melancholic incorporation of the father's mannerisms and the fetishistic appropriation of the father's fedora, in terms of how the subject relates them to her body, how she uses them to become herself?

Butler's combination of performativity and incorporation points us toward the possibility that the answer is no. We cannot take for granted that the boundary between melancholia and fetishism would be the body's surface, since that surface is itself already invested with meanings just as much as prosthetic objects are. If we cannot distinguish between the investments incorporative subjects make in their bodies from the investments fetishistic subjects make in their objects, we may no longer be able to say what's an appropriate or an inappropriate thing. In other words, given the interpretive mutability of both bodies and objects, the line between incorporation and fetishism becomes more and more indistinct. The very boundary that classical fetishism relies upon, that between the proper and improper object, begins to be called into question here. Only a very literal distinction—the object as a thing whose material is foreign to human flesh, a thing which feels no pain—seems capable of driving a wedge between the two. But the investment of care a fetishist makes in an object erodes even that thin line, for the fetishist's relation to the object is intimately tied up with not only feeling but feeling for the object. The only other distinction that still holds is that incorporation would derive from intangible objects and fetishism from tangible ones. The mechanism of each, however, disregards the factor of tangibility, so only an outsider could make such a distinction into an objection.

This troubled boundary is developed further in Butler's subsequent reading in "The Lesbian Phallus and the Morphological Imaginary," in *Bodies that Matter*, where she argues that the subject's fantasmatic map of its body is not delimited by cultural imperatives for how one should experience one's body, but through the experience and interpretation of pain and pleasure. This experience of pain and pleasure works two ways. It presses upon the subject from outside, through the pressures of social assimilation and the expectations of family or friends, and it is also produced from within the subject, from moods or nerves reporting sensations. Like fetishism, melancholic incorporation literalizes and fixes one's sense of identity not only through the fantasy, but also at the material level of the body, making the body seem to be a natural and even unchanging ground for identity. However, unlike fetishism, which inherently cannot be fully assimilated or naturalized because the fetish object exists in the world and has meaning beyond the subjective associations that the fetishist inscribes upon it, melancholic incorporation can sustain an illusion of naturalness—but only because it loses interest in the object itself. A fetishist, on the other hand, can never leave the thing behind; moreover, the object of desire is always marked as unnatural in the system of sexual differences.

In elaborating this idea of the plasticity of the body in *Gender Trouble*, Butler asserts that "the phantasmatic nature of desire reveals the body not as its ground or cause, but as its occasion, and its *object*. The strategy of desire is in part the transfiguration of the desiring body itself" (71). Fetishism is also a strategy of desire that transfigures, only it is understood to act on the *desired* body—namely the object—not the desiring body of the subject. Yet fetishism does make its effects felt on the desiring body. Whether in the narrow, strictly late Freudian sense of penis-substitution, or in the wider anthropological sense of projecting powers onto a fetish object, fetishism augments a subject's sense of capability, one's power to act or to will—and augmenting one's sense of possible actions inevitably affects how one inhabits one's body. This is true regardless of whether the fetishist is conscious or unconscious of the fetish object. While the notion of unconscious fetishism may sound like an oxymoron, given that Freud takes fetishes to be conscious manifestations of unconscious impulses, an expanded notion of the fetish must be open to the possibility of an unconscious fetish object—things we do not consciously realize we need or insist on having. In making this claim, we follow Butler's elucidation of the melancholic structure of heterosexual gender norms, which argues that not only conscious identifications shape who we are/become, but also unacknowledged or repressed identifications. Our relation to and appropriation of objects is not limited to our conscious interaction with them.

Butler's work on incorporation provides an important complication of the interpretation of being; no longer can we maintain a belief in identity as a "true" expression of an inner self. Her connection of melancholia and parody offers an incisive critique of this depth model of subjectivity, integrating the sense of conscious appropriation that is clearly resonant in "parody" with the element of unconscious or unacknowledged impulse in melancholic incorporation. Butler demonstrates that to become gendered we take on and come to embody the rules for gender from outside ourselves, dissolving, in the process, the boundary between outside and inside so as to make our gender seem to be an expression of an inner truth. Although gender is her object of analysis, Butler's argument implicitly dissolves the differences between incorporation and appropriation by moving from melancholia to parody. Thus, the implications of her argument reach beyond a new understanding of how gender works; they contaminate how we think about other identities, as well as how we can think about being, knowing, and desiring. Her text facilitates a reconsideration of how fetishism, which is similarly concerned with being, knowing, and desiring, enables subjects to negotiate these conundrums of subjectivity through the private and the public simultaneously. The nature of identity that Butler's argument elucidates cannot stop at the boundary of the subject, but must be explored through the subject's relation to objects, to materiality—in short, through fetishism.

Indeed, Butler's description of melancholia sounds strikingly like fetishism, especially as she repeatedly invokes magic to characterize melancholia's operation, thus echoing the sense of the fetish's augmentation of the subject's powers: "The melancholic refuses the loss of the object, and internalization becomes a strategy of magically resuscitating the lost object" (61). Later on, she remarks that "incorporation, which denotes magical resolution of loss, characterizes melancholy" (68). The magical elements of commemoration and resuscitation bring together both Freud's notion of the fetish as a monument to castration, and the anthropological notion of fetishism as a token of magical powers. Melancholia might seem opposed to fetishism; it is a strategy of incorporation, of assimilating an object within oneself, while fetishism is a strategy of ex-corporation, of achieving a sense of oneself by projecting onto an outside object. However, these corporeal fantasies result not from a material change (actually taking in the object or being castrated) but from an interpretive operation along a psychical border; this commonality makes them closer than they might perhaps have initially appeared. Incorporation and ex-corporation both work subjectively to redefine a boundary. More importantly, incorporation, as Butler paraphrases Freud, aids the subject in "'sustaining' the [lost] other through magical acts of imitation" (57). Thus, we should pay attention to the common denominator that melancholia and fetishism share—the magical act of imitation through a process of embodiment. The difference is whether it is the subject or object which embodies the significance.

Butler's repetition of this notion of imitation, which brings her version of melancholia closer to notions of fetishism, also raises the same issues of conscious will or volition that parody touches upon. Yet this imitation is clearly marked as emerging from the unconscious; we melancholically incorporate the lost object—the parent whom we cannot consciously desire—by returning again and again to the site of the loss. Similarly, the fetishist returns again and again to the fetish object, even if the only conscious reason he knows why is because it gives him satisfaction. This return to the site of or memorial to loss suggests that imitation rather than substitution is the key mechanism at work in fetishism. The fetish is not a simple, one-time replacement, but the creation of a new object and a new relation that is part of a dynamic process of building a subject who can express both will and desire. Fetishism thus broaches issues of volition—to what extent can one choose one's fetish object, or to be a fetishist at all? The ambivalence in fetishism between knowledge and belief, fantasy and reality, suggests that it also illustrates how conscious will is undergirded by unconscious desire.

Butler works the problem of volition through iterability. Iterability, a notion Butler inherits from Jacques Derrida's analysis of J. L. Austin's theory of speech acts, is the idea that meaning accrues through repetition, which both has a normative force and deviates from that norm. This view takes all speech, indeed all signifying practices, as performative—that is to say, they derive their meaning from the effects they produce, and they are inevitably open to being repeated, either successfully or not. However, Butler's critique pushes us even farther, adapting the fallibility of linguistic expression to classical philosophical questions of how and who we are. Whether it's the drag queen purportedly choosing a gender or the Cartesian mind choosing to doubt everything, the model of the volitional subject conceals the question of whether such a subject exists. Where there's a will, we presume, there's a self or subject, an agent acting on that will. In *Gender Trouble*, Butler is at pains to raise this question of whether such a subject, capable of conscious willing, exists. If we ourselves—and not just the things we say—are structured by iterability, then the presupposition that we could be volitional, masterful subjects becomes a crucial question.

Butler is, of course, not the first to raise this question or trouble the assumption of the volitional subject. Freud's theory of the unconscious provided an account for some of the ways subjects fail to achieve their conscious purposes, while not completely undermining belief in a willful subject. Perhaps we have reached the limits of a discourse of the unconscious, as the temptation to lapse into an individualized notion of the unconscious is too great. Butler's careful explication of how gender melancholia sustains gender parody has provided a striking model upon which to build our understanding of the limits of volition, yet to capitalize on its implications we must move beyond the consequences of her reading for subjects to think through how objects too participate in the scene of volition. Certain objects, no less than certain attributes or beliefs held by a subject, enable or constrain a subject's volition.

Butler posits that it is not essence but repetition that holds the subject together—insofar as there "is" a subject to be held together. However, it is a repetition that may not always produce the same effect; thus her reliance on iterability raises a spectre of a subject so changing as to lose coherence. Fetishism provides an antidote to this erroneous view, insofar as the subject's iteration remains in relation to an external object; thus, the fetish object sets certain parameters on meaning's change through iterability. To claim that the fetish object establishes certain parameters on interpretation is not to suggest that the material object holds some sort of special meaning that is less subject to change than the immaterial meanings of identity categories with which Butler is concerned. Rather, I mean to say that the very difference of fetish objects, precisely because they are objects rather than subjects or ideologies, gives them a different place in the system of meaning, because we normally presume that material things have fewer meanings or interpretive possibilities than subjects or ideas do.[13] While fetishists disregard this presumption and load more complex meanings onto fetish objects than nonfetishists do, even to the point of condensing an entire narrative onto the significant object, they nonetheless can still perceive the simple meanings nonfetishists impute to objects. This comparatively stable grounding of meaning is what enables the interpretive dynamic between subject and object in fetishism to be so useful.

Rather than turn to the fetish to combat this spectre, Butler relies on less tangible things to structure the subject's coherence. Integrating Lacan with Nietzsche, Austin, and Derrida, Butler's notion of identity—the "I" of who I am—posits that this "I" only comes into being as parody, through performance, action, melancholic incorporation. These processes are the same once the inner/outer distinction has been deconstructed. Butler reiterates Lacan, saying this "I" is not an exact copy of an originary "I," a precise imitation that repeats without introducing ambiguity or error; it refers according to an established code, and its referent changes as the context changes, thereby introducing an element of uncertainty in its meaning. Insofar as rules for language and performance (what gets recognized as repetition or representation) exist prior to the "I" and provide the tools for this "I"'s parodic performance, there is a kind of "original" for the parodic copy; it is, however, more of a precedent than a unique source. This model translates parody from its well-known application in literature and the arts—where it is a classic strategy of creating a new work by imitating an older one—to a context of language and semiotics.

Using signs rather than literature as the model for parody changes the interplay of parody's elements by making the associations between elements less rule-oriented; no longer is the emphasis on imitation according to a discipline, but on more free-flowing connection, recall, and citation. In Butler's argument, this change holds implications for a critique of a self-evident sexual difference. Mute bodies become meaningful texts that have no choice but to signify, even though they cannot fully nor freely will *what* they signify. This move underscores the important point that we cannot give up on the possibility of—or the political need for—interpretation, but we need not restrict ourselves to the precedents of literary interpretation. Thus, the introduction of a semiotic model of parody enables Butler to bridge her psychoanalytic critique of identity with her analysis of the broader philosophical category of identity and the problems of subversion and subjectivity in the face of a crisis of agency and will.

It may seem odd to try to discuss desire, identification, and other concepts so strongly marked by psychoanalysis without taking recourse to a notion of the unconscious. But what is particularly remarkable about Butler's account of parody is that she shifts the discussion of just these issues in the constitution of identity out of a purely psycho-analytical framework. In doing so, she shifts the level of analysis from the individual scale to the cultural and social scale. It is a shift that moves us from psychoanalysis to rhetorical analysis. This is how the term iterability gains its importance, for it bridges the gap between the individual's will or the subject's agency, and the social regulations or symbolic codes that govern the intelligibility of sexual differences. To account for the unexpected changes that inevitably occur as humans employ the shared systems of cultural rules in their daily activities, psy-choanalysis introduced the notion of the unconscious. The failure to achieve conscious aims could be attributed to unconscious wishes; in this schema, individual agency remained in place, unquestioned. Iter-ability, particularly in Butler's adaptation, likewise marks a failure, and in fact might better account for the same failings that the unconscious had accounted for.

Iterability offers a new angle into understanding subjects as em-bedded in cultural systems that shape how they come into being. Un-like the notion of the unconscious, iterability shifts the problem of agency onto the subject's context, diffusing will and intention into the situation. Strictly speaking, iterability marks the inevitable failure of an utterance to conform to the speaker's intentions, the always-open pos-sibility that an utterance will be repeated in some drastically different context that will rewrite its original meaning. J. L. Austin uses the ex-ample of a marriage ceremony to show how crucial context is: marriage is something that comes about through language, two people pledging to each other. But because of iterability, a marriage ceremony also risks failure—and this failure is not necessarily a bad thing. If the people get-ting married are performers in a play, for example, they are not consid-ered to be married to each other once they leave the stage and the performative will have failed. The fact that they repeat the same phrases that others actually use to become married means that the au-dience will recognize the characters in the play as getting married, and the performance succeeds.

In Butler's hands, iterability becomes the failure which fuels the compulsive effort to embody ideal identities. Iterability names the nec-essary and inevitable repetition which generates unpredictable differ-ences in linguistic utterances. Iterability enables citation, the act of appealing to established practice, to take place. While the notion of cita-tion is not particularly evident in *Gender Trouble*, it becomes increasingly important in Butler's subsequent book, *Bodies that Matter*. There, the em-phasis on citationality overtakes the notion of parody posited in *Gender Trouble*.[14] The shift from parody to performativity to citationality emphasizes that subjects are constituted and become intelligible through social and discursive forces rather than purely psychological and individual ones. The individual's unconscious is less important in Butler's reading than the possibilities for interpreting the law, because her interest is primarily on systems—and increasingly on regulatory systems as the shift to citationality exemplifies—rather than individuals.

However persuasive Butler's arguments are that individual will or desire is a fiction covering over the production of subjects by cultural forces of prohibition and permission, the notion of the unconscious or desire on the individual scale is difficult to give up, perhaps because it is the private and fantasmatic that we feel is most our own. Yet the notion of the individual is not only seductive for private reasons, but for public ones as well. One of the criticisms the political right has leveled against progressive cultural politics and theory is that leftist social structuring absolves people of individual responsibility. The agreeing nods that such criticism has met with—even within the Democratic party, as centrists appropriate this same rhetoric of individual responsibility—indicate something beyond simply resistance to Butler's (and similar practitioners', both cultural and political) persuasive arguments. The intransigence of the individual suggests that even after decades of intellectual critique, the individual remains a crucial node through which social forces act. Subjects are not so much the site as the switch-points in the social network. As important as it is to think through the scene of agency, it is nonetheless crucial to realize that agency is individualized, even if it is not fully individual. The scene of agency channels action through individuals; this enables power to be distributed unequally. We therefore need a theoretical model that would acknowledge this individualization without asserting individualism and denying the very valid critical elaborations of how social forces shape us.

Fetishism enables us to acknowledge this individualization by affirming the importance of fantasmatic investments in special things and simultaneously to recognize the way that our investments are shaped by our circumstances. This perspective enables us to reinterpret fetishism in a broader frame, with more emphasis on its positive aspects of creative interpretation. Butler's focus on how individuals use gender parody and melancholia to interpret the laws governing the construction of identity provides a good model for how subjects use fetishes to simultaneously negotiate and challenge norms of sexual differences (i.e., norms about both gender identity and sexual desire), because fetishes, as Freud's account shows, condense social narratives onto material objects. We can read the fetish as a thing used as a citation of power—be it a penis, a phallus, a lost feminine body, or a deity—rather than as a substitute for it. This change in perspective displaces the privilege of the original, or the "normal prototype"; it levels the hierarchical relation between the fetish object and what the fetish interprets. This leveling is important because for a fetishist, it's the *thing* that counts; not so much its public reference but its private significance. The fetishist's shoe is what holds the power for him; not its reference to the maternal phallus, even if that particular fetish stands in for the maternal phallus. But we should not be too quick to reduce fetishism down to the expression of the subject's will through the manipulation of objects; this is a protofetishism insofar as it reinforces the separation between the subject, object, and the context.[15] The fetishist would produce and experience the will of the object, because of her ambivalence between fantasy and reality, between knowing very well the object's indifference but nonetheless insisting that it matters.

I think we can retain the notion of parody from Butler's work, even if she has moved on to other considerations, to the extent that parody usefully highlights the element of interpretation, for every parody is always already an interpretation, just as every fetish is. Interpretation provides a model for a kind of limited agency, the ability of a subject to act and create meaning even within highly determined and often restrictive parameters. But parody's value is limited, outstripped by certain disadvantages that ultimately also hamstring the effectiveness of Butler's argument. Apart from its potential for being misread as a purely conscious phenomenon, as I already discussed, parody risks becoming mired in the pitfalls of relativism; parodic performances require socially significant differences of power in order to retain their edge. While parody does model well the importance of context in determining the meaning of identities, because parodies rely on the audience's knowledge of the original, this dependence leads to the need to differentiate among contexts. Butler's theory does not accommodate such nuances because she is working in a structuralist vein, elaborating general mechanisms of sexual differences as systems of meaning in which individuals are dispersed. Her analysis of gender and identity focuses on the regulatory realm and limits our perception of the artful and creative aspects of identity, the very things that make identities unique and therefore useful. Part of this obscurance is due to her need to overcome the reading of parody as a form of conscious individual agency. Yet the model of melancholic incorporation that Butler develops to counter that reading cannot save parody, because melancholia fails to offer a way to negotiate such intersubjective differences or to provide acknowledgment of the different kinds of losses subjects experience. Fetishism, in contrast, does enable a subject to satisfactorily navigate a variety of losses and power differences. I suggest that fetishism—which like parody offers insight into philosophical and psychoanalytic assumptions about subjects and objects, knowledge and desire—can break through the dead end Butler's work on parody reaches.

Even parody understood purely as performativity offers no advantage over fetishism, for the fetish too is a performative in both the classical Austinian and the deconstructed senses. In performativity lies the fetish's satisfaction, for it creates the effect that it signifies. I would even go so far as to claim that the fetish is the prototype of the performative par excellence, since it becomes what it is through its use, and cannot otherwise *be* a fetish. This point illuminates a very practical aspect of the fetish, one which has been largely overlooked—that there is no fetish that does not actually serve some purpose, even if that purpose is not publicly accessible. An object takes on its fetish quality through being used as a fetish; otherwise, it's an ordinary object.

Rereading fetishism in light of Butler's elaboration of parody and performativity calls attention to the nature of fetishism's repetition. The fixation on the fetish is generally viewed as a pathological repetition compulsion, bound up in the return to the thing which gives satisfaction and cutting the fetishist off from relation to others. But viewing the fetish as a performative suggests that its repetition is not entirely a private matter; repetition is how the fetishist relates to the outside, public world through the fetish. In light of the fetish's instrumentality, it is neither the subject nor the object that is crucial to fetishism, but the relation between them. There is a necessary sense of mutual recognition between the subject and object at work in the fetish relation. But this recognition is not exclusively for fetishists and their objects. Those who are outside the special relation to the object that the fetishist has can still recognize the object as special and powerful, even if it's not special to *them*. The fetish can thus provide useful common ground for people with very different interests, and they recognize in the particularity of the object the needs of the subjects who relate to that object. Through the intelligibility of the fetish, both fetish and nonfetish subjects can come to know something. By building the fetish relation, the fetish subject creates herself; by situating herself among others through the fetish object the subject interprets herself in a world, and can share her interpretation with others.

We would do well to view fetishism's repetition less as fixation and more as iterability, since iterability underwrites performativity, as Butler and Derrida have delineated. Iterability presents the risk of loss, as well as the risk of failure (which is how Derrida figures it). Indeed, iterability makes fetishism such a satisfying and successful strategy for negotiating loss, since it provides a structure for the fetishist to work through loss rather than avoid it. Fetishism's persistent return to the thing provides an anchor in the face of uncertainty that can support a subject in forging ahead rather than hold her back through fear. This could be as simple as wearing one's lucky shirt to a job interview, or as obscure as keeping a cracked mug from childhood at the back of one's cupboard; just knowing the object is there may give the subject a point of reference that gives her confidence in the face of uncertainty. Through a form of objective incorporation, the fetish comes to embody the threat or loss so that the fetishist does not have to experience it—or perhaps more accurately can experience it without feeling over-whelmed by it. Fetishism is a form of mastery as well as a memorial to loss; because of this memorialization, fetishism is a mastery that is grounded in an ambivalent sense of knowing better, knowing that one's mastery is limited.

The upshot of all this is that we tend to perceive identity in gen-eral and gender in particular to be an ontological issue—and *Gender Trouble*, in its particular reading of perfomativity, reinforces this under-standing. Yet we might better understand identity and especially sexual difference as an epistemological predicament, a problem of knowing and interpretation. We use identity categories as rubrics by which we expect to know a person or a thing; for example, we use gender as a cru-cial guideline to predict how a person will act, such as whether they will be accommodating or demanding. The moves that Butler makes in her argument—the shift to the performative, the reliance on melancho-lia's mechanism of incorporation, the preference for the scene over the individual—point toward an epistemological approach to thinking through identity. Gender may be only one example of knowing how, but, as Butler acknowledges, it is an example that holds important im-plications for how we organize and understand ourselves and the world. Who we are, the whole idea of having an identity or being a sub-ject, is all about the combination of what we know and desire—a volatile combination that fetishism confronts head-on. And yet Butler pulls back, to work her analysis as an ontological critique. The reading of identity and gender Butler produces is thoroughly imbued with questions of desire, but ontology, even as radically reworked as But-ler's, does not give us access to understanding desire because it blinds us to relations in its emphasis on substantive being. Epistemology, by contrast, is already contaminated by desire, for desire is what drives us to know and to convince others of what we think we know.

Butler, in fact, skirts this sticky issue of the relation between desire and knowledge, maintaining the polarity between the two by favoring desire as her analytical focus while explicitly giving up on epistemology. A radical critique of ontology such as Butler's is clearly needed, and her analysis is effective insofar as it shows how the real is not self-evident, but a phantasm, contaminated by fantasy, will, and desire. Certainly parody—insofar as it keeps its edge—is a cogent model to illustrate this contamination. But it is not enough, if it maintains the separation between reality and the things which contaminate it, or if it remains too dangerously close to conscious agency to enable a clear discussion of the problem of agency and individualism, problems which are less ontological and more epistemological.

Fetishism, on the other hand, is sufficient, not only for many of the same reasons parody provides, but also and importantly for the epistemological angle it offers. To reiterate and reinscribe the Freudian analogy, the prototype of reality is not the man's penis, as if that were some irrefutable and singularly obvious piece of evidence beyond interpretation; the prototype for reality is the fetish, the substitute for the Thing, whose very replacement induces, preserves, and supersedes the loss of the original. The fetish indicates how reality is permeated with the fantastic forces of desire, but also of knowledge—the fantasy of knowledge not only being the projection of mastery and control, but also the investment in belief that contradicts evidence or materiality. The fetishist must know before he can insist nonetheless (as Octave Mannoni's schema for fetishism depicts it). As subjects come into being they simultaneously shape the context and objects in which they will exist while incorporating and appropriating those same rules and tools to make themselves who they are. They are not stupid about how they do this, but are aware to a certain extent—though not always completely—of how knowledge and desire direct their efforts. To be smarter and stronger subjects they must work the ambivalence and contradictions more attentively; fetishism offers a way to do this.

The conclusion of *Gender Trouble* makes apparent the radical critique of how being has been theorized; this critique has been at the heart of Butler's interrogation of identity. She asserts that "Ontology is thus not a foundation, but a normative injunction that operates insidiously by installing itself into political discourse as the necessary ground" (148). She thus posits that there is little difference between how forms of being are divided and how forms of sexuality and sexual identity are divvied up: both are based in interpretive norms rather than transcendent absolutes, even though the differences thereby constituted are no less real in their effects. This interpretation of being is, as Butler notes, predicated on the distinction between subject and object, a "dichotomy, which here belongs to the tradition of Western epistemology,

[that] conditions the very problematic of identity that it seeks to solve" (144).

With this gesture, Butler seems to throw out the possibility of using epistemology to come to a new understanding of the subject-object relation. Her argument at this point inveighs against traditional epistemology—and understandably, since the constitution of identity through Western epistemological *and* ontological norms is precisely what she argues against. The alternative epistemological model of fetishism, however, counters this Western epistemological tradition to provide a new understanding of the subject-object relation. In fetishism, the subject comes into being through a relation to the object, much as Butler argues that there is no self before a subject is brought into discourse: "There is only a taking up of tools where they lie, where the very "taking up" is enabled by the tool lying there" (145). The subject's identity is not substantive in the fetish model but practical, instrumental.

It may be this very instrumentality that renders fetishism invisible to Butler's consideration. Butler argues that the "language of appropriation, instrumentality, and distanciation germane to the epistemological mode also belong to a strategy of domination that pits the 'I' against an 'Other' and, once that separation is effected, creates an artificial set of questions about the knowability and recoverability of that Other" (144). Thus by Butler's argument, it is not just the feminine that is repudiated, or the homosexual who is abjected through the process of heterosexual melancholia, but particular objects as well. But in her argument they all seem affected in the same way. This is partly due to her efforts to make us see how sexual differences and ontological differences are equally interconnected. By expanding her analysis of gender from the political or psychoanalytic register to include a critique of philosophical identity, Butler implicates the very system of Western philosophy's basic categories in the process of heterosexual melancholia. Which objects can be incorporated in order to enable subjects to come into being, and which are repudiated as objects—this is regulated by heterosexual melancholia, which Butler demonstrates centers on masculine privilege sustained through homophobia and feminiphobia. But the melancholic model leaves us without any way to address these phobias, to perceive how they are in fact contingent and to negotiate how we might acknowledge their phantasmatic existence and their real effects while not letting them overwhelm and control us. It is necessary to maintain a certain ambivalence about phobic social forces, lest we, no less than those who have bought into homophobic or feminiphobic fantasies, create a totalized sense of them as we oppose them.

Fetishism provides this instrumental ambivalence. It is effective precisely because unlike melancholia, fetishism can distinguish among different forms of loss—between partial and whole, imaginary and real, normative and perverse. Moreover, the epistemological dimensions of fetishism are connected to the desire for the object in such a way that actually enables a different ethical relation to the object than normative epistemology tends to countenance. The instrumentality of a fetish renders the subject contingent, a cooperator with the object. The fetishist reads the fetish as the thing with a greater power than herself, even if it is only the power to satisfy. Because the fetishist blurs the boundaries between subject and object in relating to the object—she construes the object to be more like a subject—there is a sense of mutual recognition at work in the fetish relation. The strategy of domination that Butler rightly locates in traditional epistemological paradigm is undermined by fetishism's ambivalent constitution of the subject and object.

Melancholia's constitution of the object offers no counterargument to the normative epistemological paradigm (and thus Butler's rejection of epistemology follows from her choice of model). Butler herself recognizes the foundational role of melancholia as a problem. Her method for working through the difficult construction of a melancholic subject or (academic) discipline is to direct us away from what she calls "an *epistemological* account of identity" to one that examines how signification produces identity (144). In doing so, she tries to establish a different grounding for how we can understand identity, one that emphasizes incorporation (in its eventual trajectory toward citationality) rather than repudiation. In this shift, agency must be reexamined "as a question of how signification and resignification work" (144). This accounts for why melancholia's mechanism of incorporation must be conjoined with parody, which is much more clearly about signification and resignification.

However, I am not so sure that epistemology, much less ontology, can so easily be left behind, particularly because Butler's reworking of the latter is so convincing, but also because epistemology is—especially on a Foucauldian view—all about agency, the exercise of power and knowledge. Where Butler effectively suggests how ontology may be transformed by emphasizing signification, an expanded notion of fetishism allows for a parallel transformation of epistemology into interpretation. If, as Butler convincingly argues, ontology and epistemology—not to mention the categories they engender—are sustained by heterosexual melancholia, then fetishism becomes even more imperative as a means of transforming them. Fetishism, because it proceeds along the lines of sexual differences as well as ontological and epistemological differences, provides an important model for understanding what an alternative epistemology might be once foundational claims to truth are productively undermined. In this regard, it exceeds the model provided by melancholia.

Butler's shift to signification and away from substantive ontology and epistemology in many ways echoes strains that have been heard in philosophy since Nietzsche. Indeed, in important ways her shift, because it insists—quite rightly—on remaining engaged in ontological issues such as identity, agency, and subjectivity, puts her in line with the tradition of hermeneutic ontology, which has evolved out of Heidegger's work in the first part of this century. Butler's move is not unique. Other feminist theorists have also characterized the postmodern turn as the move to discursive analysis from epistemological accounts.[16] But however helpful Butler's critique of the duality of constraint and creativity within the horizon of signification is, we need something more than discourse analysis alone. We still need a critical understanding of how we know, how we exercise power, and not just of how we mean. We need this understanding because there are things in the world which are not subjects, which are not capable of participating in signifying practices, but which remain both meaningful and stubbornly outside of meaning—in short, we need to relate to objects. Epistemology is still necessary—albeit as a strategy of knowing not based entirely on the tradition of metaphysical ontology. Rather, what we need is an epistemology that works through the inevitable dynamic of the creation and loss of meaning and the necessary interdependence of ontologically different things (both subjects and objects, both reality and fantasy). In the ambivalent oscillation between fact and fantasy, knowledge and desire, the model for such an epistemology is fetishism.

CODA

The Epistemology of the Object

In tackling the analysis of fetishism, we have concerned ourselves primarily with one form of how subjects relate to objects—that is, desire. But other ways of relating to objects are equally important: knowledge, too, is a prime object relation. Our culture has conditioned us to connect questions of desire to sexual differences, be it gender differences or differences in sexual practices. We are less likely to make connections between sexual differences and knowledge, although feminist philosophers have mounted impressive arguments to draw attention to this link. These feminist analyses include demonstrations of how sexual difference has been used systematically to restrict access to knowledge or to make (often incorrect) assumptions about a knower's authority, as well as arguments for understanding all knowledge as context-specific, dependent on a framework of interpretation that includes (but may not be determined by) sexual difference.[1]

But if sexual differences are epistemologically significant, as feminist philosophers have claimed, so too should we consider the epistemological significance of desire and pleasure, which are not only significant components of the system of sexual difference, but are key aspects of knowing in itself. The desire to learn, the pleasure of working out an intellectual problem—these are just two more obvious manifestations of the desire dynamic at work in the epistemological process. Instead, the connection between desire and knowledge tends to be repudiated, and the two are polarized as opposite strategies for subjects to pay special attention to objects. Butler's work in the previous chapter provides one handy example, since philosophy's traditionally stringent separation of desire from knowledge presents one important reason why Butler ultimately rejects philosophy as she works through the cultural connections between desire and identification in her critique of identity. But that rejection is not the only way to proceed.[2] Whether our concern is the analysis of the forces that shape our culture or the nature of subjectivity—and desire, knowledge, and sexual difference are certainly important in these regards—or the critical examination of desire, sexual difference, and knowledge in themselves, we need to be able to think through how all three points on this triangle are connected, and how they bear on our relation to objects and construction of our selves. This conclusion will bring out what has been intimated all along in our analysis of fetishism: the epistemological relation as the basis for fetishism.

The history of fetishism suggests that the novelty of the fetish is located precisely in the problem of the object: How can material things manifest intangible values through their social, erotic, economic, or religious powers? The answer, of course, lies in the relation to the objects, rather than the objects themselves. William Pietz argues that "the essential problem of the fetish [is] the problem of the social and personal value of material objects" (II: 35). According to Pietz, although the fetish existed for centuries in the intercultural world of Afro-European trade established in the fifteenth century between the Portuguese (and later the Dutch and English) and West Africans, a theory of fetishism did not emerge until the Enlightenment, in the work of the French *philosophe*, Charles de Brosses. This delay can be traced to a number of factors Pietz touches upon, not the least of which is the ascendancy of reason, which marked a break from the folkloric and superstitious practices of Western (and particularly Christian) Europeans.

There were also two other important and related factors, though ones that came into play before the eighteenth century. The first was the emergence of an independent secular economy based on trade, which shifted the meaning of objects from their religious or spiritual significance to their commodity value. The second was a shift in trade dominance from Catholic to Calvinist countries, which favored the belief in a direct connection to God rather than in the need for intermediaries (whether these be tangible objects like rosaries or intangible ones like saints). Intercultural trade, which provoked anxieties about value and trustworthiness, also provided a counterpart against which European rationalists could claim their superiority. Thus, fetishism split into two kinds of practice, one pragmatically commercial and one critically reflective. As Pietz describes it, the practical application of fetishes for the Portuguese and Dutch traders evolved into a system of commercial exchanges solidified by social signs indicating allegiance, trustworthiness, and identity. At the same time, the interpretation of this practice in European intellectual discussions enabled new distinctions to be made, most notably between rational or "civilized" thought and the "primitive" way of thinking that superstitiously believes in supernatural agency and thereby misunderstands the impersonal principles of causality that the "civilized" person knows (II: 42).

The rise of reason is linked to the flourishing of European trade. For objects to be exchanged as commodities requires that they take on an impersonal value, one that seems, if not actually is, transcultural.[3] Similarly, reason posits that objects, causes, and effects are impersonal, not the result of some agency larger than the human subject. As Pietz notes, "For merchants and secular intellectuals of the eighteenth century, reason was above all the capacity to apprehend the material world of nature as determined by impersonal operations (determined by the mechanistic laws of causality). In this discourse, superstition is defined as the attribution of personal intent to the events of material nature" (II: 42). Europeans deemed African society's reliance on the fetish for its organizational basis an arbitrary and irrational foundation, and concluded that such cultures produced subjects who were incapable of reason. This conclusion, not coincidentally, facilitated rather than hampered European trade and colonial expansion. Since the fetish was construed as an inappropriate substitute for the norms of law and rational thinking, the opportunity seemed to invite the introduction of "proper," that is Eurocentric and rationalist, modes of thinking and ruling as a corrective. This view of the fetish as an inappropriate social mediator resonates with the definition the fetish later takes on as an inappropriate substitute for reproductive sexual activity. But going back to the eighteenth-century emergence of the notion of fetishism in European thought brings more fully into relief the epistemological and ontological issues at the heart of fetishism. A theory of fetishism played a crucial role not only in the Enlightenment's assertion of the superiority of reason, but in the Enlightenment's construction of the impersonality of cause and effect and the objectivity of reason itself.[4] Fetishism thus has a long history of providing an alternative epistemological paradigm; it is imbricated in the early strands of Enlightenment thinking as the model of otherness. In light of the ongoing critiques of the Enlightenment since the eighteenth century, it behooves us to return to the alternative model of knowing that fetishism offers and reevaluate it in a more positive light.

The Enlightenment is of course well-known for having articulated a new conception of the subject.[5] Yet in Enlightenment and post-Enlightenment thinking, it is not just the subject that has come under consideration—it's also our relation to objects. How this relation took shape can be seen in the theory of fetishism in eighteenth-century Europe; it makes sense that we should return to this now in the age of postmodernism and the critique of reason. Feminist efforts to work through the issues presented by the Enlightenment have followed two paths: either to make good on Enlightenment promises in the face of a

perceived threat of postmodern fragmentation to the coherence of the
feminist political subject, or to critique the limits Enlightenment thinking has imposed on our understanding. Both of these lines of thought
have criticized Enlightenment rationality in terms of its emphasis on a
masculine subject; importantly, this subject has also been—sometimes
implicitly, other times explicitly—heterosexual.

But these feminist efforts have largely focused on the subject's
constitution, without much attention being given to the object, or the relation between subjects and objects. Feminist critics have wanted us to
understand epistemology as gendered and sexualized, but without going so far as to apply these characteristics to the objects (rather the simply the subjects) of knowledge. Take, for example, Butler's reworking of
the notion of the subject and her critique of ontology and identity. Her
reconceptualization of the subject through the model of melancholic incorporation clearly contributes to a new understanding of the subject.
Yet it also raises implications for the status of the object, since the object,
rather than being purely subordinate to and produced by the subject,
can now be perceived as producing the subject who is invested in the
object. In the melancholic collapse between subject and object the production of meaning becomes the focus. In Butler's analysis, this meaning is an identity category such as heterosexual masculinity; in
Schiesari's reading, the meaning produced is the gloomy genius. This
focus also prevails in fetishism; but even better than melancholia,
fetishism helps us maintain the difference(s) that sustain the production
of meaning. If a subject invests in a red sports car at midlife, this sports
car may become a fetish object that both guarantees the subject's youth
and vivacity and acknowledges her aging (if only by exercising the
power or authority that comes at midlife). As a fetish object, the car
could produce, through iteration, a subject with confidence and a
stronger sense of self in the face of the threat of loss—of death, obsoles-
cence, or waning prestige. But because the investment is in an object
with its independent existence, the renewed fetish subject will never be
confused with the object the way the man of genius is conflated with
genius. The fetish relation holds the elements apart—the car, with its
meanings, remains distinct from the owner. This is similar to how, as a
paraphilia, fetishism throws sexual difference into sharper relief against
the norm of heterosexual subject-subject relations.

Another challenge to habitual thinking about the relation to the
object also comes from the field of philosophy, but from the area of epistemology rather than ontology. In her analysis of the assumptions and
presuppositions underpinning Western epistemology, Lorraine Code
outlines the contingencies of the philosophical constitution of the sub-

ject-object relation. This relation is both the "most salient" and "most politically significant epistemological consequence" of the Cartesian model of autonomous, masculine-gendered reason (139). Code finds that two key assumptions structure this relation: "that there is a sharp split between subject and object and that the primary purpose of cognitive activity is to produce the ability to control, manipulate, and predict the behavior of objects" (139). These assumptions lead to a privileging of vision as the dominant sense for knowledge, and a presumption of a unidirectional involvement (usually through observation) of subjects in relation to objects.[6] The object is construed as unable to return the gaze of the subject. Code, however, is keen to complicate this model, which she argues is limited to only a small portion of human efforts to know, involving only the interaction of autonomous subjects—those privileged by education and culturally shared beliefs about gender, race, and other markers of social position—who confront medium-sized objects. "The rarity of [this epistemological model's] achievement should prompt denials of its paradigmatic validity," Code asserts (164).

Code's proposition of friendship as an epistemological model invites us to push her example further by considering what happens when we blur the boundaries between subject and object, as fetishism does. The ontological difference of the subject-object distinction, like sexual difference in the heterosexual opposition between masculine and feminine, undergirds conceptions of fetishism. Indeed, ontological difference reinforces fetishism's classification as deviant, whether as fetishistic sexuality or fetishistic religious practice. From the rationalist point of view, a fetishist would be someone who fails to acknowledge that he has control over the fetish object, preferring instead to submit to it for purposes of power or pleasure. A fetishist is not only a failed heterosexual (as is the case in the Freudian paradigm) but also a failed subject, whose autonomy is compromised by his [sic] dependence on an object. This assumption of self-sufficiency overlaps with the colonialist and racist judgments about the poor or puzzling object choices of "primitive" belief systems found in prepsychoanalytic definitions of fetishism as totemism. In a world view that privileges the subject over the object, the abstract over the material, the mind over the body, a fetish god would not be as valuable as an abstract god because it is closer to the object (being embodied in one) than the subject (abstracted as a mind), and compromises the believer's self-sufficiency.

As an alternative to the traditional Western epistemological model, Code proposes the epistemological paradigm of knowing other people, particularly in the context of friendship. Such a model acknowledges both the possibility of having some degree of certainty in knowing, yet requires that one remain epistemologically open to the reinterpretation of and even the possibility of being surprised by the object of knowledge. The model of friendship also recognizes the extent to which context necessarily bears upon the interpretation of knowledge. In friendship the mode of domination—that is, the assumption of the subject's superiority and control over the object—is replaced by a sense of respect, an acknowledgment that the object is not fully under the subject's control.

While conceding that the friendship model entails its own limitations, Code reflects that "it is surely no more preposterous to argue that people should try to know physical objects in the nuanced way that they know their friends than it is to argue that they should try to know people in the unsubtle way that they claim to know material objects" (165). She dismisses the objection that friends can reciprocate in ways objects cannot by pointing out that, "after Heisenberg's formulation of the 'uncertainty principle' it is no longer possible to assert unequivocally that objects of study are inert in and untouched by the observational processes" and thus "it is no longer possible to draw rigid lines separating responsive from unresponsive objects" (164). While Code would not go so far as to allow scientists to claim that "the process didn't work because the rocks failed to cooperate" (164), she does want us to recognize that there is a certain degree of reciprocity in coming to know an object, as a subject's reaction to the object changes in the course of coming to know, and that nonhuman objects of knowledge can be as resistant, recalcitrant, or surprising to an investigator as they are predictable and controllable.

Code lays the groundwork for how we can interpret fetishism as an epistemological strategy, a way to know. In contrast to the narrow Freudian interpretation, this fetishism provides a broader vision that foregrounds ambivalence between certainty and doubt or belief and knowledge, a willingness to fall out of line with traditional assumptions about ontological difference, and a belief in the necessity of the object for the subject to have knowledge or agency. This connection is most evident as she considers the work of several feminist scientists—namely, Rachel Carson, Anna Brito, and Barbara McClintock—who do interact with their objects of study as if they were subjects. Code raises the question: "Would it be merely fanciful to say that her research practice depends on a 'second person' engagement with inanimate specimens?" (152). Here, the term "second person" derives from Annette Baier's work in ethics which claims that humans become persons only after having been dependent on other persons long enough "to acquire the essential arts of personhood" (qtd. in Code, 82). In Code's translation of this notion from ethics to epistemology, she wants to emphasize that no knowledge, and no knower, is fully autonomous, but instead is developed through a network of interdependence. Thus, the feminist scientist who I would say "fetishizes" her research object becomes a knower through such a 'second-person' dependence on her object of knowledge. We can understand Barbara McClintock's research on maize in this way—as aptly captured by Evelyn Fox Keller's title of her account of McClintock, *A Feeling for the Organism*—when she characterizes the plants as her friends. The model McClintock uses for her science is not the dominating model of the conquering hero, making Nature yield her secrets, but of befriending her object of study, learning to read its idiosyncrasies and patterns as adeptly as we tune in to the idiosyncrasies and patterns of loved ones.

Code calls upon us to view all cognitive agency through the model of second personhood. In doing so, she raises questions of desire as well as identity, although she focuses explicitly only on the latter. I call this epistemological dependence on the object fetishism, rather than personification, for one important reason: the need for respect and recognition in the epistemological relation. Infusing an epistemological relation between objects and subjects with notions of respect and recognition seems like overvaluation in a context where subjects are privileged over objects; we presume to treat objects with indifference. Personification plays right into this presumption, by implying a (false) attribution or imposition of qualities not inherent in an object. It therefore remains a strategy of domination, of refusing to take the object on its own terms. In this way, personification is like pathological melancholia, which is concerned more with the relation to the object than with the object itself. Yet if there's one thing that centrally interests a fetishist, it is the object itself.

In describing this epistemological relation as fetishism, we should acknowledge Code's concern about the way that the "rhetoric of love" haunts descriptions of this scientific practice (153). For her, this rhetoric smacks of the heterosexual romance paradigm, where the woman loses her agency to disappear into her relationship with a man. But all rhetorics of love do not necessarily conform to this normative paradigm, although the danger of this assimilation is precisely (or perversely) why we should claim such scientific or intellectual engagement as fetishism. This perverse claim enables us to acknowledge the complex ways in which sexual difference and ontological difference are intertwined in desire and knowledge. Our culture's emphasis on men's desire for women has made it difficult to perceive any desire outside of that. But there's a striking parallel between formations of desire and knowledge here. Both knowledge and desire are understood in our culture in relation to norms, whether they be sanctioned and institutionalized or deviant and repudiated forms. What's more, these norms favor subjects with masculine qualities over ones coded as feminine (and not coincidentally also as objects), as feminist epistemologists have convincingly demonstrated. Fetishism is a form both of "bad" knowledge and of "bad" desire, and it thereby calls into question the limiting assumptions of the norms—their failure to accurately account for the world by preferring generalization to deviant specificity and their concomitant constraint on creativity. Because it deviates creatively from the norm, fetishism can illuminate particularly well the limits of presuming an ideal masculine subject as the only subject who can know and who can desire. Fetishism thus provides not only another model for desiring, but another prototype for knowing. Viewed as more than merely a mechanism to achieve heterosexual desire, fetishism breaks up the heterosexual romance narrative by demonstrating that one could love outside of the heterosexual imperative and love something other than a subject. Fetishism places a subject at odds with the dominant subject position, thus carving out a new perspective from which to seek to know the world.

The perverse privileging of objects over subjects disrupts the system of sexual differences and in fact makes fetishism helpful in dispelling the heterosexual romance that Code is wary of. But it also challenges the myth of the domination of the subject over the object, the indifferent control subjects are expected to exert over objects, a mastery which is of a piece with the ideal of the autonomous subject. We have shown how fetishism challenges hetero-normative assumptions about sexual difference, but fetishism also deconstructs the subject-object distinction by positing a third kind of being, one which is neither fully autonomous and rationally thinking, nor completely inert, but is instead instrumental— prosthetic and parasitic. Both the fetish subject and the fetish object take this form of being. The object is perhaps—at least from a conventional point of view—more clearly dependent on the subject both to exist and to get things done. But this instrumentality bears upon the subject's constitution, as well as the object's; believing in the object's responsiveness, the subject adopts a different relation to the object and comes to understand herself differently too. In coming to respect the fetish object, the subject may feel more humble, more aware of her limits, but also more capable because of that awareness. As an antidote to what theorists, such as Weber, have called instrumental rationality or reason, fetishism offers instrumental irrationality or unreason. This unreason is the personal and passionate investment in the object, which defies both the logic of commodity exchange and the impersonalizing pressures of rationality. Our cultural framework makes it difficult—if not impossible—to conceive of simultaneously using something (by definition impersonal, objective) and caring for something (by definition personal, subjective).

In both its psychoanalytic and anthropological interpretations, fetishism is fundamentally about purposefully augmenting one's agency. In the Freudian scenario, even in its narrowest interpretation, the fetishist does not compromise his own agency by subordinating it to someone else, and thus could be seen as experiencing the ultimate in self-sufficiency because his object-satisfaction reduces or eliminates his need for other subjects. But the only reason the fetishist's agency is not perceived to be compromised is because of his presumed heterosexual masculinity. This presumption gives heterosexual masculinity the privilege of recouping deviance into normality, thereby reinforcing the cultural power of heterosexual masculine supremacy and turning a blind eye to fetishism's creative reinterpretation of dominant paradigms. The difficulty both Freud and those who followed him, notably Clérambault, had in recognizing women or gay men as fetishists illustrates the degree to which it is of a piece with philosophical ideals about rational subjects as masculine, heterosexual, and in control of the objects around them. This intransigence also shows how important the element of agency is for fetishism, since agency is the ability of subjects to implement change in their world—including using things to do so.

Fetishism as the ultimate consolidation of autonomous agency holds true, however, only if the subject remains construed as superior to the object—that is, if the split between subject and object is reinforced in the larger context. If, however, we employ fetishism to reinterpret ontological differences as well as sexual differences—as Code's persuasive critique of epistemological models invites us to do—we will necessarily come to a different understanding of the subject and object, one that sees them as sharing characteristics rather than as radically opposed, asymmetrically related, and mutually exclusive. Fetishistic oscillation becomes productive when it changes our response to an object and thereby gives us a new angle on solving a problem or achieving a goal. We may know very well that the object of investigation, like a literary text, is not capable of acting like a subject, but if we nonetheless insist or believe that it is, we may gain important insights by using the text as a collaborator in accomplishing a larger aim rather than an opponent over whom we must triumph heroically.

Such fetishism is incipient in good close readings, for example, and indeed may account for the difficulty many people—both students and critics—have in producing workable close readings. A degree of sympathy with the text and a sense of its interpretive openness is required to produce the kind of reading that makes a text blossom; this posture is antithetical to the mode of scholarship that uses texts for evidence, punching bags, or other agonistic strategies of reading (which may have their place). This textual sympathy should not be confused with the detection of authorial intent, the confusion of text and author that leads many students in their reading to attribute to the author's agency a character's or other textual element's effect. Such readers are still operating under the assumption of a right answer or a correct reading, an assumption that remains in the thrall of normativity.

Indeed, the pitfalls in the interpretation of objects indicate precisely why psychoanalysis found fetishism to be a puzzling thing. In fetishism's overvaluation of the object, there seems to be a will to subordinate oneself, to reverse the subject-object hierarchy and put oneself on the level of the object; yet such a reversal is impossible to express in our culture because of the bias that objects are inherently subordinate. This paradox of subordination suggests why women, viewed more as objects than subjects, may not have been perceived as fetishists; if one is already subordinated, one has no leverage to play with subordination— there is no pleasure or irony in being an object.

Code's analysis of epistemological assumptions about the relation between subject and object helps us come to terms with the startling uniqueness of Freud's interpretation of fetishism as it goes against the grain of fetishism's cultural history, which turned a socially shared object relation into an individual idiosyncrasy. We can extend Code's proposition of friendship as an epistemological relation between subjects to understand the benefits of befriending—and indeed realizing a passion for—objects, for eroding the strong distinction between our things and ourselves. As determined in the last chapter, this new interpretation would have to shift away from the lack paradigm, away from the fetish narrowly understood as a penis substitute. But what the comparison with melancholia elucidates is not only the reinterpretation of fetishism through loss, but also that this shift requires us to have a new understanding of the subject-object relation—one based not in domination but in mutual recognition, the fetishistic "we." Unlike lack, which may provoke strategies of compensation or concealment, loss needs to be acknowledged, even, on occasion, narrated; it remains unbearable unless it is recognized.

The novella *Heart of Darkness* provides a useful illustration of this point, for the whole narrative emerges from Marlow's need for recognition and acknowledgment of the loss—of ignorance, of blindness to truth, of certainty—he confronted on his journey to Kurtz.[7] The negotiation of this loss produces epistemological fetishism: what happened to him was, he says, "not very clear. And yet it seemed to throw a kind of light" (10). The ambivalence in this statement oscillates between knowing and not knowing, and this split in Marlow's epistemological drive produces a new, fetish subject.[8] The boat in the Thames can be construed as the fetish object in this narrative, the object that Marlow and his interlocutors share, but to which their relations are varied and contradictory. For Marlow, this cruising yawl is a metonym for the Congo river steamboat, whereas for his companions this boat does not necessarily stand in for anything else.[9] The fetish object provides the common touchstone through which they can understand Marlow's narrative; sharing a connection to the *Nellie*, a specific instance of what the narrator calls "the bond of the sea," opens the men to the difference Marlow will confront them with, the difference of his experience which has set him apart from his earlier self, his earlier assumptions and knowledge about the world. They are "tolerant of each other's yarns, even convictions," as the narrator describes it, and this tolerance makes it possible for Marlow's loss to be acknowledged. The problem with melancholia is that it lacks this reciprocal element of mutual recognition.

   This lack of reciprocity is not limited to melancholia. As philosophy now frames it, domination is constitutive of the subject-object distinction: a subject is defined as being able to control or manipulate an object at will, without regard to the object's preferences or inclinations. Lack provides the epistemological basis for this exploitative domination: objects are manipulable by subjects because they lack their own volition; "primitive" people are inferior to "civilized" because they lack reason; women are the weaker sex because they lack a penis.[10] The lack paradigm encodes domination into the subject-object relation, because the only objects it can attend to are debased ones—either the mother or the fetish, both of which are repudiated by the implicitly masculine subject in order to claim his subjectivity.[11]

   In opening out the philosophical dimensions of fetishism (both epistemological and ontological) and moving from the lack model to the loss model, fetishism, rather than filling in for the lack of an object, comes to be seen as substituting for the loss of an object. The logic of supplementation shifts from compensation to excess. It is important to acknowledge that this loss is not a complete or avoidable loss of the object, but a partial and inevitable loss around the object of knowledge. The fetish object is special because it might be lost, and it might already have suffered loss. There is thus a sympathy between the fetish subject and fetish object, insofar as both are tainted by loss. Because of this partiality, loss provides a way to reconfigure the subject-object relation in less dominated, more open-ended terms, as something shared rather than something that divides. A static paradigm for knowing makes any sense of loss in knowing an object difficult to perceive; a loss only becomes evident once knowing is perceived as a dynamic process, which Code's epistemological paradigm shift from objects to friends makes clear.

It may help to think of this as a futural loss, not a past loss. If we think of this as a futural loss, the conservational aspect of fetishism again comes into view; only here, instead of a monument to that which has slipped away, the fetish is a memorial to what might go at any time. (The sports car fetish mentioned earlier, for example, may illustrate the loss of youthful vigor as such an impending loss, for it takes a limber body to get in and out of those low-riding cars.) Because of this contingency, the fetish is simultaneously a marker of knowing and not knowing. Epistemological loss does not look for a remedy in the recuperation of a once whole set of knowledge, along the lines of some prelapsarian model. Rather, it acknowledges the asymptotic nature of knowing, that something in the object of knowledge will always escape our grasp, no matter how close we come.

Fetishism as an epistemological strategy follows the model of theories of desire to understand knowledge as liminal. Knowledge is the responsive process of interaction between a subject and object, as the object of our knowing is transformed through the process of knowing and as it simultaneously exerts a transformational force on us.[12] If we are to keep the insight psychoanalysis provides on the sexual dimension of fetishism, yet view fetishism on its own terms, i.e., in its interest in the object, we must let go of the judgment that subject-subject reciprocity is more satisfying than subject-object reciprocity. The satisfaction that a passionate investment in an object yields is surely comparable to the satisfaction offered by a passionate connection to another person. This parity calls attention to an ethical dimension in fetishism— the subject's care for the object and presumption of being cared about by the object. Letting go of the assumption about where we can find satisfying reciprocity reveals the extent to which the division between desire and knowledge is illusory. This illusory division is supported by normative ideals that direct us to find satisfaction in desiring subjects but not objects and in knowing objects but not subjects (or rather, the kind of knowing we have about subjects is not as epistemologically valid, as the fact that Code even needs to mount her argument indicates). The assessment of proper sources of satisfaction is based on a false dichotomy between subject-subject relations, purportedly based in mutual recognition, and subject-object relations, presumed to be unilateral, unidirectional. Fetishism leads us to recognize the possibility of a mutual epistemological relation, even in subject-object relations. No longer would epistemology necessarily be divided between knowing things and knowing people, and further, in stark contrast to our Cartesian heritage, no longer would knowing be rigidly separable from desiring or seeking satisfaction through a reciprocal relationship. Rather, through fetishism, knowledge would emerge as the product of a negotiation of desire between a subject and object. Marlow's knowledge in Conrad's novella is a product of his negotiation, the epistemophilic desire to explore, and the object of that desire—be it variously interpreted as the "primitive," Kurtz, the riddle of Kurtz's last words, the empty space on the map, to name a few possibilities.

We are moving ever closer to the anthropological conception of the fetish, which views the fetish object as something augmenting the subject's power, as an apotropaïc token that has the potential to change a subject's social position. We see an example of this in the classic 1760 study, *Du Culte des dieux fétiches (On the Cult of the Fetish Gods)*, where Charles de Brosses describes a West African society that takes a particular snake as its fetish. Women who have been through a marriage ceremony that ritually unites them with the fetish-snake may subsequently be allowed to have human husbands; however those husbands "must respect them, as if they were the serpent who marked them itself, kneel to speak to their wives, and be submissive as much to their will as to their authority" ("doit les respecter, comme le serpent même dont elles portent l'empreinte, ne leur parler qu'à genoux, & être soumis tant à leurs volontés qu'à leur autorité" [42]). Here the object's intervention in the subject's life has radically altered that subject's options for conducting herself. The example suggests that the relation between subjects and objects is more like the social relation between subjects: mediated by power, full of signification, open to interpretation. I present it here to suggest that we consider not only how fetishism functions along the lines of an individualistic model, but also as a socially shared phenomenon.

Of course, the de Brosses example presents the issue of fetishism not evidently or most apparently as an epistemological one, but as a theological one—that is, based not on knowledge but on belief. Separating out knowledge from belief is a sticky issue, particularly because classical epistemology distinguishes between them, defining "knowledge" as justifiable belief and what we here have been calling "belief" as opinion. But it is precisely fetishism's ambivalence between knowledge (as justifiable belief) and belief (that is, unjustifiable belief, or—more positively—faith or fantasy) that makes it epistemologically useful at this point, for it puts the epistemological question in pragmatic terms.

Again, comparison with Code's argument for friendship helps illuminate this point. Rather than be hamstrung by punctiliousness about the difference between justifiable and unjustifiable belief, Code plays out the distinction in her analysis by comparing friendship with other, less reliable epistemological modes. The stereotype, as an example of a reductive epistemology, provides a particularly cogent model with which

Code contrasts the model of friendship. But for our consideration of
fetishism, the stereotype seems to offer more of a comparison than a contrast. The stereotype evokes a lot of the same negative connotations that
fetishism has had. Insofar as fetishism has been viewed as a rigid fixation and overvaluation that limits interpretation, it aligns quite nicely
with the stereotype—as if one were the sexual or psychological example
and the other were the epistemological or philosophical one. Code contrasts stereotypes with caricatures, noting that "A caricature proclaims
its own partiality. . . . But stereotypes tend to be presented as 'straight,' to
give 'the facts' . . . to fit this person in this slot without remainder, obscuring any other view of her. They conceal their own partiality, and the
element of truth they capture compounds the concealment" (192–93).
Stereotypes have a certain rigidity which forecloses any interpretive play
between interlocutors, a play which is foregrounded in the caricature—
and I would add, the parody. The campy fun of a drag performance
ends, for example, when it verges into stereotype, into reductive and
misogynist claims about the nature of women—claims which cannot tolerate contradiction through the counterexample of everyday women.
Yet, as Code reminds us, stereotypes are remarkably adaptable despite
their rigidity—"they stretch and shift to accommodate contradictions
and reestablish themselves" (193). This adaptability makes it harder to
undermine stereotypes, and may remind us of the adaptability inherent
in the fetishist's initial and often creative choice of object. However, its
adaptability is rooted in the fact that the fetish is designed to aid in
bringing one closer to an object—thus it facilitates rather than obstructs
knowledge of a thing and connection to it.

These convergences between fetish and stereotype perhaps suggest that while fetishism may be recuperable as a form of desire, it
cannot offer anything positive as a form of knowledge. But the epistemological linchpin for each illustrates why fetishism is more useful
than the stereotype. The fetish and the stereotype share a remarkable
ability to accommodate contradiction; however, they differ in their epistemological ends and in their appeal to a founding truth. Ultimately, the
stereotype's accommodation serves to reassure against the threat of
having to rethink one's assumptions, understanding, or knowledge.
The stereotype is the ultimate anti-epistemological trope, apotropaïcally
using a claim to know to defend against really knowing. Fetishism, on
the other hand, requires that one know and maintain that knowledge,
even if the belief or desire that the fetishist holds in tension with knowing repudiates that knowledge. Because of this complex relation,
fetishism enables us to move closer to knowing things we might not
want to know, that we might otherwise distance ourselves from know-

ing.[13] Fetishism is one way by which we can confront uncomfortable truths. It is also a useful strategy for an antifoundationalist episteme. While the stereotype claims its own truth as a foundation, the fetish eschews any claim to a foundation precisely because it is a creative and inappropriate interpretation. In its appeal to a foundation, the stereotype reaffirms cultural norms, while the fetish transgresses those same norms. The contrast between the stereotype of African American masculinity as a hypersexual identity and a transgressive and fetishistic desire for African American men by some white gay men illustrates this difference by rendering racial difference an element in a more complex scene of knowing and desiring a person. Even as the fetish provides reassurance and satisfaction, that reassurance is markedly different from that offered by the stereotype, for it is a reassurance based in transgression, irony, ambivalence, and contradiction.

At their heart, stereotypes seek to close down ambiguity, interpretive openness, and complexity. All of these aspects can be found in the negative form of fetishism, the one held in place by a rigid polarization of binary heterosexual and ontological difference. But at the same time, fetishism makes it possible to problematize this polarity. Fetishism, even in its most constricted sense, cannot jettison ambivalence or indeterminacy, even if it shuts down on ambiguity. But in the network of possibilities we have been mapping here, fetishism invites interpretive openness, introduces complexity and creativity. The vacillation inherent in fetishism is what makes it a useful epistemological strategy, because it provides a better model of knowledge, one that recognizes how knowing is both negotiated in relation to norms and a creative response to subjects' needs.

Because of her second-person friendship model, Code determines that the nature of knowing is both objective and subjective; the best strategy for knowing would oscillate between these two modes. For Code, as for the fetishist, objective and subjective modes of knowing are not contradictory to the point of canceling each other out; rather, they enable an epistemological process that knows "how to achieve an appropriate interplay between autonomy and communal solidarity" (172). Thus, her dual, ambivalent epistemology puts the knowing subject in the tension between the individual and communal identity—poles demarcated, in slightly different ways, by Schiesari's description of masculine melancholia and by Elizabeth Grosz's notion of lesbian fetishism. Code's model offers a form of knowledge that is socially embedded rather than isolated. It also offers a model that converges on Butler's notion of identity: knowledge as dynamic and iterable, since the oscillation between objectivity and subjectivity requires a constant reassertion of a claim to know, and a constant tinkering between what is known and what is believed. This link of knowledge claims to speech acts shows how they parallel performative identities; a claim to know is subject to iterability, recognizability, and intersubjectivity mediated by social norms.

This epistemological picture suggests that knowledge is more unstable than we tend to believe it to be, and that instability can indeed be threatening. If the notion of a fragmented or iterable subject seems threatening, would a similar model of knowing pose any less of a problem? Clear but controversial examples can be found by examining how marginal knowledges gain credence through reiteration, such as claims of alien abductions, recovered memories, or the so-called disgruntled-voter syndrome. Ambivalently positioning knowledge between social codes and individual perspectives seems an invitation to lose any accountability to truth. But entertaining the possibility that normal forms of knowledge are tainted by fetishism (just as Freud asserted that normal forms of sexuality are) does not immediately push us to the bottom of the slippery slope of relativism. Indeed, fetishistic epistemology offers a necessary middle ground between relativism and absolutism. Not everyone has the special relation to the fetish object that the fetishist has, although anyone can concede that the object might be special to the fetishist; we can thus both know and not know the fetish object. Claims about fetish objects thus need to be interpreted through the dynamic of fetishism, knowing that the object is not particularly or necessarily special, but believing nonetheless that it is. This strategy is at the heart of my reading of Freud's 1927 text, as well as the core of my commentary on the literary texts throughout.

The interpretations developed in these chapters show why it is so necessary to think through fetishism, rather than about it. We get nowhere by cataloging the objects taken on as fetishes, except to further pathologize fetishism as improper knowledge or desire. If we truly want to trouble social norms—and yet not collapse into a sea of meaningless relativism—we need to eschew the list in favor of the fetish object's lesson about the contingencies of our categories of sexual and ontological difference. We do not need to become fetishists, merely to accept the double vision, the ambivalent interpretation that fetishism promotes as an instrumental reading strategy. Through its particularity, a fetish provides an anchor against relativism, while at the same time its meaning does not require mediation through some transcendent Truth or in reference to some absolute standard. Fetishes provide grounds for sympathy and cooperation among subjects without requiring assimilation.

In this light, the positive reinterpretation of fetishism offers a productive model for negotiating difference in a postmodern landscape. We can take critiques of the coherency of the subject seriously without being threatened by a breakdown of identity, agency, or credibility, key elements of subjectivity that feminists rightly argue women need to continue to develop and hold onto. The changes in notions of identity, agency, and credibility are instead understood through how they operate in fetishism, along the lines we have been tracing out in this study. We can see this at work in the juxtaposition of Code and Butler in particular.

Code argues that the identity of the subject structures knowledge; yet as Butler's work shows, this identity is not a fixed point of reference but on ongoing process of incorporating and performing oneself in relation to the objects and codes around one. Despite her ultimate—and troubling—rejection of epistemology, Butler's critique of identity in fact provides an excellent model to build on for understanding in a larger sense the nature of knowledge. Knowledge is a temporally bound entity, representing both past and future possibilities; it must be conveyed through signs and interpretation, and thus it is always subject to change—whether by error or correction, deviation or assimilation. Knowledge accumulates over time, and while it may seem to be a static entity, it is always iterable and shifting, always in need of reassertion. Combining Code's and Butler's perspectives as we come to understand identity through fetishism raises the possibility that the fetishist is right: that the knowledge we come to have of subjects, the knowledge we label "identity," may not be radically differentiated from the knowledge we have of objects. Identity is a method for knowing subjects, constituted through an accumulation of past action and future potential. If we accept that knowing objects is similar, then our sense of objects will be that they are likewise an accumulation of past information and future potential. While this may seem a strange way to look at the sorts of objects that are typically used as epistemological examples—tables and chairs and hammers—it is a commonsense way of coping with the much more complex objects with which we surround ourselves and construct our lives—cars and computers and networks, objects upon which our dependence is much clearer, and knowledge of whose operation inheres simultaneously at different levels. We may be able to use the word processor or drive somewhere, but we may not be able to write the code for the processing program or figure out what's causing the engine to knock when we accelerate. We are most likely to personify the objects that defeat our mastery; the vcr flashes 12:00 because it has a mind of its own, not because its owner can't make it stop.

Changing our epistemological models does challenge the insinuation of domination in how we conceive of knowledge, and this change holds implications for how we exercise power. While we cannot extricate power and knowledge, we can transform the organization of power and paradigms of knowledge. We can move from a notion of dominance/knowledge, with its subordination of objects and the autonomy of the masterful subject, to fetishistic agency, with its mutual recognition between subjects and objects and cautious evolution of competence. In fetishism, the thing one desires and seeks to know becomes an ally in the pursuit of desire or knowledge. This transforms the position of the knower, the subject, as much as it does the position of the known, the object.

Once dominance and knowledge are no longer closely aligned, it raises the question, "can the dominated know?" Fetishism emerged in the Enlightenment to assert the answer to that question—"no." Fetishism was a substitute for knowledge, it was what "primitive" people did instead of know. Depriving people of recognition as knowers also deprives them of recognition as desirers, and ultimately as agential subjects. But as the coherency of Enlightenment ideals of self, autonomy, and power are eroded in the confrontation with postmodernism, it becomes possible to use fetishism to aver a different answer, to put forward a compelling alternative. Indeed, we would do well to affirm ourselves as fetishists, and to understand fetishism as a widely applicable paradigm for knowing, one no longer relegated to the "primitive." Because fetishism brings together contradictory impulses of desire and knowledge with a circumspect agency, it offers a coherent strategy that not only enables subjects to negotiate threatening or inconceivable differences but also provides a paradigm for new relations of power, an ethical epistemology anchored in the construction of the active self through the care of the object.

This ethical dimension helps us move from identity to agency in considering fetishism as a postmodern paradigm for feminist theory. Like most feminist theorists, Code is not interested in eliminating agency. Her work exposes the limits of the model of the autonomous, volitional masculine subject in order to confront the problem of political efficacy and responsibility. These concerns were also foregrounded in Butler's work, as we saw in the last chapter. But where Butler ends up rejecting epistemology, Code asserts that rethinking epistemology is essential if feminists are to develop theories about "subjective and cognitive agency, about displacing entrenched thought structures" (263). This effort to displace entrenched thought structures and offer new, improved forms of agency is a struggle of long standing: most recently, social-constructionist, Marxist, and poststructuralist theories have all assailed the depth model of subjectivity by critically examining how humans are inextricably enmeshed in and constituted by social, cultural, political, and economic forces. Indeed, Butler's work is itself situated in this critical tradition. Code, however, is more skeptical of the constructionist approach. While she is committed to developing a better way for subjects to act on their knowledge, Code makes clear that there are troubling limits on the answers these theories have turned up. This is evident in Code's suggestion that "seeing friendships as empowering relationships may make it possible to circumnavigate some of the neodeterministic implications of postmodern, deconstructed subjectivity" (179). Where readings of deconstructed subjectivity risk reducing individual will down to the expression of a social force, the personal and epistemological connections made through friendship open up a space for understanding how these forces fail to account for a subject's idiosyncrasies, fallibilities, and motives for acting. In short, Code's model of friendship illustrates how subjects integrate social pressures with the particular desires they have made their own.

But friendship too has its limitations, particularly insofar as it maintains the polarization between desire and knowledge. Friendship, especially how Code uses it, is an intersubjective relation that explicitly brackets questions of sexuality and desire. (Although friendship is a complicated relation that may in fact range from platonic to passionate, our concern here is with the public and paradigmatic description). Using friendship as the paradigm for knowing risks reinforcing the classical epistemological rupture between knowing and desiring or believing. In friendship there is little attention to the sort of epistemophilia that fetishism foregrounds. Code herself, as we noted earlier, explicitly backs away from any sexually charged notion of friendship, lest her argument serve to weaken rather than augment women's status as knowers. But repudiating desire in knowledge is no less shortsighted than repudiating femininity in patriarchal sexuality. We need to incorporate rather than repudiate these elements which seem so threatening to a political conception of the subject; if we are to counter the dominant and dominating paradigm of the masculine autonomous subject with a feminist subject, she needs to have agency in both knowing and desiring. Fetishism helps figure this passionate agency without reverting to the discrediting clichés about women as emotional rather than rational thinkers, thereby giving gender identities a more complex range than the binary system allows.

Gender, as Code and Butler each point out, is key to a subject's ability to be recognized as knowledgeable. In *Gender Trouble* Butler focuses on gender credibility; belief, not knowledge, makes gender performances suasive. We look for signs in someone's self-presentation to clue us in about a person's gender, and only if the signs conflict do we seek "knowledge" through signs that have been guaranteed to verify gender identity—genitals, chromosomes, hormones, government documentation. But because signs of gender have to be enforced by other signs which cannot sustain the myth of two genders, this ultimately renders genders—and by extension identity—epistemologically unstable. There is no single arbiter of gender that can assure knowledge, only an infinite regression which must be resolved by belief. This view of knowledge renders fetishism even more clearly necessary as an alternative epistemological paradigm. Gender—as a case in point, particularly when it comes to fetishism—is a "performative accomplishment which the mundane social audience including the actors themselves, come to believe and perform in the mode of belief" (Butler 141). As we come to believe, so we come to think we know.

Code pursues the issue of credibility from a different angle than Butler, though she is no less wary of the ways that belief backed by power can overrule knowledge. Her analysis of the problem of women as knowers points to the fact that not only is knowledge not a neutral entity with regard to gender or other identity categories, but that intelligibility is intertwined with credibility. The lesson to draw from Code's work is that recognition is absolutely crucial to agency—that agency is not something a subject inherently has, an expression of an inner truth that is part of being a subject, but that it is something accorded a person through intersubjective acknowledgment. This insight helps arbitrate the claims by some feminists that the notion of the agential subject is being dissolved right as certain marginalized groups began to gain autonomy and agency. This model of the agential subject, however, is not so much threatened by a move to postmodernism as it is complicated by how that recognition would work in postmodernism. What such critics of postmodernism crave is the authentic, full recognition that they believe was promised by Enlightenment-inspired political movements. Such complete recognition is no longer possible—if ever it once were—because it is recognition without loss, without difference. It requires a pure knowledge that has no need of belief to sustain it. This epistemological ideal is impractical for the ways in which we claim to know the world, since the world itself is not straightforward but rather contradictory. What we need is a different ideal for subjectivity, constructed through a more rigorous and pragmatic epistemological paradigm, as Code and Butler's analyses point toward.

Fetishism provides this alternative form of subjectivity; it complicates the model of an autonomous, volitional subject with an ambivalently dependent-independent subject, but one who is still capable of acting with and through particular objects. Through fetishism, we can gain that mutual recognition, as we strategically employ fetishes as points of mutual interest and exchange, in the intersection of which we can come to acknowledge each others' differences. A fetish subject creatively and passionately negotiates between belief and knowledge, acknowledging the threats presented by the world but instrumentally disavowing them in order to move forward. Fetishism can serve as an epistemological model not only because it provides an example of agency through the fetishist's creative interpretation of his world to satisfy his own aims, but also because it provides an anchor of meaning and understanding through objects that remains open to reinterpretation as well as to ontological difference. It is crucial not to conflate otherness with ontological difference. Between subjects—and especially between friends—there is no ontological difference; however much there may be otherness, the two are the same kind of being. Between subjects and objects, however, there remains ontological difference, even though fetishism may disavow it.

It is this difference which makes fetishism useful, for it provides the leverage for the revaluation of ontological difference we have explored in this conclusion. This difference can be figured as the object's impassivity. A subject can never be completely impassive, but will always react to another subject (although that reaction may be suppressed, e.g., when there is a great difference in power between the two subjects, or when the subject impersonates an object). The impassivity of the object remains a factor, however much the fetishist disavows it by lavishing care and attention on the object or insisting that the object responds; indeed, this impassivity is simultaneously and ambivalently disavowed and acknowledged in fetishism. The object's indifference makes it shareable and communicable, while the object's difference— both from itself over time, and at once from the subject—makes it special, often in exclusive or private ways. This ambivalence between difference and indifference may be a truism as an illustration of the mechanism of desire, but it also works at the heart of knowing; it is what makes knowledge useful. We can act on knowledge because it is complexly constituted as both individual and social; fetishism mimics this complexity more closely than does friendship, and provides a sounder basis for agency and action, especially among different people. The ambivalence inherent in fetishism acknowledges that subjects and objects *are* ontologically different, but also disavows that knowledge for instrumental reasons, to achieve a particular end.

But can we really live as fetish subjects? Perhaps at best we are failed fetishists, striving to be more fetishistic. We would like to live in a world where we are not threatened but are instead satisfied. Yet we turn to sameness rather than difference for reassurance in the face of a threat. This turn, which is the reductive formula for fetishism, takes us away from the real insights fetishism offers, away from its negotiation of difference by introducing more difference, changing the relations between the original binary terms. The nature of our failure as fetishists is that we cannot successfully negotiate epistemological loss, and we close down interpretive openness as a result. We prefer to disavow our inability to know, to seek satisfaction in the insistence that we can have the whole picture, rather than in the ambivalent embrace of objects that mark—and share—our loss or incompleteness. We lapse into the illusory and static reassurance of our beliefs, at worst being overtaken by a sense of righteousness, instead of becoming (use)fully ambivalent.

We also fail as fetishists by believing too much in the impassivity of the object and not enough in the object's responsiveness. We do not impute enough personal, private value to our objects, and instead we cave in to the pressures of capitalist rationality that insists on the impersonality—the exchangeability, the lack of specialness—of the object. Yet exchange is not based on sameness, but on difference and indifference, on a willingness to lose something in order to gain something else. By disavowing the loss inherent in exchange, we focus on sameness rather than difference, on assimilation rather than creation. In doing so, we lose some of our own specialness, since our identities are ontologically tied to our objects, both tangible and intangible; we incorporate ourselves out of the materials surrounding us. These losses of difference and particularity are much more damaging than the loss of a center or of certainty, and we need to be able to perceive that difference. Because fetishism allows us to yearn for something other than oneness, to create deviant interpretations that are more pragmatic and fantastic than the preordained patterns cut from whole cloth, it enables us to perceive that difference. Through fetishism, we can survive the loss of wholeness, developing a sense of the world that embraces difference, loss, incompleteness, and contradiction.

Our failure at fetishism is ultimately part of a faustian bargain, one that gives up satisfying and productive partiality for the promise— ever deferred, ever frustrated—of completion. If we are to succeed at being fetishists—or at least not fail quite so badly—we would do well to remember that the loss that has been supplemented by the fetish is a loss of the concrete, the real, the original that never was.

NOTES

Introduction

1. Pietz's elaboration extends across three separate articles, published as parts under the general title "The Problem of the Fetish." All citations to this work in the text will be listed by the part and the page number (e.g., II: 6).

2. Gloria Hull edited this landmark volume with Patricia Bell Scott and Barbara Smith.

1. How to Do Things with Fetishism

1. Because I am working with different translations of Freud as well as different essays, I will cite quotations from Freud by volume and page number of the *Standard Edition*, hereafter called *SE*, or by the name of the translator and page number. The German citations come from the *Gesammelte Werke*, hereafter called *GW* in the text.

2. This disturbance can be interpreted a number of ways. Sander Gilman suggests in *Freud, Race, and Gender* that Freud's writings about women are in fact discussions of Jewish males in Europe. In summing up his account of Sander Gilman's argument in a recent review article, Daniel Boyarin provides us with one resolution of this textual sexual indifference: "Freud's reinscription of the clitoris as male, then, is a code or cipher for the reinscription of the circumcised penis as male, and thus of the Jewish man as male as well" (31). I believe that the introduction of racial difference, especially as Boyarin uses it to argue for a different formulation of gender that breaks apart a simple, biologically based binary system, is important here. Nonetheless, I want to take a slightly different tack toward the same end, and locate the instabilities that emerge if we try to retain a binary framework here.

3. I would like to thank Matthew Potolsky for calling my attention to this distinction. To underscore this point in English, we might entertain the notion of translating "reale" with the word "veritable," a Latinate term that, while not as obviously imported as "reale," is less common than "real," and would furthermore eliminate the colloquial emphasis.

4. Some psychoanalysts have already examined the intersection of sexual difference and fetishism in a way that might provide a different under-

standing of how women have access to fetishism. Michael Balint's discussion of fetishism suggests a fundamental indeterminacy at the heart of the fetish-object's interpretation. Balint points out that "The interpretation of these objects as the vagina and the womb respectively is quite as obvious as the penis interpretation of the use of the body itself or part of the body" (172). If we followed this reading, then we might understand that the fetish-object could be interpreting and supplementing either male or female genitalia. Yet this reading, like the reductive Freudian one, maintains an uncritical attitude toward binary sexual difference and its consequences in our culture by not interrogating the extent to which anatomy is itself always already interpreted.

5. Some feminists and queer theorists have recently been doing this work of deconstructing gender—for example, Teresa de Lauretis in *Technologies of Gender* and *The Practice of Love*, Judith Butler in *Gender Trouble* and *Bodies that Matter*, and Anne Fausto-Sterling in *Myths of Gender*, among many others. They are hardly working *ex nihilo*. Indeed, not only has Freud's own work made this possible, but he was arguably influenced by the complexities of biologizing discourses working on defining not only gender and sexuality but also race and class at the turn of the century. Sander Gilman notes that "little attention has been given to what Freud could have understood about the powerful model of homologous structures, which argued that the male and female genitalia were absolutely parallel" (38). Critics have, instead, assumed Freud was working within the same framework of binary, heterosexual difference that dominates twentieth-century Western thinking. But because Freud, in Gilman's view, was affected by the racialized discourse that marked Jewish men as both a different race *and* gender, it is reasonable to think that such an assumption is unfounded.

6. Indeed, Freud acknowledges that although many fetishes "would be such as appear as symbols for the penis in other connections as well," this is not necessarily the case (*SE* 21: 155). This assertion, several pages before the final sentence, makes the idea that the man's penis is the model for the fetish even odder than it already is.

7. We see this in "Some Psychical Consequences of the Anatomical Distinction between the Sexes," where, for example, Freud's whole theory of penis-envy hinges upon the little girl's realization of the inferiority of her clitoris in comparison to the boy's penis; thus implicitly there is an analogy at work. More explicitly, he tells us that her "masturbation, at all events of the clitoris, is a masculine activity" (*SE* 19: 255). In "Female Sexuality" he remarks that the clitoris "is analogous to the male organ" and also talks about "the clitoris, with its masculine character" (*SE* 21: 228). Gilman points out that this confusion exists within the culture at large, since in Viennese slang at the turn of the century the clitoris was referred to as *der Jude* (the Jew), thus establishing a "relationship between the body of the male Jew and the body of a woman" (39). Although this relationship feminized the male Jew, Gilman argues, Freud took up the clitoris as a sign of masculinity, which "stands in relation to the intact male" (Gilman 39).

8. In just this article the list has ranged from expected or clichéd objects such as the foot or a shoe to the famous shine on the nose (the first fetish mentioned), or a "suspensatory belt which can also be worn as bathing drawers" (one of the last listed [SE 21: 156]).

9. Specifically, *Three Essays on the Theory of Sexuality*, "Some Consequences of the Anatomical Distinction between the Sexes," "Female Sexuality," "The Question of Lay Analysis," and "Femininity." This inferiority is clearly framed as a question of value, as the following passage makes clear: "But we have learned that girls feel deeply their lack of a sexual organ that is equal in value to the male one; they regard themselves on that account as inferior" (SE 20: 212).

10. The notion of fetishism is mentioned not only in the texts that we might expect, such as "Fetishism" and *Three Essays on the Theory of Sexuality*, but Freud discusses aspects of it in quite a few texts before 1927, such as *Delusions and Dreams in Jensen's* Gradiva, his discussion of Leonardo da Vinci, and the essay on "Repression."

11. The fact that this penis is lost, rather than found to be lacking through castration, will become important later in this study, in the third chapter's argument that loss, rather than lack, is the foundation for fetishism. We can see here in the last sentence of this passage some evidence to ground this claim.

12. The clearest explication of this may be Jacqueline Rose's reading of Lacan. For Lacan, as Rose tells us, the penis is not the phallus because "the phallus stands at its own expense"; thus any man who presumes to have the phallus by virtue of having a penis is an impostor (69). She also emphasizes that for Lacan, it is interpretation that counts: "sexual difference is then assigned according to whether individual subjects do or do not possess the phallus, which means not that anatomical difference *is* sexual difference (the one as strictly deductible from the other), but that anatomical difference comes to *figure* sexual difference, that is, becomes the sole representative of what sexual difference is allowed to be" (66).
Jane Gallop has argued that the effort to distinguish the penis from the phallus is doomed to fail, precisely because we can never sever the phallus from the penis (see "Beyond the Phallus" in *Thinking Through the Body*, esp. 126–27). However, if we acknowledge that anatomical difference is merely a *figure*, and that figure is ambiguous (as it is in the last sentence of "Fetishism") then we can perhaps introduce other grounds for figuring who has and who is the phallus. Judith Butler discusses the phallus along these lines in "The Lesbian Phallus and the Morphological Imaginary," in *Bodies that Matter* (57–91).

13. This deferral has another interesting effect, in that it puts off any connection between substitute for the maternal phallus, viewed by the child, and the mother's own perspective on her penis substitute, which in "Femininity" Freud posits as a child. If the mother and child concurred with Freud about the

maternal phallus substitute being a child, we might come to understand fetishism as a narcissistic investment, since the child would see himself in/as the fetish object.

14. This difference between the boy and the man is yet another nuance of sexual difference which is concealed in the workings of fetishism. While fetishism has classically been understood as the elision of sexual difference between men and women, that is, an elision of a narrowly defined but broadly applied binary anatomical difference, fetishism can be read in other ways. For instance, its connection to castration, read through Gilman and Boyarin as a figure for circumcision, suggests it also reinterprets the difference between Jewish and Gentile men; in Freud, fetishism also rather significantly serves to blur the distinction between hetero- (those who find women appropriate sexual objects) and homosexual (those who do not) men.

15. Freud's certainty here also compares with his earlier certainty, that to declare the fetish to be the maternal phallus substitute would be a disappointing revelation. His certainty here, however, contains a more persuasive force; his surety is part of his effort to convince us of something we probably do not know, rather than his resignation that we probably already know what he is trying to tell us.

16. See Whitney Davis's argument that this backwards move is necessary for the development of true fetishism.

17. Freud makes the point that "Aversion from the female genitals . . . is never lacking in any fetishist" (*SE* 21: 154). This assertion has a number of consequences. First, the very idea that women cannot be fetishists rides on the assumption that one could never be averse to oneself, a point implicitly contradicted by Freud's claim at the end that the clitoris is the prototype of an organ felt to be inferior. Second, like Freud's apparently unrigorous slippage between the "penis" and the "phallus," it seems to conflate the difference between the "real" or anatomical given and the "symbolic," or interpretations of that morphology. While men's relation to castration could produce a number of quite different effects in Freud's formulation (to become heterosexual, homosexual, or fetishist), women's relation is implicitly reduced to one teleology, and their potential ambivalence—or outright desire for another end—is elided here. Why entertain the notion that women would fear what they must become? To do so introduces the notion that women may not want to be feminine any more than men do, and furthermore that the heterosexual matrix could fail in its operation to position subjects.

18. This overvaluation as a result of acquiring knowledge of sexual difference provides an interesting bridge between fetishism and Freud's short piece "Family Romances" concerning neurotics (*SE* 9: 237–41). Here, the scenario of the child's discovery of sexual practices, which clearly entails the discovery of sexual difference, is connected to the economy of overvaluation

through loss; only this time, the parents are the object of this process, not the penis.

19. See her *Gender Trouble: Feminism and the Subversion of Identity*.

20. In *Of Grammatology* Derrida writes, "For the concept of the supplement . . . harbors within itself two significations whose cohabitation is as a strange as it is necessary. The supplement adds itself, it is a surplus, a plenitude enriching another plenitude, the *fullest measure* of presence. . . . But the supplement supplements. It adds only to replace" (144–45). The context of this commentary is Rousseau's view toward masturbation as a dangerous supplement. This view could easily be transposed a century or so later to late-nineteenth- and early-twentieth-century taxonomies of sexuality, where indeed the fetish and the clitoris each figure as a dangerous supplement, providing something beyond genital heterosexual practice narrowly construed in reproductive terms as the insertion of the penis into the vagina.

21. In the earlier but similar essay, "Female Sexuality," Freud asserts that the clitoris "continues to function in later female sexual life in a manner which is very variable and which is certainly not yet satisfactorily understood" (*SE* 21: 228).

22. This difference implicitly aligns femininity with male homosexuality. As Kaja Silverman has shown, Freud's formulations of male homosexuality are inconsistent, yet two of his three paradigms involve either identification with or desire for a feminine object. See the chapter "Femininity in Male Homosexuality" in *Male Subjectivity at the Margins*, 339–88.

23. The underlying assumption of reproductive heterosexuality which structures Freud's notion of the sexual aim bears comparison with the Eastern practice of tantric sex, which while still heterosexual is not genitally focused: instead, sexual feeling is directed throughout the body, away from the genitals and along the spine to the brain.

24. Freud, *SE* 21: 154. Overvaluation is also critical to Marx's notion of commodity fetishism in vol. 1 of *Capital*. The difference between these two texts, however, brings out the inflection of "overvaluation": in Marx, value is loaded with economic significance, whereas in Freud it carries a moralistic charge. This difference underscores the tacit privileging of a certain form of sexual aim in Freud; that aim is based not on the satisfaction one receives from engaging in a certain practice, but on whether one's practice accords with a specific form of activity widely recognized as "normal." Overvaluation, in the Freudian sense, is merely what is most worthwhile or satisfying from the fetishist's standpoint.

25. In this light, it is feasible to construe penis-envy as fetishism par excellence, even if (as Irigaray has pointed out in her reading of Freud's "Femininity" ("The Blind Spot in an Old Dream of Symmetry" in *Speculum*) the man overvalues his own penis as the object of desire. The feminine heterosexual

woman, like the fetishist, seeks an object outside her body—here, the man's penis, or later in Freud's narrative, the child—to substitute for the threatened loss of her own penis, the clitoris. If we understand that, contrary to Freud's lapses into the biologistic rhetoric of his day, this envy is symbolic envy of something we not only already have but also already lack—if we exploit the instabilities inherent in the text's notion of "penis" and "clitoris"—then perhaps we can begin to perceive the great extent to which the heterosexual matrix of difference constrains and produces fetishism, and we can begin to wonder how that fetishism could change and be more productive as that matrix is deconstructed.

26. Eve Sedgwick discusses the imbrication of shame and identity in "Queer Performativity": "Shame floods into being in a moment . . . in a circuit of identity-constituting identificatory communication" (5).

27. See also Freud's "Some Psychological Consequences of the Anatomical Distinction between the Sexes," 193.

2. The Travesty of Clothes Fetishism

1. This lecture was edited and translated by Louis Rose, and can be found under the title "Freud and Fetishism: Previously Unpublished Minutes of the Vienna Psychoanalytic Society," in *Psychoanalytic Quarterly*.

2. This ideology of sameness in women in fact conceals the diverse range of physical differences among women's bodies.

3. Page numbers in the text refer to the version that appeared in *Poetics Today*.

4. In addition to Rivière's work, Luce Irigaray advanced thinking about masquerade by contrasting it with "mimesis," in which a woman uses femininity to emphasize that she is not limited to the feminine, rather than to compensate for having stepped out of her expected feminine role. Masquerade and mimesis are of course not restricted to clothes, though they foreground the role of clothes; rather, they are centrally concerned with how a subject presents femininity. While each of these theories has foregrounded women's practices of dressing—and the concomitant processes of identification that inform sartorial choices—they also have implications for cross-dressing in its various forms, recent attention to which might be viewed as a sort of "second wave" of masquerade theory.

5. Garber's comments are from her essay on transsexuality, "Spare Parts," 140.

6. This lack of a political charge provides an interesting contrast between Schor's work and Judith Butler's later notion of gender parody, about which I will have more to say in the third chapter.

7. Other feminists have followed Schor in emphasizing travesty as a—if not the—form of female fetishism: Jane Marcus, for example, analyzes the significance of clothes worn by suffragettes as a form of feminist fetishism, while Jann Matlock examines both clothing obsessions (seeking sexual satisfaction from a piece of cloth) and costume obsessions (finding sexual satisfaction in relating to a partner's particular garb) as forms of fetishism, and shows that female transvestism is analogous to male fetishism in nineteenth-century views. Within the framework of her study of nineteenth-century French male writers' use of fetishism in their depictions of femininity, Emily Apter draws explicit parallels between feminist discussions of masquerade and fetishism, suggesting that female clothes fetishism offers a corrective to feminist theories of masquerade, in *Feminizing the Fetish*, 98. Even feminists who do not devote attention exclusively to female fetishism have taken up Schor, as Marjorie Garber does in her discussion of "Fetish Envy," which explicitly interconnects fetishism and cross-dressing.

8. De Lauretis's reading comes from *The Practice of Love*, 268.

9. See the first essay in Freud's *Three Essays on the Theory of Sexuality*.

10. Although Noun was Indiana's foster-sister (15), she was her maid (30), and thus clearly subordinate to Indiana. Thus, even within her character, modern readers might find a certain class ambivalence.

11. From our historical vantage point, the significance of her class transgression pales in comparison to the perceived difficulty of a cross-gender or cross-racial travesty. But rather than illuminate some truth about the inherent difference between social identity (such as class) and other identity-elements construed to be biological (such as race and gender), this perception merely shows how entrenched our notions of gender and race as immutable remain, even as class may be idealized as changeable. There is no "My Fair Lady" for gender or racial transition.

12. Homi Bhabha has elaborated connections between the psychoanalytical understanding of fetishism and its function in the colonial context in *The Location of Culture*. His reading situates the use of the fetish against the background of a colonial fantasy of ruling which is fundamentally split in its constitution of knowledge and exercise of power. Although my reading of *Indiana* similarly links fetishism to racial and class difference, it differs from Bhabha's in that the background against which Indiana's fetishism plays out is dominated by the heterosexual romance narrative. *Indiana*, of course, is not some purely romantic tale, since it is indeed tainted by issues of colonialism; however, the focus of the narrative on individual desires emphasizes the system of sexual difference rather than cultural or national differences.

13. In the early eighties feminist criticism was gaining a foothold in the academy, making its impact on curricula and hirings. The strategic ambivalence that Schor notes is at work in feminist criticism of the 1980s through themes of doubling—double-voiced, double vision, palimpsest, the oscillation between

theory and practice, between France and the United States, between becoming an "insider" discourse and remaining marginal—reflects these gains. However, the usefulness of this ambivalence does not automatically make it fetishism.

14. The spectre of fetishism is evident at a fundamental level, as feminists, unable to unequivocally choose one, strive to negotiate the quest for equality, with its implications of sameness or common identity, and the acknowledgment of differences among women, including differences of power and interest that work against claims for equality.

15. In *Come as You Are*, Judith Roof argues that identification is a complex process through which a subject uses sameness as a guise to negotiate difference "whose crafting into ego results not in any unified whole entity or identity, but rather into the split subject and multiple fragmented identities" (160). Fetishism is important to this process because it provides a strategy to cope with this fragmentation and nonetheless sustain a sense of self.

16. The little girl's differentiation from her mother is a puzzle for Freud, precisely because of his emphasis on binary sexual difference. In "Femininity," Freud finds it not only necessary but a compelling question to think through how a daughter would turn against her mother, and thereby differentiate herself from her. He is, however, unable to answer this question without appeal to "penis-envy." While for the little girl it may seem that sexual difference is not a means for differentiating herself from her mother, in fact this is not necessarily the case. The girl's sexual difference may be one of virginity versus sexual experience, to name the perhaps most obvious form (another might be the sexual difference of a lesbian daughter from a heterosexual mother).

17. To say nothing of how Camhi reinforces Schor's thematization of female fetishism as a theft. This parallel provides a different and still interesting reading of Marx's notion of fetishism; here, theft [in this particular form] is both made possible by capitalism and is capitalism's counterdiscourse or evil twin. Unlike the classical commodity fetishist, who comes to alienation through fetishism, a thief enters into a relation with a (stolen) object in a bid to escape alienation, as a way to try to participate in the economic system.

18. Like the lesbian, the category of pleasure drops out entirely from the scenario of fetishism, however much it remains on the level of rhetorical fetishism. Grosz asserts that "whereas the fetishist [in the classical Freudian scenario] is the most satisfied and contented of all perverts, the masculine woman remains the least content" (51). According to Grosz, the lesbian fetishist's desire, expressed through the fetishism of the femme and an ambivalent attitude toward her own castration that makes that desire possible, brings her no pleasure, only dissatisfaction with her social context. But fetishists seek their objects because they give pleasure and satisfaction; this is an important lesson to learn from fetishism. Grosz's rhetorical fetishism not only eclipses the lesbian in the text, it also forecloses upon finding satisfaction in the text, since ultimately she remains unresolved about the question of lesbian fetishism.

19. Of course, this desire for the masculine woman is not limited to "the feminine woman" figured in this sentence, but could extend to butch-butch desire, or a desire for male-to-female transsexuals or transvestites, or even a seemingly heterosexual man's desire for a masculine woman (quite apart from the orthodox account of fetishism).

20. To be sure, we should guard against conflating lesbian desires and desire for the mother, especially since psychoanalysis has a history of being unable to distinguish the two, much to the detriment of conceptualizing women's desires in general.

21. Furthermore, the scenario de Lauretis describes remains uni-directional within the butch-femme framework; there is no opening for a femme lesbian to experience this bodily dispossession.

22. That this difficulty could be dismissed on the basis of an erroneous confusion between the phallus and the penis is equally specious. Remember, de Lauretis has also determined that "the phallus—as representative of the penis" does not play a role in the constitution of the girl's sense of self (241).

23. In our current cultural context, lesbian desire is not normative, although certainly within lesbian subcultures it has its norms; despite correspondences in individual lives with normative injunctions (adherence to monogamous patterns of relationships, or to ideals of romantic love, for example) lesbian desire remains outside the dominant script.

24. In addition to Schor's interchanging of these ideas, and the interconnection Matlock discusses between them, de Lauretis notes that "The connection between (male) fetishism and (female) masquerade was first suggested by Joan Rivière and subsequently reformulated by Lacan" (270).

25. Freud makes this distinction in *Three Essays on the Theory of Sexuality*.

26. Judith Butler reminds us that "the body in the mirror does not represent the body, as it were, 'before the mirror; the mirror, even as it is instigated by that unrepresentable body 'before' the mirror, produces that body as its delirious effect" (*Bodies that Matter*, 91). The notion that the image in the mirror is productive complicates de Lauretis's reading of Stephen's self-confrontation.

27. And these masculine things are fetishized as signaling desire for a femme, thus as a way to recover the lost feminine body; this frame renders little difference between such objects and how a butch might fetishize a femme's accoutrements as a prelude to having the femme herself.

3. The Language of Loss

1. Irigaray makes this argument in "The Power of Discourse and the Subordination of the Feminine" in *This Sex Which Is Not One*.

2. In fact, if we take de Lauretis's model of lesbian fetishism, which posits the fetish's origin in the fantasmatic loss of a female body (231), back to the heterosexual male model of Freud's 1927 fetishism, we might begin to understand the fetish as acting atropopaïcally against incest, rather than against homosexuality. By making the sexual partner more like his mother (whom the incest taboo has made inaccessible; thus her body is lost to him), the fetishist makes her acceptable to himself. He can still have it both ways, but in this case the both ways is having the mother and not having the mother. On this view, the fetish is not necessarily standing in for a penis at all, but rather a special attribute of one's mother.

3. See, for example, his essay "Femininity."

4. It is perhaps interesting to note that the word "real" rather than the word "wirklich" crops up here, as it did in the final sentence of "Fetishism." Both times, Freud is talking about an object's hypothetical condition—either as a "reale" penis, or not really dead.

5. Because the phallus seems to resolve these kinds of contradictions in patriarchy, it seems inextricable from fetishism.

6. This privilege is underscored, as chapter one shows, in Freud's comparison of the man's (unmarked and unremarked) penis and the woman's "real small penis, the clitoris," which is rendered all the less real for its string of adjectives that qualify the clitoris as a penis.

7. That excess is the distinguishing feature here is notable in light of the idea that melancholia is a drag version of mourning, since drag is often marked as an exaggerated or excessive imitation.

8. We can see this particular confluence of fetishism and melancholia around the process of identification in Mary Kelley's work, "Post-Partum Document," which she describes as centrally concerned with female fetishism. The work, which Emily Apter called a "maternal reliquary," is a collection of a child's everyday objects gathered by its mother as memorabilia ("Splitting Hairs," 115). As Kelley describes this collecting, "the way she saves the lock of hair, the tooth, or school reports . . . signals a disavowal of the lack inscribed by separation from the child" (353). But such collecting is also a melancholic memorial to a lost love object, the baby or young child, whose arrival at each new developmental stage also marks a loss that the mother mourns, if only unconsciously. She is no longer the mother of a baby, or a toddler, or a school-age child. The mother's identification with the child as part of herself must undergo transformation, and the objects facilitate that, both fetishistically and melancholically. In a similar way, Teresa de Lauretis's rewriting of fetishism as a reaction to the narcissistic wound imposed by the threat of castration-as-bodily-loss suggests the connection between melancholia and fetishism, especially through its reliance on narcissism.

9. This dissolution extends beyond the individual to the cultural situation of melancholia; not only is the individual melancholic unable to distinguish between psychical loss and real loss, the cultural privilege accorded melancho-

lia makes it harder to perceive the difference between melancholic and other, more real and tragic, losses. The melancholic's loss trumps any others' loss, because his value as outsider genius provides the standard measure for what counts as inside or included. (Ophelia's grief is eclipsed by Hamlet's, for example.) The pathology of melancholia, its inability to distinguish between inside and outside, is thus reinforced by its social cachet.

10. This is also true of those lawmakers, who in rewriting welfare legislation elide the systemic obstacles that welfare recipients often face, in favor of a ideology of heroism, of pulling oneself up by the bootstraps, that places too heavy an emphasis on the subject and does not give enough consideration to the relations in which the subject is entangled. There is no regard for dire loss under welfare acts that limit lifetime benefits to five years, no differentiation among how subjects may be institutionally or socially positioned.

11. Drag, however, turned out to be a troubled example for Butler. In her review of *Gender Trouble*, Susan Bordo complains that Butler did not draw on actual drag queens for her argument, but remained on the level of the abstract. Drag, though it plays a pivotal role in concretizing Butler's discussion of gender parody, does not loom large enough in the book to warrant an entry in the index; its discussion coalesces around pages 136–38. Butler gives more attention to the subject of drag in her subsequent book, *Bodies that Matter*, even devoting an entire chapter to the film "Paris is Burning" which brought the drag subculture of Latino and African Americans in Harlem to the big screen and to the attention of a wider audience. Such attention may seem to be a response to critics, like Bordo, who want to see real drag queens. If that were the case, we might see some irony in the fact that Butler makes a point of examining how "realness" works as a normative standard in judging the drag contests, as well as in the "real" world, where subjects are made intelligible according to norms of sexual, racial, and class identities. In doing so, she expands her analysis from *Gender Trouble* to include identities other than gender, while honing her point about the troubling issues of intelligibility and embodiment that all subjects encounter.

12. Although she shares Grosz's and de Lauretis's psychoanalytically informed understanding of the connection between prohibition and desire, Butler does not impose a binary gender grid through which this dynamic operates. Instead, she posits that the prohibition of desire for one particular parent results in the loss that produces melancholia. Butler acknowledges that this prohibition comes from social injunctions that produce sexual norms, but leaves room for the possibility that a subject may creatively or deviately interpret these injunctions in relation to herself.

13. This presumption can be seen in the examples philosophers tend to choose to explain elementary epistemology—the question of whether we know what a table is, or whether a chair exists, rather than who a person is. I will explore this more fully in considering Lorraine Code's work in the coda.

14. This takeover occurs in the introduction to *Bodies*, as early as the second page but perhaps most clearly on p. 12, where we find the heading "Perfor-

mativity as Citationality." In the shift marked by this title, Butler emphasizes that in contrast to the connotations suggested by the term parody, performativity is neither singular, nor an act of free will, but something done repeatedly and under compulsion, according to the laws at work in producing the subject. For example, Butler notes that the institution of heterosexuality forces us to take on one of two sexes, and this requirement simultaneously produces the category of sex: "this 'assumption' [of sex] is *compelled* by a regulatory apparatus of heterosexuality, one which reiterates itself through the forcible production of 'sex'" (12). A subject thus comes to perform her sex and to produce it at the behest of a system of signification that sorts subjects into one or another binary options.

15. I call the manipulation of objects by subjects a protofetishism in order to highlight the subject-object relation as the basic building block of fetishism; fetishism adds the dimensions of ambivalence and contradiction on these basic elements.

16. See, for example, Nancy Fraser, "Pragmatism, Feminism, and the Linguistic Turn," 157.

Coda

1. See, for example, Donna Haraway's chapter on "Situated Knowledges" in *Simians, Cyborgs, and Women*, Elizabeth Spelman's *Inessential Woman*, Naomi Scheman's *Engenderings*, and Lorraine Code's *What Can She Know?*; feminist standpoint epistemology, best exemplified in the work of Sandra Harding, is a major advocate of the epistemological significance of sexual difference.

2. Freud is one of the few thinkers who has bridged the connection between desiring and knowing, through his notion of epistemophilia, the drive for knowledge. Lynne Joyrich calls our attention to how this notion slides in Freud's formulation from a child's research into the origins of life to the child's research into sexual difference; this slide also transforms the child from any child to only some boys. This transformation is similar to the changes in Freud's text, discussed in chapter one, regarding the sufficiency of the clitoris as an instrument for knowing about the penis.

3. In this light, commodity fetishism is rather an oxymoron, since commodities are impersonal objects and fetishes are highly personal ones. My thanks to Jane Gallop for bringing this distinction to my attention.

4. Arguably, this notion of reason has been overextended into what Weber labeled instrumental rationality, which Wendy Brown posits "is one of the strongest contemporary forces erasing both the standing and significance of the subject"—far more so than postmodern fragmentation (66).

5. I am using the notion of the Enlightenment here rather schematically, because it has become an important benchmark for theorists in the late twenti-

eth century; the thinkers who contributed to this sea-change in human self-conceptualization did not all concur on a single model of the subject.

6. This dynamic is clearly played out in Freud's 1927 analysis of fetishism, where the origin of the fetish is situated in the *sight* of the mother's genitals. It is striking that when the origin of fetishism is narrowed to the visual field, rather than the partial repression of other senses such as smell (as was the case in the 1909 lecture), the fetishist also becomes exclusively male.

7. There are many interpretations of what Marlow loses in his journey; the loss of the sense of distinction between Europeans and Africans or between the "civilized" and the "primitive" would be particularly key here in relation to fetishism's cultural history.

8. The narrator attests to Marlow's epistemophilia by contrasting him to the sailors who do not wander, but remain "sedentary," at home on their ships, indifferent to the changes travel presents to them. Marlow also later talks about having a passion for maps, and this connects to his drive to explore, to his sense that "I must get there by hook or by crook" (12).

9. The narrator waxes associatively on the other boats borne by the tidal current, but these function metaphorically rather than metonymically.

10. This relation of domination founded on theories of lack is the model many feminist film theorists have drawn upon for their critical analysis of fetishism. This model of fetishism, however, has served more as a focal point to work against than a paradigm that productively opens up the field of interpretive possibilities. Fetishism need not entail domination.

11. On this view, fetishism is a failure because of the incomplete repudiation of the mother, which is viewed as necessary to the development of an autonomous masculine subjectivity.

12. This reciprocal arrangement of mutual recognition invokes not the Freudian or Lacanian models of subjectivity, but those of D. W. Winnicott and Jessica Benjamin. Jane Flax argues that Winnicott's object-relations theory differs from Freudian and particularly Lacanian psychoanalysis precisely in its focus on intersubjectivity and sociality, in contrast to what she perceives as the narcissistic or solipsistic notion of the subject that has been the dominant psychoanalytical theoretical model taken up by critical and postmodern theorists. Rather than do away with the valuable insights of psychoanalysis, an epistemological fetishism would integrate the insights of object-relations theories too.

13. Anne McClintock has described fetishes as "compromise objects" ("Return," 4), and this formulation seems particularly apt here for thinking about compromised knowledge. The play on "compromise" illuminates the notion of epistemological loss, that all our knowing is a compromise with partiality, yet this does not compromise our sense of having certainty about the world.

WORKS CITED

Adams, Parveen. "Of Female Bondage." *Between Feminism and Psychoanalysis*. Ed. Teresa Brennan. New York: Routledge, 1989. 247–65.

Apter, Emily. *Feminizing the Fetish: Psychoanalysis and Narrative Obsession in Turn-of-the Century France*. Ithaca: Cornell UP, 1991.

———. "Splitting Hairs: Female Fetishism and Postpartum Sentimentality in the Fin du Siecle," in *Eroticism and the Body Politic*. Ed. Lynn Hunt. Baltimore: Johns Hopkins UP, 1991. 164–90.

Apter, Emily and William Pietz, eds. *Fetishism as Cultural Discourse*. Ithaca: Cornell UP, 1993.

Austin, J. L. *How to Do Things with Words*. Cambridge: Harvard UP, 1975.

Baier, Annette. *Postures of the Mind: Essays on Mind and Morals*. Minneapolis: U Minnesota P, 1985.

Balint, Michael. "A Contribution on Fetishism." *Problems in Human Pleasure and Behaviour*. London: Hogarth, 1957. 171–73.

Benjamin, Jessica. *The Bonds of Love: Psychoanalysis, Feminism, and the Problem of Domination*. New York: Pantheon, 1988.

Berg, Elizabeth. "The Third Woman." *Diacritics* 12 (1982): 11–20.

Bersani, Leo and Ulysse Dutoit. "Fetishisms and Storytelling." *The Forms of Violence: Narrative in Assyrian Art and Modern Culture*. New York: Schocken, 1985. 66–72.

Bhabha, Homi. *The Location of Culture*. New York: Routledge, 1994.

Bordo, Susan. Review of *Gender Trouble: Feminism and the Subversion Identity*. *Feminist Studies* 18.1 (Spring 1992): 159–78.

Boyarin, Daniel. "Épater l'embourgeoisement: Freud, Gender, and the (De)Colonized Psyche." *Diacritics* 24.1 (1994): 17–41.

Brown, Wendy. "Feminist Hesitations, Postmodern Exposures." *differences: A Journal of Feminist Cultural Studies* 3.1 (1991): 63–84.

Butler, Judith. *Bodies that Matter: On the Discursive Limits of "Sex."* New York: Routledge, 1993.

————. *Gender Trouble: Feminism and the Subversion of Identity.* New York: Routledge, 1990.

Camhi, Leslie. "Stealing Femininity: Department Store Kleptomania as Sexual Disorder." *differences: A Journal of Feminist Cultural Studies* 5.1 (1993): 26–50.

Clérambault, Gatian de Gaëtan de. "Passion érotique des étoffes chez la femme." 1906–08. *Oeuvres Psychiatriques.* Vol. 2. Paris: PU de France, 1942. 683–720.

Code, Lorraine. *What Can She Know?: Feminist Theory and the Construction of Knowledge.* Ithaca: Cornell UP, 1991.

Conrad, Joseph. *Heart of Darkness and The Secret Sharer.* New York: Bantam, 1981.

Davis, Whitney. "HomoVision: A Reading of Freud's Fetishism." *Genders* 15 (Winter 1992): 86–118.

de Brosses, Charles. *Du Culte des dieux fétiches: ou Parallèle de l'ancienne Religion de l'Egypte avec la Religion actuelle de Nigritie.* Westmead: Gregg, 1972.

de Lauretis, Teresa. "The Technology of Gender." *Technologies of Gender: Essays on Theory, Film, and Fiction.* Bloomington: Indiana UP, 1987. 1–30.

————. *The Practice of Love: Lesbian Sexuality and Perverse Desire.* Bloomington: Indiana UP, 1994.

Derrida, Jacques. *Limited Inc.* Trans. Samuel Weber and Jeffrey Mehlman. Evanston, Northwestern UP, 1988.

————. *Of Grammatology.* Trans. Gayatri Chakravorty Spivak. Baltimore: Johns Hopkins UP, 1976.

Doane, Mary Ann. "Film and the Masquerade." Reprinted in *Femmes Fatales: Feminism, Film Theory, Psychoanalysis.* New York: Routledge, 1991. 17–32.

Fausto-Sterling, Anne. *Myths of Gender: Biological Theories about Women and Men.* Revised ed. New York: Basic Books, 1985.

Feinberg, Leslie. *Stone Butch Blues.* Ithaca: Firebrand Books, 1993.

Flax, Jane. *Thinking Fragments: Psychoanalysis, Feminism, and Postmodernism in the Contemporary West.* Berkeley: U of California P, 1990.

Fraser, Nancy. "Pragmatism, Feminism, and the Linguistic Turn." *Feminist Contentions.* Ed. Seyla Benhabib, Judith Butler, Drucilla Cornell, and Nancy Fraser. New York: Routledge, 1995. 157–71.

Freud, Sigmund. "Family Romances." *The Standard Edition of the Complete Psychological Works of Sigmund Freud.* Trans. and ed. James Strachey. Vol. 9. London: Hogarth, 1964. 237–41. 24 vols. 1953–74.

————. "Female Sexuality." 1931. *The Standard Edition.* Vol. 21. 223–43.

———. "Femininity." 1933. *The Standard Edition*. Vol. 22. 112–35.

———. "Fetischismus." *Gesammelte Werke*. Vol. 14. Frankfurt a. M.: S. Fischer, 1969. 311–17.

———. "Fetishism." 1927. *The Standard Edition*. Vol. 21. 147–57.

———. "Fetishism." *Sexuality and the Psychology of Love*. Trans. Joan Rivière. New York: Collier, 1963. 214–19.

———. "Freud and Fetishism: Previously Unpublished Minutes of the Vienna Psychoanalytic Society." Ed. and trans. Louis Rose. *Psychoanalytic Quarterly* 57 (1988): 147–66.

———. "Mourning and Melancholia." 1917. *The Standard Edition*. Vol. 14. 243–61.

———. "The Question of Lay Analysis." 1926. *The Standard Edition*. Vol. 20. 179–258.

———. "Some Psychical Consequences of the Anatomical Distinction Between the Sexes." 1925. *The Standard Edition*. Vol. 19. 241–58.

———. "The Splitting of the Ego in the Defensive Process." 1938. *The Standard Edition*. Vol. 23. 275–78.

———. *Three Essays on the Theory of Sexuality*. 1905. *The Standard Edition*. Vol. 7. 123–243.

———. "Trauer und Melancholie." *Gesammelte Werke*. Vol. 10. Frankfurt a.M.: S. Fischer, 1969. 428–46.

Gallop, Jane. *Thinking through the Body*. New York: Columbia UP, 1988.

Gamman, Lorraine and Merja Makinen. *Female Fetishism: A New Look*. New York: New York UP, 1995.

Garber, Marge. "Fetish Envy." *Vested Interests: Cross-Dressing and Cultural Anxiety*. New York: Harper, 1993. 118–27.

———. "Spare Parts: The Surgical Construction of Gender." *differences: A Journal of Feminist Cultural Studies* 3.1 (1989): 137–59.

Gilman, Sander. *Freud, Race, and Gender*. Princeton: Princeton UP, 1993.

Grosz, Elizabeth. "Lesbian Fetishism?" *differences: A Journal of Feminist Cultural Studies* 3.2 (1991): 39–54.

Haraway, Donna. *Simians, Cyborgs, and Women: The Reinvention of Nature*. New York: Routledge, 1991.

Harding, Sandra. *Whose Science, Whose Knowledge? Thinking from Women's Lives*. Ithaca: Cornell UP, 1991.

Hull, Gloria, Patricia Bell Scott, and Barbara Smith. *All the Women Are White, All the Blacks Are Men, But Some of Us Are Brave: Black Women's Studies*. Old Westbury: Feminist Press, 1982.

Ian, Marcia. *Remembering the Phallic Mother: Psychoanalysis, Modernism, and the Fetish*. Ithaca: Cornell UP, 1993.

Irigaray, Luce. *Speculum of the Other Woman*. Trans. Gillian C. Gill. Ithaca: Cornell UP, 1985.

———. "The Power of Discourse and the Subordination of the Feminine." *This Sex Which Is Not One*. Trans. Catherine Porter. Ithaca: Cornell UP, 1985.

Joyrich, Lynne. "Elvisophilia: Knowledge, Pleasure, and the Cult of Elvis." *differences: A Journal of Feminist Cultural Studies* 5.1 (1993): 73–91.

Kaplan, Louise. *Female Perversions: The Temptations of Emma Bovary*. New York: Anchor, 1991.

Keller, Evelyn Fox. *A Feeling for the Organism: The Life and Work of Barbara McClintock*. San Francisco: W. H. Freeman, 1983.

Kelley, Mary and Emily Apter. "The Smell of Money: Mary Kelley in Conversation with Emily Apter." Apter and Pietz 352–62.

Kofman, Sarah. "Ça cloche." *Les Fins du l'homme: à partir de Jacques Derrida*. Ed. Phillippe Lacoue-Labarthe and Jean-Luc Nancy. Paris: Galilée, 1980. 89–116.

Lacqueur, Thomas. "Amor veneris, ve; Dulcedo Appeletur." *Fragments for a History of the Human Body*. Part 3. Ed. Michel Feher with Ramona Naddaff and Nadia Tazi. New York: Zone, 1989. 91–131.

Mannoni, Octave. "Je sais bien, mais quand même . . ." *Clefs pour l'imaginaire ou l'autre scène*. Paris: Editions du Seuil, 1969. 9–33.

Marcus, Jane. "The Asylums of Antaeus: Women, War, and Madness—Is There a Feminist Fetishism?" *The New Historicism*. Ed. Aram Veeser. New York: Routledge, 1989. 132–51.

Marx, Karl. *Capital: A Critique of Political Economy*. Vol. 1. 1867. Trans. Ben Fowkes. New York: Vintage, 1977.

Matlock, Jann. "Masquerading Women, Pathologized Men: Cross–Dressing, Fetishism, and the Theory of Perversion, 1882–1935." Apter and Pietz 31–60.

McClintock, Anne. *Imperial Leather: Race, Gender, and Sexuality in the Colonial Contest*. New York: Routledge, 1995.

———. "The Return of Female Fetishism." *New Formations* 19 (Spring 1993): 1–21.

Morrison, Toni. *Beloved*. New York: Knopf, 1987.

Pietz, William. "The Problem of the Fetish, I" *Res* 9 (Spring 1985): 6–17.

———. "The Problem of the Fetish, II," *Res* 13 (Spring 1987): 23–45.

———. "The Problem of the Fetish, IIIa" *Res* 16 (Autumn 1988): 105–23.

Poe, Edgar Allan. "The Purloined Leter." *The Portable Poe.* Ed. Philip Van Doren Stern. New York: Viking, 1945. 439–62.

Rivière, Joan. "Womanliness as Masquerade." Reprinted in *Formations of Fantasy.* Ed. Victor Burgin, James Donald, and Cora Kaplan. London, Methuen, 1986. 35–44.

Robinson, Sally. "Misappropriations of the Feminine." *SubStance* 59 (1989): 48–70.

Roof, Judith. *Come as You Are: Sexuality and Narrative.* New York: Columbia UP, 1996.

Rose, Jacqueline. *Sexuality in the Field of Vision.* London: Verso, 1987.

Sand, George. *Indiana.* Trans. Georges Burnham Ives. New York: Howard Fertig, 1975.

Scheman, Naomi. *Engenderings: Constructions of Knowledge, Authority, and Privilege.* New York: Routledge, 1993.

Schiesari, Juliana. *The Gendering of Melancholia: Feminism, Psychoanalysis, and the Symbolics of Loss in Renaissance Literature.* Ithaca: Cornell UP, 1982.

Schor, Naomi. "Female Fetishism: The Case of George Sand." *Poetics Today* 6.1–2 (1985): 301–10. Reprinted in *The Female Body in Western Culture: Contemporary Perspectives.* Ed. Susan Rubin Suleiman. Cambridge: Harvard UP, 1986. 363–72.

Sedgwick, Eve Kosofsky. "Queer Performativity: Henry James's *The Art of the Novel.*" *GLQ* 1.1 (1993): 1–16.

Silverman, Kaja. *Male Subjectivity at the Margins.* New York: Routledge, 1992.

Spelman, Elizabeth. *Inessential Woman: Problems of Exclusion in Feminist Thought.* Boston: Beacon, 1988.

Stoller, Robert. *Sex and Gender.* New York: J. Aronson, 1974–76.

Traub, Valerie. "The Ambiguities of 'Lesbian' Viewing Pleasure." *Body Guards: The Cultural Politics of Gender Ambiguity.* Ed. Julia Epstien and Kristina Straub. New York: Routledge, 1991.

Yingling, Thomas. "Fetishism, Identity, Politics." *Who Can Speak?: Authority and Critical Identity.* Ed. Judith Roof and Robyn Wiegman. Urbana: U of Illinois P, 1995. 155–64.

INDEX